THE
DEMAGOGUE'S
PLAYBOOK

ALSO BY ERIC A. POSNER

Radical Markets: Uprooting Capitalism and Democracy for a Just Society

Last Resort: The Financial Crisis and the Future of Bailouts

The Twilight of Human Rights Law

The Executive Unbound: After the Madisonian Republic

THE
DEMAGOGUE'S
PLAYBOOK

THE BATTLE FOR AMERICAN DEMOCRACY FROM THE FOUNDERS TO TRUMP

ERIC A. POSNER

ALL
POINTS
BOOKS

NEW YORK

First published in the United States by All Points Books, an imprint of
St. Martin's Publishing Group

www.allpointsbooks.com

Designed by Omar Chapa

Library of Congress Cataloging-in-Publication Data

Names: Posner, Eric A., 1965– author.
Title: The demagogue's playbook : the battle for American democracy
    from the founders to Trump / Eric A. Posner.
Description: First edition. | New York : All Points Books, 2020. |
    Includes index.
Identifiers: LCCN 2020002693 | ISBN 9781250303035 (hardcover) |
    ISBN 9781250303028 (ebook)
Subjects: LCSH: Political leadership—United States—History. |
    United States—Politics and government. | Political culture—United
    States—History. | Populism—United States—History. | Democracy—
    United States—History. | Power (Social sciences) | Trump, Donald,
    1946– | United States—Politics and government—2017–
Classification: LCC E183 .P785 2020 | DDC 306.20973—dc23
LC record available at https://lccn.loc.gov/2020002693

First Edition: 2020

10   9   8   7   6   5   4   3   2   1

for Emlyn, Nathaniel, and Jacob

CONTENTS

THE
DEMAGOGUE'S
PLAYBOOK

INTRODUCTION

At dawn, the night was interrupted by the growl of thirteen cannons, which brightened the dark sky and signaled the start of the momentous day. By late morning, enormous crowds filled the grounds of the Capitol. Though they came from all classes and walks of life, the people in this immense mass stood as one as they waited with barely suppressed anticipation for the appearance of their new leader.

They stood before the majestic façade of the Capitol, its design inspired by a Greek temple and the Roman Pantheon, which evoked the country's debt to the ancient inventors of democracy and constitutional law. Standing on First Street, those on the fringes of the crowd could barely make out the figures walking out the door of the Rotunda, partly obscured by the columns of the East Portico. Moments later, a roar erupted as those at the front of the crowd recognized a figure, somberly dressed in black, surrounded by dignitaries, emerge from the building. The sound surged backward through the crowd, swelling in volume until the noise overwhelmed spectators. "The very heavens were rent with the shout which greeted the long expected vision," wrote an observer. The cannons thundered again as President-elect Andrew Jackson took his seat.[1]

The crowds were expected to disperse after the inaugural speech and the taking of the oath. But they did not. As Jackson rose to depart, well-wishers pressed through the barricades and eagerly pushed toward him from all directions. For a moment he was engulfed by the jubilant, heaving crowd. His guards, flanked on either side, ushered a path for him out of the mob, and he took flight on a white steed down Pennsylvania Avenue.

Word got around that a reception was being held at the White House, and soon huge streams of people were pouring toward it from every direction, enveloping the government buildings along the way and then the White House itself. Those lucky enough to make it into the executive mansion pushed and shoved one another, many scrambling up on furniture in their muddy boots for a glimpse of the president, who was being pressed against the wall by a mass of supporters. Servants, day laborers, prostitutes, and pickpockets struggled with foreign ambassadors and society matrons for access to the cakes and refreshments. Punches were thrown, noses bloodied, tables overturned, china smashed into a thousand pieces. As Jackson vanished within a circle of guards, White House servants lured the crowd out the doors and through the windows by removing the punch bowls from the interior to the White House lawn.

One Margaret Smith, reflecting on what she had seen, observed that "ladies and gentlemen only had been expected at this Levee, not the people en masse. But it was the People's day, and the People's President, and the People would rule. God grant that one day or other, the People do not pull down all rule and rulers."[2]

The day after Donald Trump was elected president, I received a phone call from a reporter who asked me whether Trump would become a dictator. He then told me that, as far as he was concerned, "this was a Warsaw Ghetto moment." I thought his reaction was extreme. While I didn't vote for Trump, and didn't like him, I thought the reporter had lost all sense of proportion. The Warsaw Ghetto uprising against the Nazis in 1943 ended in the death of tens of thousands of Jews who were killed during the battle itself or murdered in concentration camps to which they were transported.

The idea that Trump's presidency would introduce authoritarian rule, or worse, received a great deal of attention. Several authors wrote books warning of such an outcome, and commentators had a field day.[3] While one group insisted that Trump would be a dictator, another group argued that he was insane and therefore should be removed under the Twenty-Fifth Amendment. And yet in some ways, this was nothing new. The slanderous claim—made by Trump, among others—that Barack Obama was born in Kenya implied that he was not a legitimate president because of the constitutional requirement that the president be a natural-born citizen. Many Democrats argued that George W. Bush was not a legitimate president because the Supreme Court threw the 2000 election to him. The Republican Congress impeached President Bill Clinton because it believed that he had shown himself unfit for office as a result of his lies and obstruction of justice in connection with a sex scandal. Significant efforts were also made to investigate and impeach Ronald Reagan and George H. W. Bush because of their involvement in the Iran-Contra affair in the 1980s. A decade before that, in 1974, Richard Nixon was forced to resign the presidency. Significantly, before Nixon, no president was ever forced from office, and hardly any faced serious investigations for personal wrongdoing, with the exception of Andrew Johnson, who was impeached but not removed from office in 1868. The impeachment proceedings against Trump, which began in 2019, seem hardly surprising in light of this pattern.

Something is wrong with the presidency, but what exactly? The extraordinary negative reaction to Trump's election—by conservative intellectuals as well as by liberals and Democrats—reflects something more than ordinary partisan and policy disagreements. It reflects genuine fear about the vitality of our constitutional system. The sheer number of books and articles published since 2016 accusing Trump of an authoritarian, or even fascist, agenda provides evidence of this anxiety. But rather than a diagnosis, the dictatorship argument seems more like an inarticulate attempt to express—in constitutional terms—an uneasiness. What actually is wrong with Trump?

A better place to start may be with another epithet that is frequently used to describe him: that he is a "demagogue" or a "populist demagogue." While America has never experienced a dictator, it has had many populists and demagogues, so an exploration of these terms may offer insight into how they may apply to Trump. The Founders, reaching back to classical precedents, feared that their experiment in republican self-government could produce a demagogue: a charismatic leader who would gain and hold on to power by manipulating the public rather than by advancing the public good. Demagogues are often accused of populism because populism has come to mean a kind of uncontrolled mass activism that rejects deliberative, pluralistic government and the political, legal, and constitutional institutions that maintain it. Trump, who has played to the mob and attacked institutions from the judiciary to the press, may seem to embody these ideas.

The problem is that these two terms have become all-purpose political epithets, flung so frequently against so many different politicians that they have all but lost their meaning. The terms often mean "a politician I don't like." As the New Deal lawyer Thurman Arnold put it:

> There is no difference between the demagogue and the statesman, except on the basis of a judgment as to the desirability of the social ends and social values which move the one or the other. The man with the social values you do not like, you will call the demagogue. You will say that he appeals to emotion and not to reason. This, however, is only because "reason" is the respectable end of the two polar terms, "reason" versus "emotion," and you instinctively want it to point toward your own organization.[4]

The overuse of the term has made those who use it vulnerable to the charge of demagoguery themselves, opening them to accusations that they call anyone a demagogue whose policies they disagree with or whose manners fall short of those of the educated elite. Inevitably, after Barack Obama called Trump a demagogue in a speech, a commentator said no, it was Obama who was the demagogue. Meanwhile, shortly after the death of George H. W. Bush, a headline blared: "GEORGE H. W. BUSH CAMPAIGNED AS A DEMAGOGUE. TWICE."[5]

Similarly, the term "populist" has been sapped of any meaning. The term first appeared in the late nineteenth century, referring to the farmers who created the "People's Party" to counter the indifference of the Republicans and Democrats, who when not refighting the Civil War were preoccupied with business and urban issues—or "power and plunder," as the populists argued. While populists nursed legitimate grievances, they often spoke in wildly apocalyptic terms that resonate even today. As one populist tract put it, "The fruits of the toil of millions are boldly stolen to build up colossal fortunes for a few, unprecedented in the history of mankind; and the possessors of those, in turn, despise the republic and endanger liberty. From the same prolific womb of governmental injustice we breed the two great classes—tramps and millionaires." This proclivity for bombast has led commentators to refer to populism as a political attitude that opposes parties and other political and civic institutions, pluralism, and bureaucratic regularity and traffics in conspiracy theories that blame the elites (another all-encompassing epithet that's been flung around with high frequency) for every problem. Populism was blamed for Britain's exit from the European Union in 2017. The explanation was that British voters were tired of being bossed around by European bureaucrats, while refusing to appreciate the advantages of the Union. Nigel Farage, the pro-leave leader, used typical populist language when he said, after the referendum, "This will be a victory for real people, a victory for ordinary people, a victory for decent people. We have fought against the multinationals, we have fought against the big merchant banks, we have fought against big politics, we have fought against lies, corruption and deceit."[6] Populism has also been blamed for the rise of authoritarianism in Poland, Hungary, Turkey, and Russia.

But "populist" has also been used positively to refer to politicians who care about ordinary people and oppose institutions that favor an entrenched ruling class. Used this way, it's worn as a badge of honor by certain right-wing critics of the political establishment, like former White House adviser Steve Bannon. The term has been applied favorably to people on the left as well, like Bernie Sanders. Populists, understood this way, argue that they are right to oppose parties and other institutions because those institutions are controlled by the elite and maintain the status quo.

The purpose of this book is to put some historical flesh and blood on these terms. Both demagoguery and populism are meaningful ideas that identify inherent problems with constitutional democracy. A constitutional democracy is a form of government that gives political power to ordinary people while subjecting their exercise of that power to fairly rigid constitutional structures. These structures give rise to institutions—the courts, the bureaucracy, the press—that are almost always controlled by specialists or professionals, including elected politicians, political appointees, and civil servants. Populist critics often refer to them collectively as the "elites"—though this term, as we will see later in the book, can be quite broad and amorphous, sometimes referring to corporate leaders, financial titans, or the merely rich, and sometimes referring to university professors, scientists, professionals, and other highly educated people with technical expertise. The institutions of our constitutional democracy are necessary for translating the people's interests and values into policy choices and, it is generally assumed, to prevent people from exercising their political power in a way that is self-defeating or contrary to their own interest. But because the institutions are controlled by specialists whose values and interests may differ from those of ordinary people, the institutions may end up thwarting the popular will. Populists argue that the specialists instead advance their own interests as the expense of the public interest.

Thus, constitutional democracy faces two challenges: from below and from above. The challenge from below is the traditional populist attack on institutions. "Populism," as I use the term, refers to a political attitude that distrusts established institutions on the assumption that they thwart popular will. The populist's attitude should be distinguished from that of a reformer. Reformers may believe that particular institutions are badly run or captured by special interests, but they advocate reform of the institutions—not their wholesale destruction. The logic of populism, in contrast, pushes toward the more radical view. The populist tends to believe that institutions are inherently corrupt because they are so easily captured by "elites." Of course, populism varies in its extremity; more moderate forms of populism edge onto reformism, while more extreme forms can seem (at least to moderates) almost nihilistic.

Populism can also vary in its choice of targets. Today, left-wing populists most frequently target businesses, market institutions, and the "1 percent." Right-wing populists target government bureaucracy, courts, and the press. Trump himself provides the best example, with his fulminations against the "deep state," "biased" judges, and "Fake News." Some thoroughgoing populists target both groups, and all populists complain about the two major parties. There are two common themes. Populists are antipluralist. They see the political landscape as a zero-sum game: an apocalyptic battle between the "people" and the "elites." The people are assumed to not be divided; or, if divisions are acknowledged, those divisions are assumed to be of far less significance than the divisions between the people and the elites. Second, populists are frequently (though not inevitably) attracted to leadership by a single person.

The second point is related to an inherent problem with populism. There is no direct way for the people to rule in the American system. They must rule through someone. If the people distrust the existing constitutional institutions, believing them controlled by the elites, then it is natural for them to seek representation from a person or institution outside the political establishment. And if populism denies pluralism, it is natural to look for a representative in a person rather than in an institution, which will inevitably be composed of squabbling individuals.

This gives rise to the problem of demagoguery. A demagogue is someone who attempts to exploit this vulnerability in order to amass power. Despite its overuse, the word "demagogue" has a core meaning that has remained stable over millennia. It refers to a charismatic, amoral person who obtains the support of the people through dishonesty, emotional manipulation, and the exploitation of social divisions; who targets the political elites, blaming them for everything that has gone wrong; and who tries to destroy institutions—legal, political, religious, social— and other sources of power that stand in their way. The demagogue is frequently considered to be (and in many cases actually is) crude, vulgar, and violent—contemptuous of manners, civility, and norms, which the demagogue sees as structures that keep the elites in power. Huey Long, the demagogic governor of Louisiana, wore his pajamas when he met ambassadors, while another southern demagogue, the Arkansan Jeff Davis, called his opponents "Aunt Puss" and "Sister Hinemon." The fear of demagoguery is closely related to distrust in democracy, but in moderate form it reflects the historically grounded recognition of the risk that, from time to time, the people can be misled— because they are (sometimes) unwise, ignorant about many things, or susceptible to (transitory) passions, especially in times of crisis. A demagogue skillfully exploits all these vulnerabilities on the way to power.

Once in power, the demagogue abuses it. Demagogues try to entrench their power by undermining competing power centers and interfering with elections; they are likely to throw politics into turmoil and damage the public interest. The table below offers ideal types of the demagogue and what I call a "statesman," or simply an ordinary politician.[7]

	APPEALS TO	SEEKS	CHARACTER	CLAIM TO AUTHORITY	PUBLIC GOAL	STYLE	ATTITUDE TO INSTITUTIONS AND EXPERTISE
DEMAGOGUE	Negative emotions like fear and hatred, prejudice	Personal power	Amoral, narcissistic, violent	Connection to people	Abstract (national greatness; elimination of corruption)	Vulgar, angry, divisive	Hostile
STATESMAN	Reason, interest, values, positive emotions like solidarity	Public good	Virtuous, prudent	Expertise, experience, virtue	Concrete (tax reform, public health, etc.)	Technocratic, unifying	Respectful or reformist

The last column in the table is the most important. Demagogues almost always attack the dominant political and civic institutions, which they see as standing in the way of their own power and which they portray as elite-controlled institutions that arrogantly lord it over the public. Demagogues thus claim authority by virtue of a close connection with the people, while in fact dividing people by directing negative emotions—hate, anger, fear—against vulnerable groups like foreigners or a minority population. Because their ultimate goal is personal power and glory, they are unaffected by the scruples that most ordinary professional politicians have, and often they are not interested in policy specifics or do not have a coherent view of the world.

Demagoguery and populism have always been thought to be serious problems for democracy. The Founders tried to counter demagoguery by limiting the influence of ordinary people in political matters, but their efforts sparked a populist backlash. As we will see in chapters 2 and 3, out-of-power politicians courted ordinary people by promising them greater influence, expanding the franchise, and reforming the Electoral College, which eventually paved the way for Andrew Jackson, the only demagogic president before Trump. Jackson's presidency also produced the modern two-party system, which was co-opted by a new generation of elites and led to another round of populist criticism. Talk of demagoguery reflects a basic anxiety about the stability of democracy.

The term's overuse is also readily explained. In any great political contest, the losers are apt to blame their loss on the other side's demagoguery. After all, if the losers are sure of their political convictions, but the majority of the people reject them, then a ready explanation is that the people were led astray by the charismatic demagogues on the other side. Thus, liberals are sometimes tempted to label anyone who does not promote liberal values a demagogue, and this posture is mirrored by other ideological groups as well. This temptation must be resisted: demagoguery is foremost a problem for democracy, not merely an epithet to be flung at ideological opponents.

The view of demagoguery and populism I have described can be contrasted to a more extreme view: that the people are hopelessly ignorant, unable to know their own interests, unable to organize, and unable to recognize good leadership. A popular leader is thus always a "demagogue," so when the public enthusiastically supports someone, we should always be skeptical. This idea can be traced all the way back to Plato, a critic of democracy, who believed that the masses were easily swayed by rhetoric delivered by a charismatic rabble-rouser. In a famous parable, he writes of a crew that mutinies against the ship's captain. Every sailor "is of opinion that he has a right to steer, though he has never learned the art of navigation and cannot tell who taught him or when he learned, and will further assert that it cannot be taught, and they are ready to cut in pieces anyone who says the contrary." Once they gain control of the ship, they "make free with the stores; thus, eating and drinking, they proceed on their voyage in such a manner as might be expected of them." Lurking in the background is the demagogue:

> Him who is their partisan and cleverly aids them in their plot for getting the ship out of the captain's hands into their own . . . , they compliment with the name of sailor, pilot, able seaman, and abuse the other sort of man, whom they call a good-for-nothing; but that the true pilot must pay attention to the year and seasons and sky and stars and winds, and whatever else belongs to his art, if he intends to be really qualified for the command of a ship, and that he must and will be the steerer, whether other people like or not—the possibility of this union of authority with the steerer's art has never seriously entered into their thoughts or been made part of their calling.[8]

Many other literary illustrations of the hazards of demagoguery exist. In Shakespeare's play *Julius Caesar*, Antony uses a few well-turned phrases in iambic pentameter to turn a crowd that had a moment earlier proclaimed its loyalty to his rival, Brutus.

The concept of demagoguery as I use it assumes that self-government is possible, and is vulnerable because the people are sometimes susceptible to demagoguery. Constitutional democracy thus depends on a knife-edge view that people can be trusted sometimes to act in their interest but not all the time. In this view, demagoguery poses a challenge to democracy and, echoing Plato, questions whether democracy can survive its assault.

Constitutional democracy may also be challenged from above. The idea that the "elites" may seize control of government and rule in their own interest at the expense of the people is as old as democracy itself. Democratic forms are maintained—eligible people can vote, for example—but political outcomes are not determined by the people. In the past, a chronic fear was that a landed aristocracy would bribe and manipulate popular leaders. Today, the anxiety is that government officials—elected politicians, bureaucrats, judges—are either entirely unconstrained and maintain power without paying much attention to the public, or are controlled by outside groups. The populist Left fears that the government is controlled by finance and big business. "Let us wage a moral and political war against the billionaires and corporate leaders, on Wall Street and elsewhere, whose policies and greed are destroying the middle class of America," says Bernie Sanders.[9] The populist Right fears that the government is controlled by a "deep state" of liberals, cosmopolitans, and minorities.

The potency of anti-elite sentiment can scarcely be exaggerated. Ordinary people resent the suggestion that they need to be governed by a superior body of people (even if this superiority is entirely based on educational and professional accomplishments that qualify them for policymaking authority, rather than the old criteria of blood and wealth). Politicians know this. While today anti-elite rhetoric is more closely associated with the conservative political movement than with liberalism, that has not always been the case. Today, liberalism is on the defensive because of its association with elite control of government bureaucracy.

But not even conservatives really want to demolish elite institutions. They want to replace liberal control with conservative control, or elite-dominated public institutions with elite-dominated private institutions like the church. Hence the enthusiasm in conservative circles for programs like school vouchers, which would allow parents to move children from government-run public schools to religious or secular private schools, and the long-standing belief that business leaders (typically, these days, graduates of Ivy League business schools) should run the government. But the populist rhetoric resonates with the public and hence has proven irresistible even to conservatives who would not be seen dead at a tractor pull.

Still, the idea that elite control of the government has led to policies that harm the public interest is not confined to the right. Some liberals and others on the left have taken up this view as well. When Elizabeth Warren says "the system is rigged," she's quoting Trump. Unfortunately, it is extremely difficult to evaluate this claim. A study from a few years back found that "economic elites" have more influence on government policy than ordinary people do. This study actually suggests a story of control by the wealthy rather than by intellectuals or bureaucrats, as the authors define "economic elites" to mean citizens above the ninetieth percentile of income. But even if the study's conclusions can be generalized to all elites, or relevant subgroups, it does not prove elite control is excessive. To evaluate this claim, we would need to know what policy would look like if elites held less control, and no one knows.[10]

But my goal is not to ask whether "elite control" or "popular control" is better for democracy in the United States. My goal is to ask whether the "demagogue" is a meaningful political category, rather than simply a term we assign to politicians we don't like, as Arnold argues. My conclusion is that it is—the ancients got it right. It is a style of political action that—independent of the demagogue's agenda—poses a threat to democracy and effective government. If the American president is a demagogue, the country faces a constitutional problem, well beyond the ordinary turmoil of acceptable politics.

1

THE FOUNDERS' VISION OF ELITE GOVERNANCE

(1774–1797)

History will teach us . . . that of those men who have over-turned the liberties of republics, the greatest number have begun their career by paying an obsequious court to the people; commencing demagogues, and ending tyrants.

—ALEXANDER HAMILTON, *FEDERALIST 1*

In the summer of 1787, the newly independent American states were in shambles. The national government could not protect its territorial borders, which remained vulnerable to hostile Indian tribes, the British, and two other empires, Spain and France. It could not pay its debts. It could not build roads and canals. It could not put down rebellions except with difficulty, as an uprising led by Daniel Shays in Massachusetts had just revealed. It could not protect diplomats or foreign travelers or American shipping.

The nation, as it stood, was ungovernable.

Under the Articles of Confederation, which the states had ratified in 1781, the national government, which consisted entirely of a Congress made up of delegates from the thirteen states, could get little done. It lacked a powerful executive to enforce the law, represent the government overseas, and lead the nation in war. It lacked a federal court system. The states could rarely agree with each other, and since the Articles of Confederation required them to act with a large majority or unanimously, Congress was frequently unable to act—even in the most pressing circumstances.

Fifty-five Americans met in Philadelphia to hash out a new Constitution. George Washington, the Revolutionary War hero, presided, but the leading figure was James Madison, a Virginia delegate who would later serve as the country's fourth president. Other luminaries included Alexander Hamilton (New York), Benjamin Franklin (Pennsylvania), George Mason (Virginia), Gouverneur Morris (Pennsylvania), and James Wilson (Pennsylvania). John Adams and Thomas Jefferson, serving overseas, were not present but later played a vital role in the development of the constitutional system.

Americans worship the Founding Fathers. Today's lawyers and judges look to their work for solutions to our constitutional problems, as if the Founders had left coded messages for posterity, and their biographies regularly top the bestseller lists. The Founders, or most of them, were impressive people. They were highly educated, deeply learned, experienced in politics and business, devoted to their new country, and, in some cases, touched by genius. Thomas Jefferson, for example, was a scientist, architect, and inventor (as well as the author of the Declaration of Independence and third president of the United States). No other generation of politicians in American history can match their achievements.

But they were not saints and, brilliance aside, were hardly infallible. As commander of the Revolutionary army, Washington was more lucky than talented. Franklin had made significant contributions to the scientific understanding of electricity and is known for several inventions (the lightning rod, bifocals, and the Franklin stove among them). But during the ratification debates, he was in his eighties and long past his prime. Hamilton would later be blackmailed after conducting an extramarital affair and then died prematurely in a senseless duel with then-sitting Vice President Aaron Burr. Adams's presidency would be a failure; Jefferson would serve a disastrous term as governor of Virginia. Most of the Founders were extremely wealthy, and their own interests were not far from their deliberations. The southerners among them owned slaves, mostly knowing slavery was wrong but unwilling to sacrifice their luxurious lifestyles to correct injustice. Washington, one of the richest presidents in American history, freed his slaves only on his deathbed. Jefferson, one of history's most eloquent defenders of human freedom, denounced slavery and signed a bill to outlaw the import and export of slaves but nonetheless kept hundreds of slaves on his plantation and in the White House. He sired children with Sally Hemings, whom he owned, and freed only a handful of slaves over his lifetime.

These men did not agree on very much—none was very happy with the Constitution they produced, each believing it full of flaws—but they were willing to compromise. After ratification, they quickly divided into factions and quarreled over the spoils of power. Hamilton and Jefferson became enemies. Jefferson and Madison despaired when Washington fell under Hamilton's influence. The unlikely friendship between the tall, aristocratic

Jefferson and the short, rotund Adams collapsed. Hamilton, brilliant but arrogant, would eventually repel even his own allies, like Adams. Their views about the meaning of the Constitution shifted with the political winds, often based on no principle other than political expediency.

Still, we need to take seriously their opinions and accomplishments. We inherit the Constitution they created, and their decisions continue to influence our own politics.

What is the nature of this inheritance? It is common to say that the Founders created a "democracy." But most of the Founders would have blanched at the term. It is true that they rejected the systems that today we contrast with democracy—monarchy, dictatorship, aristocracy. They had committed themselves earlier on, during the Revolution, to the principle of popular sovereignty—the people rule. As they wrote in the Declaration of Independence, "All men are created equal . . . ; Governments are instituted among Men, deriving their just powers from the consent of the governed." The Founders complained that the American colonies lacked representation in the British Parliament, so it was natural to acknowledge that Americans—"We the People," as the Constitution says—were entitled to representation in the new government. Moreover, popular sovereignty was a rallying cry, used to persuade the common people to take up arms against the hated imperialists.

However, the Founders did not want to create a democracy, as the term was understood at the time. "Democracy" meant rule of the common people, or mob rule. Athens' democratic institutions produced its disastrous defeat by Sparta in the Peloponnesian War. Democracy in Athens and other Greek city-states meant incessant turmoil, frequently leading to wars and cycles of authoritarian rule. John Adams noted in a letter to John Taylor, a leading political theorist, that "the Athenians grew more and more Warlike in proportion as the Commonwealth became more democratic. I need not enumerate to you, the foolish Wars into which the People forced their wisest Men and ablest Generals against their own Judgments, by which the State was finally ruined, and Phillip and Alexander, became their Masters." It was also democracy that gave power to demagogues who undermined the ancient Roman Republic. Adams observed with typical gloominess, "Remember, democracy never lasts long. It soon wastes, exhausts, and murders itself. There is never a democracy that did not commit suicide." Even Madison agreed that "democracies have ever been spectacles of turbulence and contention; have ever been found incompatible with personal security or the rights of property; and have in general been as short in their lives as they have been violent in their deaths." He worriedly observed the tendencies toward democracy in the failing experiments of self-governance in the American states.[1]

What was wrong with "democracy"—rule by the people? Drawing on classical history, the great English political theorist Thomas Hobbes, writing toward the end of the English Civil War in the mid-seventeenth century, argued that democracy was inherently unstable because it incites competition for power among the people. Hobbes's amusing portrayal of legislative assemblies as "a triall of wits" among the "Eloquent" before people who are largely ignorant of public affairs, one that "breeds that most destructive of human characteristics, proclivity to the profitless contentions that vain-glory engenders," would have struck a nerve with the Founders. Most Americans in 1787 received little or no formal schooling, lived in remote villages and on isolated farms, believed in religious dogmas that had been debunked by the scientific revolution and Enlightenment philosophy, and lacked access to newspapers or books that provided adequate information about the wider world. As the historian Richard Beeman explains, most newspapers of the time were about four pages long. At least two of those pages were devoted to advertisements for fabrics, furnishings, ship passage, servants, and land. The others might contain poems, public announcements, and a bit of news—not always accurate. As a result, ordinary people knew next to nothing about foreign affairs, or even conditions in the neighboring state. And they knew even less about how economic and political institutions functioned.[2]

Most ordinary people were dependent on others for their livelihoods, which meant that they lacked political independence. Living in tiny settlements, villages, and cities, they were vulnerable to the opinions of their neighbors. The ballot at the time was public, so it took significant character and independence to avoid the crushing local conformism that prevailed in most places. Moreover, as leading philosophers in France and Britain had demonstrated, there were paradoxes and problems of aggregation that could interfere with efforts to derive the public good from democratic voting even when people were informed.

The solution, as we shall see, was not to return to the ways of aristocracy but to ask the common people to delegate their political power to an elite class of gentlemen, from whose ranks would be drawn bureaucrats and elected officials. What about the risk that this class would govern selfishly rather than in the public interest? The people would retain a check—in the form of a limited right to vote and run for office—and certain unalienable rights. But policymaking would be carried out by the elite, or those with the education and training to make informed decisions.

The Founders did not invent democracy, or even create a democracy. Their accomplishment was to create a lasting system of government that combined elements of democracy and elite rule. The elites would govern, but ordinary people would retain a residual power to check them if they ruled badly.

Or such was the theory.

THE CONSTITUTION

In the sticky heat of the Philadelphia summer, the delegates agreed that the new national government would need to be stronger than the existing government. Strong enough to put down internal rebellions, oppose foreign powers like Britain, France, and Spain, and protect the frontier from Indian tribes. Strong enough to knit together local economic systems into a national economy, protect American merchant shipping on the high seas, enforce tariffs, and finance roads and canals. Strong enough to protect religious dissenters and to resolve disputes among citizens and groups. Many of the Founders harbored visions of a great empire, while others hoped only to cultivate a virtuous citizenry. Nearly all of them agreed, however, that a powerful national government would play a vital role.

At the same time, they were worried that a national government could cause great harm. Majority rule could mean "tyranny of the majority" that ran roughshod over individual liberties or the interests of vulnerable groups. At the Constitutional Convention in Philadelphia, Madison pointed out that when debtors gained control of the Rhode Island legislature, they passed laws that blocked creditors from collecting on their debts. In other states, legislatures confiscated the property of people who had been loyal to Great Britain. These events showed that legislative control might be seized by a "faction" that used the government to advance its interest at the expense of the public.

The major source of division was economic. Southerners

wanted to preserve their slavery-based plantation economy. To advance commerce, northern merchants favored tariffs to protect manufacturing and internal improvements like canals. But tariffs would raise costs for southerners, who also did not see much to gain from internal improvements.[3]

As the debate proceeded, the now-familiar contours of our system emerged. The government would be divided into a legislature, an executive, and a judiciary—reflecting a widespread view of the period that a government divided into branches posed less of a threat to liberties. The legislature, or Congress, was given power over taxation, the budget, commerce, declarations of war, and much else. It was divided into a House and a Senate. The House would represent the common people, who were allowed to elect representatives who oversaw districts of roughly equal population. It was established to support the principle of popular sovereignty. But the Founders also worried that a powerful legislature dominated by the people might make foolish decisions. Thus, to counter the House, they conceived of a separate body, the Senate.

George Washington famously (and perhaps apocryphally) explained the Senate as a device for ensuring that transient popular enthusiasms did not produce bad law:

"Why did you pour that tea into your saucer?" asked Washington. "To cool it," said Jefferson. "Even so," responded Washington, "we pour legislation into the senatorial saucer to cool it."

Because senators enjoyed six-year terms, compared to the two-year terms of members of the House, they would not be as vulnerable to popular passions, or so the theory went. The senators differed in another respect: they were not elected by the people. (This remained true until the Seventeenth Amendment, ratified in 1913, which allowed the public to choose senators through the ballot.) They were instead chosen by state legislatures, which themselves were dominated by professional politicians and the merchant or planter classes in most states. (The planters were the wealthy plantation owners of the South.) The senators were meant to be drawn from a kind of aristocracy of experienced politicians, who would take a more deliberative approach to legislation and ensure that traditional institutions—above all, property rights, including (among southerners) rights to slave ownership—were respected. Because senatorial representation was not proportional to population, with each state entitled to two senators, the slave states could preserve their system even if southern members of Congress were outnumbered in the House.

The delegates reached consensus about Congress relatively quickly. They also agreed that a Supreme Court should lead a federal judiciary, and that federal law should prevail over state law. The delegates had more difficulty with the presidency. They started with radically different ideas. Roger Sherman, a delegate from Connecticut, argued that the executive should be a kind of clerk—"an institution for carrying the will of the Legislature into effect."[4] James Wilson, from Pennsylvania, forcefully advocated a powerful presidency that was independent of the legislature. The delegates debated whether the executive should be "plural"— meaning that a committee would preside over the executive branch, or that different components of it would be assigned to different officers—but abandoned the idea. Article 2, section 1 of the Constitution thus announces that "the executive power shall be vested in *a* President of the United States of America." But what exactly is "executive power"? The Founders did not define this term, and indeed went on to mention only a few of the president's powers: to command the army and navy, to make treaties (with Senate consent), and to appoint officers (also with Senate consent). Executive power included enforcement of the law, collection of taxes, expenditure of funds, and supervision of government employees, but the exact and even rough contours were highly ambiguous at the time. The Founders also imposed on the president a number of obligations: to report to Congress, to receive ambassadors, to "take care that the laws be faithfully executed." Elsewhere, the president was given the power to veto bills and issue pardons. Historians who have scoured the debate at the Constitutional Convention and other contemporary sources have found little to fill in the gaps.

This has led to wildly divergent interpretations of the presidency. At one extreme, the president is little more than a clerk who is charged with carrying out Congress's will, like a police chief or sheriff—albeit one commanding an army in times of war. An important figure, to be sure, but not someone with the authority to make policy, or a true leader of the country. At the opposite extreme, one could see him—and many did see him—as an "elective monarch." He would be only slightly less powerful than a king and, beholden to elections, be more accountable to the people. As Patrick Henry, the Virginia radical, put it, "Among other deformities, [the Constitution] has an awful squinting: it squints towards monarchy." Henry was one of a group of critics, known as Anti-Federalists, who opposed ratification of the Constitution. Many of them spoke in even blunter terms. One Anti-Federalist sneered, "The President-general, who is to be our king after this government is established, is vested with powers exceeding those of the most despotic monarch we know of in modern times."[5]

While Alexander Hamilton would go on to defend and

expand presidential power as secretary of the treasury during George Washington's administration, he took pains during the ratification debates to counter these objections by portraying the president as no more threatening than the governor of New York—and certainly a far cry from the British king. "What answer shall we give to those who would persuade us that things so unlike [namely, the US president and the British king] resemble each other? The same that ought to be given to those who tell us that a government, the whole power of which would be in the hands of the elective and periodical servants of the people, is an aristocracy, a monarchy, and a despotism." In Hamilton's view, the Anti-Federalists were raving.[6]

What accounts for such conflicting views of the American presidency? Two factors. The first was that the delegates disagreed about presidential powers, and also could not rely on a good historical model to help them envision the role. The great democracies and republics of the past, including Athens and Rome, mainly ruled through bodies of citizens to whom the officials or magistrates—chosen by lot or elected—were considered subordinate. The governors in the states were too weak; the king of England was too strong. (Actually, at the time, the British king, George III, was not very powerful, but other kings—the French king Louis XVI, for example—were.) The second was the presence of George Washington. So popular and highly respected was Washington, everyone knew that he would be the first president, including Washington himself. The delegates believed that Washington, once elected, would help define presidential powers, and thus were able to spare themselves the awkward task of debating the risks of a too-powerful chief magistrate in his presence.

Washington would indeed define the contours of the office. He established that the president would be the leading figure for determining foreign policy, and that he would exert considerable control over subordinates in the executive branch. But Washington was a special case. With a few exceptions, including Thomas Jefferson, Andrew Jackson, James Polk, and Abraham Lincoln, presidents were relatively weak and subordinate to Congress—until the twentieth century. Starting with Teddy Roosevelt, presidents amassed power to an extent unimaginable to the generation that conceived of the role.

THE ELITES, THE COMMONS, AND THE DEMAGOGUE

Educated people in America in the late eighteenth century were steeped in the classics. They read Homer, Sophocles, Plato, and the other great Greek poets, dramatists, and philosophers. They read Cicero, Seneca, Virgil, Catullus, and other great Roman poets and political thinkers. The Founders, especially so. At a tender age, eight or thereabouts, they began their studies of Latin and ancient Greek, which were literally beaten into them under the pedagogic methods of the time. The entrance examination at Harvard in the 1750s required applicants

> extempore to read, construe, and parse Tully, Virgil, or such like common classical authors, and to write Latin in prose, and to be skilled in making Latin verse, or at least in the rules of the Prosodia, and to read, construe, and parse ordinary Greek, as in the New Testament, Isocrates, or such like, and decline the paradigms of Greek nouns and verbs.

Adams, Madison, Hamilton, Jefferson, and other members of the founding generation kept reading the classics long after they completed their formal education; they drew inspiration from them and quoted them in letters, speeches, and pamphlets. They flung classical allusions at each other during the Philadelphia convention, quoted the classical authors in the ratifying debates, and kept at it long into retirement.[7]

The political models that the Founders admired came mainly from these texts. In contrast, the dominant form of political organization after antiquity was the monarchy. Monarchies came in many variations, some more appealing than others, but none could serve as a model for the US Constitution. The Founders were committed to Enlightenment principles, including political equality, which were incompatible with monarchy. Even constitutional monarchies, like Britain's, gave enormous power to a hereditary landed aristocracy, which could not be reconciled with American traditions of self-government.

To find inspiration for self-government, the Founders reached back further. Some city-states in Italy during the Renaissance enjoyed various forms of self-government. But the great example was the ancient Roman Republic, which was the greatest, most powerful civilization of antiquity and survived for five hundred years. Before Rome, ancient Greece provided more examples of powerful city-states in which self-government prevailed—above all, Athens, which ruled an empire and originated many of the political, philosophical, and cultural ideas of Western civilization. Classical myths, philosophy, and art inspired the founding generation. The architectural legacy of the ancients can be seen in the Founders' mansions, like Thomas Jefferson's Monticello, and the official buildings of Washington, DC, to this day.

It is no wonder, then, that the Founders and their critics not only cited the lessons of ancient civilization but donned classical monikers when they wrote pamphlets and newspaper articles. Hamilton, Madison, and John Jay wrote the *Federalist Papers* over the signature Publius. Others signed their names Brutus, Cato, Cicero, or Cincinnatus. Even their critics, the Anti-Federalists, frequently used classical pseudonyms. But their readings of ancient history were not entirely reassuring. All the great republics had, after all, collapsed into civil war, degenerated into anarchy or tyranny, or fallen to a conqueror—a fate that was never far from the minds of the Founders. They faced the formidable task of creating the first large-scale republic since Rome, and hoped to avoid the mistakes of their heroic predecessors, from Pericles to Cicero.

In diagnosing the failures of the classical republics, the Founders returned again and again to a single theme: the problem of factions. Ancient Athens was a democracy in which citizens met in an assembly and voted on all matters of public policy, and could even vote to put people to death or exile them from the city. But even a pure democracy like Athens needs leaders, and therein lies the problem. If democracy means self-rule, what is the role of the leader?

In 415 BC, a military fleet of over a hundred ships left Athens for Sicily. It would end in disaster, with the ships destroyed and nearly the entire force—thousands of soldiers—killed or captured. The Sicilian debacle was a turning point in the war between Athens and Sparta, and the great ancient Greek historian Thucydides blamed it firmly on the demagoguery of Athens' leading citizens. The trouble started with a conflict between two Sicilian city-states, Segesta and Selinus. Segesta sought help from its ally Athens. An Athenian general and political leader named Nicias offered wise advice to the Athenian assembly. He pointed out that the expedition would leave Athens poorly defended; that "the Sicilians, even if conquered, are too far off and too numerous to be ruled without difficulty"; that earlier victories had given the Athenians an unwarranted feeling of invincibility;

that many supporters of the expedition merely sought personal gain; and that skeptics of the expedition were worried that if they publicly opposed the mission they would be regarded as cowards and shunned by their fellow citizens.[8]

Nicias's words made a strong impression, but then Alcibiades arose to address the crowd. Thucydides informs us that Alcibiades was a sybarite who lived beyond his means and hoped to conquer Sicily so as "to gain in wealth and reputation by means of his success" resources he could use to pay his sizable debts and finance further disreputable adventures. Improbably, Alcibiades claimed that his own extravagance redounded to the glory of Athens, then painted an exceedingly optimistic picture of success. The crowd reveled in the imagined glories. The older men saw no possibility of disaster, while younger men "felt a longing for foreign sights and spectacles," and "the idea of the common people and the soldiery was to earn wages at the moment, and make conquests that would supply a never-ending fund of pay for the future."[9] Of course, the reader knows that disaster ensues.

Earlier in his great work, Thucydides described the character of Pericles, the leading citizen of Athens at the start of the war.

> Pericles indeed, by his rank, ability, and known integrity, was enabled to exercise an independent control over the multitude—in short, to lead them instead of being led by them; for as he never sought power by improper means, he was never compelled to flatter them, but, on the contrary, enjoyed so high an estimation that he could afford to anger them by contradiction.[10]

By contrast, his successors—including Alcibiades and a Trump-like merchant named Cleon—were "more on a level with one another, and each grasping at supremacy, they ended up committing even the conduct of state affairs to the whims of the multitude . . . , producing a host of blunders, and amongst them the Sicilian expedition."[11] While modern scholars have expressed some skepticism about Thucydides's account, which he may have used to settle scores with his enemies, the Founders did not benefit from modern scholarship, and in any event would have seen a moral that jibed with many other classical sources.

Athenian thinkers were pessimistic about the role of popular leaders in a democracy. Thucydides believed that Pericles was a great statesman because he could control the mob, but Thucydides also believed that Pericles was exceptional. Normal politicians like Cleon and Alcibiades were demagogues. They gained power by playing to the mob and then, dependent on the mob for their power, found that they could not defy it, which produced disastrous results. Plato was even more pessimistic about democracy. Appalled by the prosecution and execution of his great teacher, Socrates, who had offended the citizens of Athens by questioning their values and beliefs, Plato put no trust in the wisdom of the masses. For Plato, pretty much any popular leader in a democracy was a demagogue. Plato focused on the dangers of oratory, the way that the masses—undisciplined, often lacking in virtue, ignorant—could be easily deceived. Thus, Plato had little good to say even about Pericles. While Aristotle believed that in some conditions self-rule was possible, he also thought that the people, especially the poor, were susceptible to the lure of a demagogue, who could cause the polity to degenerate into mob rule.[12]

In ancient Rome, the danger of demagogues was ever present, and indeed a pattern developed. The Roman constitution gave most power to the aristocrats but some power to common people, who also exercised significant political power merely through their numbers—they controlled the streets in a city without police officers. From time to time, a leading figure of the aristocracy—often a successful military leader with great wealth and prestige—would seek power by presenting himself as a man of the people: a *populare* ("populist" in Latin). Lucius Sergius Catilina (also known as Catiline) came to power in just such a way. He was a Roman aristocrat who sought to overthrow the Roman Republic, at the time led by Cicero. While Cicero managed to thwart the Catiline conspiracy by tricking the leaders into revealing themselves and then having them strangled to death, it was a near thing. What was most troubling about Catiline was not that he was a traitor; it was that he was immensely popular among Roman citizens. Although an aristocrat from an ancient family, he amassed power by promising to cancel the debts of poor farmers and give land to veterans. What he really sought to do, at least according to the Roman historian Sallust, was to establish himself as a dictator.

Catiline was not the last demagogue to threaten the ancient Republic. Julius Caesar, another aristocrat and general, gained power by exploiting his prestige among his soldiers and other Roman citizens. He was a man of extraordinary talent, self-confidence, and intelligence. While in his teens or early twenties, he was kidnapped by pirates. Young Julius complained to them that the ransom they demanded was not commensurate with his stature and insisted that they raise it, while also promising that after his release he would hunt them down and kill them, which he did. Caesar would subsequently win a series of stunning military victories over Germanic tribes in Gaul, then ignited a civil war when he returned to Italy with part of his army in violation of the law. He swiftly defeated his enemies, including the great Roman general Pompey, and established himself as the leading figure in Rome. While under the constitution of the Roman Republic the major offices were supposed to rotate among leading citizens, usually on an annual basis, Caesar was able to consolidate power, becoming a king in all but name. Caesar possessed tremendous political gifts, an illustrious family, and a triumphant record of military conquest. But like Catiline and so many others before him, Caesar achieved power by presenting himself as the voice of ordinary people (despite his aristocratic origins) and in favor of redistributing wealth from the rich to the plebs. His attacks on the aristocracy to which he belonged, on behalf of commoners with whom he had nothing in common, followed by his elimination, once in power, of the Roman institutions through which those commoners exercised power, marked him as a demagogue in the eyes of the Founders. His assassination by Roman aristocrats who saw themselves as defenders of the republic led to another civil war, the collapse of the republic, and the emergence of a monarchy under Augustus.

What did these demagogues have in common, and what distinguished them from ordinary politicians? Don't all politicians tell lies and make promises that they can't keep? It may be tempting to take one of two extreme positions: that a demagogue is simply any politician in a democracy who causes harm to the public through misrule; or that a demagogue is a good politician who is called a demagogue by the political establishment because he sides with the people against them.

But there is a better view. What is special about demagogues is that they seek to exploit and undermine rather than work through established political and civic institutions. The recurrent theme in all discussions of demagogues from ancient times to the present is their willingness and ability to deceive and manipulate the public—to set people against one another, persuade them to act against their own interests, and put their trust in the demagogue rather than in more established leaders. While democracy depends on independent thought, reason, and commitment to compromise, the demagogue makes a religion of himself, inspiring slavish devotion. Thus, the essence of democracy—its reliance on the wisdom of the people—becomes its chief vulnerability.[13]

In seeking to divide society, demagogues often target the most vulnerable groups: foreigners, immigrants, and a whole host of racial, ethnic, and sexual minorities. They also target another minority, statistically speaking: the very wealthy and powerful. In ancient Rome, the major division was between the rich and the poor, but there were also related disputes over the rights of military veterans, farmers, and the urban masses. And while many politicians try to exploit "wedge issues," the demagogue is distinctive in claiming that the people on the other side of the issue are corrupt, subhuman, or otherwise lacking in political legitimacy. The demagogue is uncommitted to democratic (or what the Romans called "republican") institutions. The demagogue wants power above all else, and if he maximizes his own power by destroying democratic institutions, then so be it. In later eras, demagogues would target institutions that protect people's rights, like courts, and that offer sources of opposing power, such as the press, the civil service, the party system, and the legislature. Demagogues seek to obtain control over these institutions when they can, and to destroy them when they can't. By contrast, most politicians, whatever their ideology and however badly they want power, are willing to work within the system.

The demagogue was a problem unique to democracies and republics. The dominant political systems of the founding era— the hereditary monarchy or aristocracy—were vulnerable to tyranny but not vulnerable to demagoguery because ordinary people lacked political influence: they were denied the right to vote. While demagogues would usually cite legitimate grievances of the people, they came to power by exploiting crowd psychology and the public's general lack of sophistication. The Founders understood that most people knew little beyond their villages or farms, rarely venturing beyond their boundaries. Travel was difficult in an era before paved roads, railroads, and airplanes; most people sustained themselves by farming and trading within small communities. Even highly intelligent people in such circumstances are hard-pressed to recognize the words of a demagogue for what they are. Such people are still beguiled by lies and promises and stirred up by angry words. They are overly impressed by military exploits; they are charmed by charismatic leaders who flatter them. Nor do the people understand that power can be trusted only to leaders who are virtuous; or, if they do, they are not good at evaluating the virtue of a public figure from afar. There is a strong tendency in crowd psychology, visible even today, to worship the rich and the powerful, and even big men who promise an authoritarian solution to the frustrations of self-government. By contrast, the elites, whatever their own limitations and stupidities, are rarely impressed by claims by one of their own tribe to be a tribune for the common man.

This worried the Founders. George Washington's favorite play, Joseph Addison's *Cato: A Tragedy*, depicted the triumph of the demagogue Caesar and the collapse of the Roman Republic in lushly sentimental terms. Cato says of Caesar (to Caesar's envoy, Decius):

> Alas! thy dazzled eye
> Beholds this man in a false glaring light,
> Which conquest and success have thrown upon him;

Did'st thou but view him right, thou'dst see him black
With murder, treason, sacrilege, and crimes
That strike my soul with horror but to name them.

The Founders believed that Rome collapsed not (as so often argued at the time) because the Romans had ceased being virtuous but because the Roman constitution had become unbalanced, giving too much power to ordinary people, who were vulnerable to the wiles of demagogues. This is what Hamilton meant when he spoke of politicians "paying an obsequious court to the people; commencing demagogues, and ending tyrants." Or, as John Adams put it, "In Rome, from the time of Romulus to Julius Caesar, the commons were growing by degrees into power, gaining ground upon the patricians, inch by inch, until at last they quite overturned the balance, leaving all doors open to popular and ambitious men, who destroyed the wisest republic, and enslaved the noblest people, that ever entered on the stage of the world." To be sure, this wasn't some arcane feature of ancient republics. Wherever self-government was tried, demagogues came to power or disrupted politics. Consider the city-states of the Italian Renaissance, whose republican institutions collapsed one after another as the public threw its weight behind charismatic leaders, or the constitutional monarchy of Britain, which suffered through Oliver Cromwell's dictatorship in the seventeenth century.[14]

And in the years leading up to the Constitutional Convention, many leading figures thought they saw similar patterns in the American states where demagoguery led to political turmoil in legislatures. In many cases, ordinary people wanted legislatures to cancel their debts and redistribute property, and the legislatures were glad to accommodate them. Here was demagoguery again, but writ small: ordinary people, with poor manners and little

experience, persuaded their neighbors to elect them to a legislature, where they served the narrow, short-term interests of the
people who elected them at the expense of the public interest.
No economy can function if property and contract rights are
constantly being violated. The Founders saw in these actions the
threat of *legislative* tyranny, at the basis of which was a fear that
ordinary people, if given political power, may use it unwisely, and
possibly to devastating effect.[15]

Perhaps the most alarming example was Pennsylvania's radical system of government. In 1776, Pennsylvanians adopted a
new constitution that embodied the radical spirit of the Revolution. To avoid influence by any "aristocratic" elements, it gave
significant power to a unicameral legislature, which dominated
both the executive and the judiciary. A council, rather than a
governor, was given executive power. Property restrictions on the
franchise were abolished. Legislators were given one-year terms.
The idea was to give maximum power to the people by limiting
the ability of elites—lawyers, professional politicians, and admin-
istrators—to check legislation. Opponents feared that this constitution could only lead to anarchy, and local opposition, led by the
elites, ultimately undermined it.[16]

The last straw came on August 29, 1786, when several hundred armed farmers and townsfolk under the leadership of two
Revolutionary War veterans, Joseph Hines and Joel Billings, confronted three judges at the courthouse door in the western Massachusetts town of Northampton and blocked them from holding
judicial hearings. As the uprising spread, its leadership was taken
over by another veteran, Daniel Shays, and it became known
as Shays's Rebellion. The rebels were unhappy with the state's
baroque legal system, taxes, and the policies of an indifferent state

legislature that favored (in their view) the Boston elite. Shays had been a soldier in the Continental Army. His military background and his objections to tax and debt collection on behalf of ordinary people marked him out as a demagogue to authorities. It also made him a hero among many farmers and townspeople in western and southern Massachusetts. Few people were killed in the rebellion, which seems tame by modern standards. One likely apocryphal story tells of the rebels borrowing a yarn-beam from the loom of a Mrs. Perry, placing it on wheels, and directing this "cannon" at the approaching troops of the government, who fled in fright. Although the rebellion had petered out by the spring of 1787, Shays provided yet another example of the risks of demagogic leadership in a democracy.[17]

The political logic of demagoguery was simple, and it hasn't changed much. It depends on a class structure—a huge group of commoners and a tiny elite. In ancient Rome, the commoners were farmers, soldiers, tradesmen, manual laborers. The elites were wealthy people, or people with access to wealth through family connections—and very often military leaders. In the founding era, the commoners were also mainly farmers and urban laborers, while the elites were planters, merchants, professional politicians, financiers, and heirs to fortunes. Today, the commoners are the huge mass of the working class and low-level white-collar workers, while the elites are a varying mix of business leaders, media personalities, university professors, powerful lawyers, scientists, professional politicians, and the ultra-rich. In all cases, the demagogue seeks power by appealing to the masses. Usually, people are sensible enough to resist—that's why democracy has lasted as long as it has—but in times of hardship, the demagogue's appeal may be too powerful to overcome.

CONSTITUTIONAL SOLUTIONS

The conundrum before the founding generation was simply put: How do you create a democracy if you don't trust the masses? The answer is equally simple: you don't create a democracy. The Founders called their handiwork a "republic," and, like the Romans before them, they were careful to create a system that did not give too much power to ordinary people. "The grand secret of forming a good government, is, to put good men into the administration," observed a commentator of the time named Pelatiah Webster. Hamilton thought of government officers as "the guardians" of the interests of the people who can tell when "the interests of the people are at variance with their inclinations" and can act "to withstand the temporary delusion." Madison defended representative democracy by observing that the public good is less likely discerned by "the people themselves" than by "a chosen body of citizens, whose wisdom may best discern the true interest of their country, and whose patriotism and love of justice will be least likely to sacrifice it to temporary or partial considerations." That was one way to see it. Another was to observe that the effect of the Constitution was "to increase the influence, power and wealth of those who have it already," as John Quincy Adams put it. Most power would rest with the elites.[18]

To understand this idea, go back to ancient Greece. In Athens, rule by people—democracy—led the country into a ruinous war, made all the worse by the terrible decisions that were made about how to conduct it. It eventually became clear that the people made bad decisions for numerous reasons, but the most important was that they did not always understand the policy choices at hand, especially with respect to choices requiring military expertise. They frequently panicked, misinterpreted events, changed their minds, or ignored precedents and tradition while placing their faith in demagogues. This is just what Hamilton was referring to:

> It is a just observation, that the people commonly INTEND the PUBLIC GOOD. This often applies to their very errors. But their good sense would despise the adulator who should pretend that they always REASON RIGHT about the MEANS of promoting it. They know from experience that they sometimes err; and the wonder is that they so seldom err as they do, beset, as they continually are, by the wiles of parasites and sycophants, by the snares of the ambitious, the avaricious, the desperate, by the artifices of men who possess their confidence more than they deserve it, and of those who seek to possess rather than to deserve it.[19]

Writing in a newspaper, Hamilton was careful to attribute to the people his own view about the risks of the demagogue. But the meaning was plain enough. Greek thinkers disparaged democracy as mob rule and insisted that a successful polity required a balance between the common people and the aristocracy. This system came to be known as a "mixed constitution." Rome's celebrated constitution gave the aristocracy domination over the Senate, while reserving to the plebeians various offices like that of the tribune. The latter was also given a veto over legislation and other powers that were designed to protect the masses.

Under the British constitution at the time of the Glorious Revolution, which took place in 1688, the common people shared power with the aristocracy and a hereditary monarch. The masses were (at least in theory) represented in the House of Commons in Parliament, while the aristocracy wielded power in the House of Lords. The monarchy itself provided another balancing element, a source of stability while the Lords and Commons reached compromises over policy. The idea was partly to balance the interests of the people and the aristocrats, partly to ensure that the aristocrats—the most excellent and virtuous people, or so it was thought—would take the leading role in governance.

The Founders were children of the Enlightenment. Many of them were self-made and recalled from their early lives the sting of contempt for the masses among the upper class. Benjamin Franklin, for example, was apprenticed to a printer before running away and starting a business in Philadelphia. John Adams's father was a farmer and shoemaker. Alexander Hamilton was born out of wedlock, received a spotty education, and worked as a clerk for a merchant when he was a teenager. With financial help from friends and neighbors, he was later able to study for the bar and support himself as a lawyer. The Founders rejected a hereditary aristocracy, and most of them rejected monarchy. They tried, not always successfully, to shake off the eighteenth-century prejudice against common people—the "grazing multitude" (Washington), the "common herd" (Adams), the "unthinking populace" (Hamilton), the "hackneyed rascals of every country" (Jefferson). "A choice by the people themselves," Jefferson asserted, "is not generally distinguished for its wisdom."[20]

Yet they also believed that some people were more talented and virtuous than others, and certainly that some people were more educated and experienced than others. These people formed a social class, the gentry. They did not have superiors and enjoyed independence from the day-to-day duties of work. They could thus speak and act freely without obligation. This was the natural ruling class, the elite—"those who have received a liberal education" (Adams), the "aristocracy of virtue and talent" (Jefferson).[21]

The talented, virtuous, educated, experienced people should rule, albeit subject to a check from the common people. While the Founders did not have a very clear idea of who the elites were, they meant people like themselves: lawyers, merchants, planters—the highly educated and successful people of the day. The identity of the elites would change over time, but they would always compose the more influential members of society.

The Founders believed that the elite must rule but committed themselves to popular sovereignty. How to reconcile these commitments? The trick was to give ordinary people political power ("self-government") but ensure that they chose elites to rule them. Various institutions were put into place to ensure that the government could not be taken over by rabble-rousers or used in ways that advanced narrow political interests at the expense of the long-term good of the public.

One of the chief methods for ensuring elite control is now so familiar as to be invisible: the system of representative government, which resulted in the creation of a specialized class of politicians who would manage the government, along with an appointed judiciary with lifetime tenure. This was hardly inevitable. The Athenian assembly consisted of citizens who voted on all matters of policy and conducted trials. Officers were selected by lot and governed during limited terms. This was a form of direct democracy that lingers today in the United States in the watered-down form of popular referendum, which exists in some states but not at the federal level. The Roman system was less direct than the Athenian, but the Romans, too, relied on assemblies consisting of ordinary citizens to pass laws and adjudicate disputes. The Founders' system was a strongly representative system, without term limits, virtually guaranteeing that the legislature and the presidency would be held by specialized politicians, while the judiciary would become an aristocracy of distinguished lawyers.

This representative system was also not entirely representative: while the common people were allowed to elect public officials to serve in the House of Representatives, they were not allowed to elect senators. Senators would be selected by state legislatures. The state legislatures were staffed by professional politicians, most of them with significant political experience. These local elites would ensure that the senators in the national government were qualified, which meant being members of the elite themselves.

To ensure that the president would be drawn from the elites, the Founders invented the Electoral College. Today, many people are unhappy with the Electoral College because the distribution of electors favors less-populated states, enabling some candidates—such as George W. Bush and Donald Trump—to win the presidency despite losing the popular vote.

But there is another feature of the Electoral College that concerns us. The Founders did not trust the people to choose the president directly. As George Mason put it, "It would be as unnatural to refer the choice of a proper character for chief Magistrate to the people, as it would, to refer a trial of colours to a blind man. The extent of the Country renders it impossible that the people can have the requisite capacity to judge of the respective pretensions of the Candidates."[22] Unlike the system today, in which electors are required by state law to vote for the winner of the popular vote in the state, in the founding design the electors were to be selected for their wisdom and were expected to exercise discretion in choosing among presidential candidates.[23] The Electoral College system thus avoided putting excessive reliance on the wisdom of the common people. But citizens could be expected to identify the best people in their local community even if they could not evaluate presidential candidates. As Hamilton explained:

> It was equally desirable, that the immediate election [of the president] should be made by men most capable of analyzing the qualities adapted to the station, and acting under circumstances favorable to deliberation, and to a judicious combination of all the reasons and inducements which were proper to govern their choice. A small number of persons, selected by their fellow-citizens from the general mass, will be most likely to possess the information and discernment requisite to such complicated investigations.[24]

These grandees, being educated, experienced, and propertied, would find no attraction in a Catiline or a Caesar who sought power by promising to redistribute wealth. Worried that even the electors might be overawed or cowed by a dashing young military leader or a foreign usurper, the Founders also agreed that the president must be at least thirty-five years old and a natural-born citizen.

The Constitution also relied on property restrictions for the franchise, which were common in the states. They varied across location, but by 1790 only 60–70 percent of white men were eligible to vote, while women and slaves were disenfranchised. The Founders were not entirely comfortable with the property restrictions, but it was possible to rationalize them. John Adams, for example, believed that people who are dependent on others are unable to exercise independent political choice, and thus should be denied the vote. This was a common view of the day among the elites. Madison, similarly, took a pragmatic view:

To restrain [the right to vote] to the land owners will in time exclude too great a portion of citizens; to extend it to all citizens without regard to property, or even to all who possess a pittance may throw too much power into hands which will either abuse it themselves or sell it to the rich who will abuse it.

However, many of the Founders, including Adams, also believed that property ownership would spread, and so eventually nearly everyone would be able to vote. In the Philadelphia debate, proposals for property restrictions were rejected by the majority as inconsistent with the prevailing democratic ethos of the time, but no effort was made to overrule the restrictions in state law.[25]

The Electoral College, along with the state franchise restrictions and other requirements, composed the major guarantee of elite rule and constitutional barrier against the demagogue. The Founders also hoped that the separation of powers would work against a demagogue who managed to achieve the presidency. The president, after all, can rule only with the support of Congress, which makes the law and supplies the budget. Congress was also given the power to impeach the president, and the courts could rule against him if he violated the liberties of citizens. So a president who obtained power through demagoguery would be, in theory, restrained from using that power to harm the public. But this idea was a fraught one, as it was in tension with the goal of creating an effective president in the first place.

COUNTERATTACK

The Founders' commitment to elite rule was also their major vulnerability in the ratification debates. The Anti-Federalists argued that the Constitution would create a governing elite or aristocracy that acts in its own interest and disregards the well-being of the common person. Commenting on the proposed Congress, an Anti-Federalist who called himself the Federal Farmer complained:

> The people of this country, in one sense, may all be democratic; but if we make the proper distinction between the few men of wealth and abilities, and consider them, as we ought, as the natural aristocracy of the country, and the great body of the people, the middle and lower classes, as the democracy, this federal representative branch will have but very little democracy in it. Even this small representation [in the House of Representatives] is not secured on proper principles.[26]

Another Anti-Federalist, this time a fellow who called himself Montezuma, put the matter more starkly, sardonically observing:

> In fine, this plebian house [the House of Representatives] will have little power, and that little will be rightly shaped by our house of gentlemen [the Senate], who will have a very extensive influence, from their being chosen out of our genteeler class, and their appointment being almost a life.[27]

Writing under the pseudonym Publius, Madison argued that the Senate was necessary for various reasons of abstract public policy. It gave representation to the states, composed a repository of political wisdom, and ensured that members of Congress would not be carried away by "sudden and violent passions." But privately Madison said the Senate was needed to protect landowners from the redistributive impulses of the masses. No one was really fooled. The Senate was to be an aristocratic body composed of the elites, like its Roman namesake. To forestall the worst objections, the Founders gave the House alone the power to originate money bills.[28]

The trouble was partly due to disagreement about the nature of elite rule. For the Founders, nothing could be more obvious than that educated, experienced people should lead the government. Madison had attended the College of New Jersey (now Princeton), while Adams had attended Harvard. Washington, Jefferson, and James Monroe attended the College of William and Mary. Jefferson was so proud that he had founded the University of Virginia that he had this accomplishment carved into his gravestone (which also mentioned his authorship of the Declaration of Independence but omitted his presidency). Yet university education at the time was available to only a handful of people. Many of the Founders were lawyers, and it was widely accepted that only someone who undergoes intense training should practice law. Because Congress makes law and courts interpret law, it would hardly be surprising if many of the most powerful government officials were trained lawyers rather than farmers and laborers. Running a business or a plantation also required significant experience (even if not a formal education), and it made as little sense for a messenger or road worker to run the government as it would for them to head a bank. Similarly, how could one participate in government if one knew nothing of Pericles, Cicero, and Cato?

The Anti-Federalists saw all this as a ruse. The simple premise—that educated and experienced people should rule—seemed always to lead to the conclusion that old and wealthy families should rule. As Adams acknowledged in 1787, "Gentlemen will ordinarily, notwithstanding some exceptions to the rule, be the richer, and born of more noted families." The logic may be familiar.

Wealthy families have the means to educate their children that poor families lack. The children of wealthy families also enjoy social connections that double as political advantages. Wealthy people, once in power, govern in ways that favor their own class. And then, sooner or later, as illustrated by Adams's remark, the political class rationalizes its dominance by claiming to be of superior stock.[29]

This is not to say that the Anti-Federalists were modern-day egalitarians. Many of them agreed with the Founders that an elite—a "natural aristocracy," as it was sometimes called—was inevitable. Many of them believed that the best defense against mass rule was state sovereignty, which allowed control by a *local* aristocracy. Anti-Federalism, in this respect, should be understood as simply localism. Madison's theory that a large republic could control factions was an ingenious effort to turn this traditional view on its head.[30]

But anti-elitism played a large role in Anti-Federalist thought, and especially among the common folk who were not even local elites but middling farmers and traders. These Anti-Federalists objected to a Constitution that gave the natural aristocracy special political and legal advantages (in effect, if not formally). They distrusted the elites, who could use their power to advance their interests at the expense of the people. And there was considerable resentment toward a group that may have not deserved its status. As one anti-Federalist put it:

> If any person is so stupidly dull as not to discern who
> these few [the aristocracy] are, I would refer such to nature
> herself for information. Let them observe her ways and
> be wise. Let them mark those men whom she has endued
> with the necessary qualifications of authority; such as

the dictatorial air, the magisterial voice, the imperious tone, the haughty countenance, the lofty look, the majestic mien. Let them consider those who she hath taught to command with authority, but comply with disgust, to be fond of sway, but impatient with controul; to consider themselves as Gods and all the rest of mankind as two legged brutes.[31]

Hence the power of the Anti-Federalist critique.

While most Anti-Federalist thought veered toward localism—the view that the national government should be weak, and the states should retain most of their power—some Anti-Federalists did see advantages in a powerful president. As "A Farmer" argued:

The only remedy the ingenuity of man has discovered for this evil [that is, aristocracy] is a properly constituted and independent executive—a vindex injuriarum—an avenger of public wrongs; who with the assistance of the third estate [the House of Representatives] may enforce the rigor of equal law on those who are otherwise above the fear of punishment; and who may expose to public view and inquiry, those who screen their peculations under the sanction of office.[32]

In short, a powerful chief executive could serve the interests of the common people by opposing the elites in their stronghold in the Senate. What the author saw as the saving grace of the president was exactly what the Founders feared from a demagogue. We've come back around to the logic of a Catiline or a Caesar. It had not lost its power across the centuries.

Yet the founding-era debates did not focus on the risk that the president might become a dictator—which came to be known as "Caesarism"—though the issue was not far from anyone's mind. The Anti-Federalists obsessed about the risk that the Constitution would establish aristocratic government, but their focus was on the Senate. Given America's weak international position, the failure of Pennsylvania's constitution, Shays's Rebellion, and all the other forces of disorder, the proponents of the Constitution ultimately prevailed. Rather than replace the British landed aristocracy with a radical democracy, the Founders created a "natural aristocracy" of "virtue and talents," as Jefferson called it: rule by the elite.

WHY THE ELITES PREVAILED OVER THE POPULISTS IN THE FOUNDING ERA

In approaching constitutional reform, the Founders faced a paradox. They had established the nation based on the principle of popular sovereignty, but they did not believe that the masses could govern, at least not in a direct way. Most of the Founders not only believed but assumed that the elite political class would continue to govern as it always had. But they needed to reconcile their commitment to elite rule with the principle of popular sovereignty, which was the ideological basis of the Revolution and had seized the imagination of the masses.

The solution took two forms. First, the Founders redefined elite rule as "rule by the most talented" rather than "rule by a hereditary aristocracy." This was an easy step to take, so easy that its importance is frequently overlooked. But this step was politically significant because it amounted to a promise to the masses that they or their children could ascend to the political class if they possessed enough talent. A route to political power was thus opened up to the general public, which helped reconcile ordinary people to the less democratic features of the Constitution.

Second, the Founders built into the Constitution numerous bulwarks against populist rule—or, what amounts to the same thing, commitments to elite (talented) dominance. As we have seen, the Founders assumed that only members of the elite would be elected to the Senate and to the presidency. Local elites who dominated government in the states would decide on senators and presidents. Legal and bureaucratic elites would staff the major judicial and executive offices in the government. Ordinary people would exert a check on elite government through their influence on the House of Representatives. But given franchise restrictions, the better sort of ordinary people would play a greater role than others.

The system thus fell between aristocracy and democracy. The Constitution was really a "mixed constitution" of the sort advocated by the ancient Greeks and Romans, one that tried to reconcile the interests of different classes of people while giving leadership to those considered most worthy. The major difference between the Founders and their predecessors in Greece, Rome, and even Britain is that the Founders (or most of them) saw class more fluidly. The elite class was based on talent rather than on social connections; the children of today's elite would not necessarily be the elites of tomorrow. The Anti-Federalists opposed ratification because they believed that the Constitution gave too much power to the elites, an aristocracy in different clothes. Some Anti-Federalists believed that the elite class would entrench itself; others believed that this exclusive club, whatever its membership, would always serve itself over the interests of the common people. Why was this iteration of the Constitution ratified, then? Let's consider the reasons.

First, the proponents of the new Constitution—and above all

George Washington—enjoyed immense prestige because of their role as victors in the Revolutionary War. Their support for the Constitution and their ideas more broadly were taken very seriously.

Second, proponents of the Constitution benefited from natural political and organizational advantages. The country seemed to agree that the Articles of Confederation were a failure. During the ratification debates, even reasonable dissent provoked a ferocious response in many places. After an anonymous author writing in the Philadelphia *Freeman's Journal* complained about some rather minor provisions in the Constitution—for instance, the proportion of representatives to the population—an eighteenth-century version of an internet troll suggested in the *Independent Gazetteer* that this "Antifederalist" be "honor[ed] with a coat of TAR and FEATHERS."[33] Yet even the first author thought the Constitution should be ratified! Both believed that the country was in crisis and that something needed to be done. If the Philadelphia Constitution was not ratified, then it would be back to the drawing board.

Moreover, because the Constitution was the handiwork of members of the political class, they could draw on all their resources to support it: existing relationships of patronage and power, control of the state legislatures, and dominance over the newspapers. And the political class happened to include a number of brilliant people, among them Hamilton and Madison, who took the lead in organization and intellectual support. Advocates of a strong national government initiated the Philadelphia convention and dominated its membership. The opposition was scattered and disorganized. And yet the political class was flexible enough to accommodate its critics. One of the major objections was the absence of a bill of rights. At the Massachusetts convention, where a fistfight broke out between two delegates, ratification was made conditional on proposed amendments that guaranteed certain rights. Other states soon followed suit. While Madison had opposed a bill of rights as unnecessary, unenforceable, and possibly mischievous, he reluctantly gave his consent. He would support it, as he grumpily explained at the first meeting of the House of Representatives, so that "our constituents may see we pay a proper attention to a subject they have very much at heart."[34]

Finally, while the nation firmly rejected hereditary aristocracy, it was not yet populist. Once it was agreed that the aristocracy was based on talent rather than birth, it seemed to follow that ordinary people should retain their habits of deference—albeit deference to the talented rather than deference to the well-born. Not everyone agreed with this, of course, but old habits die hard. The nation was not—at the time—populist in its political sensibility.[35]

The upshot of the elite victory of 1787 was elite rule for the next generation, accompanied—perhaps not surprisingly—by a level of excellence in the federal government administration that was envied by the most advanced nations of the time. This accomplishment was not without controversy. A populist counterattack, which we will discuss in the next chapter, was under way by the 1790s. But it was beaten back—or, more precisely, quickly absorbed and manipulated—by a new elite led by Thomas Jefferson.

2

THE ANTI-ELITE BACKLASH OF
JEFFERSONIAN DEMOCRACY

(1797–1809)

The danger to be apprehended, as all past history teaches us, in governments resting in all their parts on universal suffrage, is the spirit of faction, and the influence of active, ambitious, reckless, and unprincipled demagogues, combining, controlling, and abusing the popular voice for their own selfish purposes.

—JAMES KENT, *COMMENTARIES ON AMERICAN LAW* (1826)

WASHINGTON ENTERS OFFICE

George Washington's fledgling government faced many problems, but none greater than the national debt. The debt incurred by the Revolutionary government and the states had reached $80 million. Much of it consisted of notes given to soldiers as pay for their services and to merchants who had provisioned the troops.

The barely functional Continental Congress was plainly unable to guarantee that these debts would be repaid, and so many of the original recipients had sold them for a pittance to speculators. This also meant that the public credit of the new United States was in tatters. No one would lend to the national government if the country could not pay off its debts, and this would put the country in peril if war broke out again with Britain or any other great power. Nor could the government simply pay down the debt. Tax revenue, mostly from tariffs, amounted to only $2.8 million per year, not enough to pay interest on the debt. This meant that the principal would continue to grow indefinitely.[1]

To solve this problem, Hamilton, the secretary of the treasury, proposed a debt renegotiation with creditors that would guarantee payment—by earmarking tax revenues to debt service—on a nondiscriminatory basis (so that speculators were paid the same as soldiers who had kept their notes), albeit at a lower interest rate than most creditors had been promised. Madison, who believed that the speculators should not be rewarded, was outraged at the nondiscrimination provision, while others believed that the lower interest rate violated the contractual rights of the creditors. But Hamilton persevered. People would not buy government bonds unless they could resell them, and they would not be able to resell them if the buyers couldn't be sure that they would be paid in full. As for the other objection, the renegotiation would be voluntary. Any creditor could reject it.

The other aspect of Hamilton's plan was the assumption of state debts. While the states had done most of the borrowing, the federal government would repay their debts. Through assumption, Hamilton hoped both to improve the nation's credit by centralizing repayment, so that the federal government's growing credit among lenders would benefit the entire country, and to give the creditors—mostly, by this time, wealthy commercial interests—a stake in the survival of the national government. The Republicans were outraged. The plan would reward the profligate states at the expense of those that had responsibly serviced their debts. Worse, as Jefferson pointed out, the plan would give the elite commercial interests not only a stake in the survival of the federal government but an incentive to influence the federal government—with bribery if need be—so that it adopted policies that served the interests of the bond market rather than the values of the public. Hamilton further inflamed passions by proposing a national bank and a program of tariffs to spur industrial development.

With Washington's backing, Hamilton won these battles, and the nation greatly benefited. But the controversy left political scars. While Washington anticipated criticism, he was taken aback by its violent tone. Critics argued that the national government was growing too rapidly and becoming too powerful; that Washington's economic and financial programs benefited northeastern bankers and merchants at the expense of southern and western farmers; and that Washington's foreign policy favored the hated British over the French, America's former ally and heir to America's revolutionary spirit.

One of Washington's most strident critics, the Republican journalist and publisher Benjamin Franklin Bache (the grandson of Benjamin Franklin), launched his attacks shortly after Washington's reelection in 1792. One article, titled "Forerunners of Monarchy and Aristocracy," described the efforts by Washington to elevate the dignity of the government by holding ceremonies and bestowing titles on government employees, and argued that Washington acted like "the omnipotent director of a seraglio" or "as if he sat upon the throne of Industan." Another article stated that "the President began his political career as if he had inherited a kingdom, his port has been that of a Monarch, and the customs which he introduced are those of a Sovereign." And yet another: "Will not the world be led to conclude that the mask of political hypocrisy has been alike worn by a CAESAR, a CROMWELL and a WASHINGTON?" The verbal assaults on Washington's successor, John Adams, were even more ferocious. His chief tormentor, James Callender, a crony of Jefferson, pressed forward the notion that Adams, like Washington, sought to raise a monarchy from the infant republic.[2]

Callender's argument, though exaggerated, was based on some truth. Many of the Founders had supported a powerful presidency even before Washington took office. Hamilton had wanted to make the presidency a lifetime position, while Adams hoped to clothe the presidency in the trappings of royalty. Later, Adams tried to persuade Congress to bestow the title of "his Highness" on the president, and in a letter to a friend suggested "his Majesty." (Jefferson called Adams's aspiration "the most superlatively ridiculous thing I ever heard of.") While virtually all the Founders distrusted ordinary people, and harbored doubts about whether they could govern themselves, some of them, like Adams, incautiously made their views known to the public. Adams did not believe in hereditary aristocracy in the British sense, but he thought people were naturally talented or untalented and that the former group formed a kind of natural aristocracy. And because he thought that talented parents tended to raise talented children, if only because of the advantages of wealth and personal connections, his view—a belief in a kind of hereditary meritocracy—was not much different from the British version. For Adams, this natural division of society between the elites and commoners—natural because it would emerge even without the support of legal institutions—should be acknowledged not just implicitly in the design of political institutions but forthrightly in public discourse and in the theatrics of politics. In a book called *A Defence of the Constitutions of Government of the United States of America* and a series of newspaper articles, he criticized revolutionaries in France for abandoning that country's aristocratic traditions and establishing a new government on classically republican principles. Many observers understandably believed that Adams wanted to create an American aristocracy and to bring the US Constitution into line with the British mixed constitution, which he admired. Ceremony and protocol would express the superiority of the governing class and—at least in theory—instill habits of deference in everyone else.[3]

Sensibly, Washington resisted the calls for aristocratic forms of government. But he reasonably believed that even a republican government benefited from ceremonies and norms that would honor its officials and bestow dignity on its proceedings. This was all the ammunition that Bache and the other critics needed. Any effort to elevate the governing class could be presented as an aristocratic plot to downgrade the people.

By the end of his presidency, Washington bitterly complained he had never expected "that every act of my administration would be tortured, and the grossest, and most insidious mis-representations of them be made (by giving one side *only* of a subject, and that too in such exaggerated and indecent terms as could scarcely be applied to a Nero, a notorious defaulter, or even to a common pickpocket)."[4] Even more surprising to Washington, the opposition organized itself as a kind of party. Worse, this party was led by Washington's erstwhile allies Thomas Jefferson and James Madison, even though Jefferson was Washington's secretary of state for most of his first term. This nascent party would present itself as a populist alternative to the aristocratic party of Hamilton.

PARTY TIME

Early in Washington's presidency, divisions opened up in Congress and within the executive branch itself. A group of Anti-Federalists were elected to the First Congress and advanced a strict interpretation of the Constitution, especially with respect to executive power—even arguing that Congress lacked the power to authorize the president to designate a day for thanksgiving, which seemed European and monarchical to them. But the major issue was Hamilton's plan for the national government to assume the debts of the states, which the Anti-Federalists vigorously opposed. While Jefferson and Madison ultimately acquiesced to the assumption scheme, they were deeply troubled by it.[5]

With the conclusion of the First Congress, in 1791, Madison and Jefferson withdrew to lick their wounds. They had suffered significant political damage among their own constituents in Virginia, having underestimated southern opposition to the federal government's assumption of debts. They responded by adopting the rhetoric of the Anti-Federalists—an extraordinary volte-face for Madison, who had been the Constitution's major early proponent and an advocate of executive power, which he had helped advance as late as the just-concluded session of Congress. But Madison and Jefferson now believed that Hamilton was seeking to create a national government modeled on the British system, with a powerful executive supported by a financial elite. Having failed to influence the administration or prevail in Congress, Madison and Jefferson adjusted their tactics. They sought to create a political movement among officials and prominent people at the local level. These people, after all, could influence the national government by electing senators and the president himself and could influence existing national officeholders through the threat of withdrawing support for them in future elections. Madison and Jefferson thus embarked on a tour of Virginia and other parts of the country, seeking out these local dignitaries for consultation. A network of like-minded people was extended, strengthened, and infused with purpose.[6]

Opponents of the Hamiltonian policies became known variously as Jeffersonians, Republicans, Jeffersonian Republicans, or Democratic Republicans. (I will call them Republicans.) Meanwhile, Hamilton organized a Federalist Party to oppose this newly established Republican Party. Hamilton's Federalists were drawn from the merchant and financial elites concentrated in the Northeast.

The new party system cut across the entire apparatus of government, with lasting implications. In the Founders' earlier thinking, factions were fluid, often temporary and ill-defined groups that would reflect various interests and in a general way influence officeholders and voters from time to time. Instead, two parties emerged and ossified into apparently permanent institutions in which citizens invested their passions and loyalty. Factions would exert influence mainly through the parties, and the parties would exert influence through the officeholders, who were required to ally themselves with one or the other.

This meant that the Framers' imagined political relations between Congress and the executive did not materialize. Washington kept his distance from the Senate rather than working closely with it (as was contemplated by the constitutional obligation to obtain the "*advice* and consent" of the Senate on appointments and other matters). The more general notion that Congress and the executive would check each other gave way to a more complex idea, later expressed by political scientists as the distinction between unified government—when both houses and the presidency were controlled by the same party—and divided government. Unified government meant that there was no real check on the governing party, except possibly from the courts or public opinion. Divided government implied the possibility that the entire system could grind to a halt, unable to function.

Despite the novelty of the party system, the division between the Federalists and Republicans can be traced back centuries. In Britain, in the late seventeenth century, a cleavage had opened up between the "Court"—the king and his ministers—and the "Country." The Country consisted of the landed gentry, oriented toward agriculture, who feared that the king and his ministers used bribery and other forms of corruption to sway Parliament. The glitter and luxury of the Court were the obvious manifestations of this corruption, to be contrasted with the (supposed) simplicity and virtue of country ways. As commercialization and then industrialization proceeded through the eighteenth century, the Court was more and more associated with wealth, the corrupting effects of "new money," and the urban environment characterized by the extreme imbalance of wealth and poverty, with the poor living in moral and physical squalor and the rich corrupted by luxuries.[7]

The defenders of the Court did not really contest the moral and political premises of the Country but argued in terms of practicalities. Britain was an empire with vast commercial interests around the world, and it faced enormous military challenges. These exigencies called for a powerful executive, to counter the centrifugal tendencies of Parliament, and for a vast financial system, so that money could be quickly raised to fund war efforts. This in turn required the government to rely on the great merchants—where wealth was concentrated, it could be most easily borrowed—and hence to compensate them with monopolies and offices. So powerful were these arguments, and so successful was the British government in advancing British power and wealth, the Country view made little headway in that nation.

But the Country view was immensely influential in the American colonies. This view would feed into the ideology of the Revolution, which similarly accused the Crown of corruption and contrasted the commercial, oligarchic, military orientation of the empire with the simple, agricultural, republican purity of the colonies. Without a landed aristocracy and an inherited crown, it was easy for the newly freed states to put Country principles into practice. The states assigned political authority to democratic legislatures, which reflected dominant rural interests, and minimized the power of any executive authority.

Unfortunately for the colonists, these experiments failed. The initial remedy was supposed to be the Constitution itself, with its provision for a powerful national government led by a significant executive. But the Constitution was an abstract document. While the Anti-Federalists worried that it would re-create the sort of corrupt elite system that prevailed in Britain, their fears could be brushed aside. All this changed when Hamilton proposed his ambitious program.

Hamilton unerringly hit every sore point of the Country ideology. The Country feared a powerful executive; Hamilton sought to create one. The Country criticized vast national debt; Hamilton believed that a national debt would unify the country and grease the financial system. The Country hated monopolies, including the central bank, the Bank of England. Hamilton created the Bank of the United States, which was given a monopoly over national deposits. The Country favored agriculture; Hamilton's system of tariffs was designed to promote manufacturing at agriculture's expense. The Country opposed standing armies; Hamilton pushed for a permanent professional army that could be used, under the president's authority, to suppress rebellions, protect the country from invasion, and unify the nation. The list goes on. The underlying tension was the same. Hamilton believed, correctly, that a powerful national government was required to advance the security and prosperity of the nation. His critics believed, also correctly, that a strong national government can favor one interest over another and become a force of its own, seeking to maximize its power at the expense of individual liberty.

The major defect in Hamilton's program was that it was more oriented toward national greatness than toward the interests of particular groups and people—the people whose votes Federalists needed to retain power. His program was only popular in the Northeast. Hamilton needed to raise taxes to support his vision, and people, then as now, did not like paying taxes. Thus, the Republicans built their opposition through planters and farmers in the South and the middle of the country, whose interests were not being met. They opposed the centralization of power in the national government at the expense of the states, and the strengthening of the executive branch at the expense of Congress. Part of this opposition was happenstance: Republicans enjoyed more political power in Congress. But the president himself was moving toward accepting Hamilton's reforms.

To counter the Federalist policies of the national government, opponents organized. Partisan newspapers kept party members informed and coordinated political action, and attracted and persuaded others who might join or support a particular coalition. Madison and Jefferson persuaded a talented rogue, Philip Freneau, to edit the *National Gazette*, in 1791. Madison subsequently published a series of essays justifying the creation of the Republican Party, whose members were the "real friends of the Union," as opposed to the Federalist friends of monarchy.[8] This required quite vigorous backpedaling from his position in the Federalist Papers, in which Madison staked out the traditional anti-faction position. But the new political realities required it. With the national government in danger of falling under the control of financiers and monarchists, an opposition party was needed to save the Union.

Things quickly deteriorated. In 1792, Hamilton took advantage of the pro-administration sympathies of the *Gazette of the United States*, edited by John Fenno, to launch a counterattack against the Republicans. The divisions between Hamilton and the Republicans, exacerbated by military setbacks from the Indians, economic turmoil, and other reverses of Hamilton's program, burst out into the open. The friendly personal relations that allowed Hamilton and Madison to collaborate in the ratification debates were replaced by animosity. Hamilton and Jefferson became enemies. Jefferson fell out with vice president John Adams as well. In the towns, tensions between Republicans and Federalists sometimes broke out into violence. Washington was so distressed that he almost refused to run for reelection. The elections at the end of the year pitted candidates who increasingly identified themselves with the Hamiltonians or with the Republicans. Washington barely escaped being politically damaged by this battle, as his sympathy with the Federalist cause was widely known. Nonetheless, the electors again chose him unanimously.

Then, in 1793 and 1794, groups of men formed political associations, which came to be known as Democratic Societies or Democratic-Republican Societies. The first was apparently the German Republican Society, which formed in April 1793 in

Philadelphia. A few weeks later, the Democratic Society of Pennsylvania was created. Dozens more sprang up like mushrooms over the next year. These groups were inspired by the revolutionary events in France and promoted themselves as instruments for discussing political events, expressing patriotism, and advancing republican principles. They also reflected dissatisfaction with the policy choices of the Washington administration, especially Hamilton's financial system, and so took the character of opposition groups. These groups frequently allied themselves with the Republicans or were seen as Republican-dominated organizations.[9]

The Democratic Societies provide early examples of populist political organization. They were typically led by and composed of self-made men and other political outsiders, who sought to play a greater role—or any role—in the experiment in republican self-government. But for this reason they were viewed with skepticism not just by the elitist Federalists, who were predisposed to be suspicious of any opposition, but by Republican leaders as well. A Democratic Society in western Pennsylvania lent support to the Whiskey Rebellion in 1794, earning a rebuke from President Washington, who blamed Democratic Societies for stirring unrest. Also in 1794, the Democratic Societies unsuccessfully opposed the Jay Treaty, which normalized relations between the United States and Britain. By the end of the 1790s, they were a spent force, regarded as ineffectual and no longer dangerous to the elite-led opposing coalitions. But they also showed how popular enthusiasm could be channeled into political organization, and organization into influence—a process that would culminate in the party system.[10]

The significance of the party system for our story is that the party provided a mechanism for ordinary people to participate in politics. It forged links between public officials on whom ordinary people had leverage—members of the House, and state elected officials—and those on whom they lacked leverage, including the president and the senators. This is why the party system became a vehicle for mass democracy and therefore—as we will see in later chapters—a back door through which the demagogue, so carefully shut out of the political system by the Founders, could reenter it.

THE ALIEN AND SEDITION ACTS

By the end of George Washington's tenure in office, there were two well-defined parties. The Republicans by now had established a network of fellow travelers—opponents of the Hamiltonian policies of the Washington administration. Though Washington refused to join any party, the Federalist Party was effectively the party of the administration.

During the 1796 election campaign, the two parties advanced multiple candidates for president. On the Federalist side, the leading nominee was John Adams, Washington's vice president. On the Republican side, the leading nominee was Thomas Jefferson, Washington's former secretary of state. Former members of Democratic Societies and Republican officeholders and politicians formed Republican organizations to get out the vote. They used newspaper articles, handbills, petitions, and other materials to publicize the names of Republican electors and urge voters to support them. They printed ballots, held meetings, and gave speeches.[11] Adams won a majority of the electoral votes, and Jefferson came in a close second—which meant, under the rules of the time, that Adams was elected president and Jefferson was elected vice president. The Federalists gained a majority in the House and maintained their majority in the Senate. But the Republicans made deep inroads in state legislatures throughout the country. Formally a member of the Adams administration,

Jefferson maintained a low profile and worked behind the scenes against the Federalists.

While the Federalists were able to govern successfully for the first couple of years, they soon faced scrutiny over their foreign policy decisions. In the wake of the Jay Treaty, the French navy and French privateers had begun attacking American merchant ships. In 1798, after a failed effort to broker a diplomatic resolution, the Adams administration obtained authorization from Congress to construct a small navy and use military force against the French. (War was not formally declared; hence the hostilities were known as the "Quasi-War.")

Once at quasi-war, the Federalists saw Republican criticisms of the government as seditious rather than merely partisan, and really seditious rather than quasi-seditious. It was one thing to criticize the president for adopting tariffs that favored northern merchants. It was another to criticize the commander in chief while the cannons of French warships blasted away at American merchant ships, seizing or sinking thousands. Even more alarming, French refugees and other immigrants flooded into the country, along with Irish nationals who fled a thwarted rebellion in Ireland against the British. These foreigners—the Francophile French and the Anglophobe Irish—were natural allies of the Republicans. Many of the immigrants saw themselves as international revolutionaries and took part in Republican opposition to the policies of the Federalist national government. Government leaders believed that national unity was essential during times of war, even quasi-war. There was also concern that foreign revolutionaries would destabilize the country.

In 1798, Adams signed four laws known as the Alien and Sedition Acts. Three of the laws addressed the problem of French and Irish influence, and foreign influence more broadly. The

Alien Friends Act and the Alien Enemies Act gave the president the power to deport foreigners who posed a threat to national security. The Naturalization Act increased the length of time before foreigners who resided in the United States could be naturalized as American citizens. Although the laws were framed in neutral terms and reflected a genuine concern about national unity, they also advanced a partisan interest in limiting the support that the Republican Party received from immigrants and other foreigners.

The fourth law, the Sedition Act, generated the greatest controversy, as it made it a crime to publish or utter "any false, scandalous and malicious" statement about the US government, Congress, or the president or "to stir up sedition." The law applied to US citizens as well as foreigners and seemed to conflict with the recently adopted First Amendment, ratified in 1791, which prohibited Congress from "abridging the freedom of speech."

Today, this law seems like a shocking breach of the First Amendment. At the time, matters were more complicated. While the First Amendment loomed in the background, there was enormous controversy and confusion about what it meant and was supposed to do. The common law already recognized a crime of seditious libel, and common law actions had been brought against some agitators even before the Sedition Act was passed. It was commonly thought that the First Amendment did not abrogate common law sedition, which meant that the First Amendment permitted restrictions on subversive speech. Federalists argued that the First Amendment barred only the most extreme forms of censorship by Congress. When the Republicans took power in 1801, they allowed the Sedition Act to expire, but Jefferson himself did not object to continued state sedition prosecutions under the common law or state statutes.[12]

The Alien and Sedition Acts stirred up significant opposition in part because Republicans saw them, pretty accurately, as a partisan and ideological measure. The Federalists sought to deprive the Republicans of a position from which they could benefit politically—support for the still-popular French. And the Federalists sought to embed into law and the constitutional structure their vision of a powerful national government—with which the Republicans disagreed. Thus, the major justification for the law—the need for national unity at a time of (quasi-)war—seemed like a pretext. The Federalists were really targeting Republican political leaders, including officeholders in Congress, by prosecuting the press, which acted as their mouthpiece. Outraged, Jefferson and Madison (anonymously) drafted resolutions that were issued by the Virginia and Kentucky legislatures. These resolutions declared the laws unconstitutional.[13]

But this response initially failed. No other state legislature followed Kentucky and Virginia; indeed, most repudiated the resolutions because they implied that states could unilaterally disregard the Constitution—an explosive claim that would be made good sixty years later with the eruption of the Civil War. Over the remainder of the Adams administration, the national government brought fourteen indictments under the Sedition Act.[14] While the number of prosecutions was low, they were aimed for high impact—at the publishers of the major Republican newspapers, several of whom were tried, convicted, and punished with jail and fines. Some papers were forced to shut down. The Federalists hoped not only to silence their critics but to persuade the public that the Republicans were in fact seditious—that their support for the French threatened the nation.

But the prosecutions backfired. The trials gave Republicans

a platform for their views, enabling them to portray the national government as authoritarian; even more important, they exposed the Federalists as abusive, clumsy, and arrogant. Matthew Lyon, an obstreperous Republican businessman from Vermont who had finally been elected to Congress after numerous failed efforts, was convicted for, among other things, saying that Adams had "an unbounded thirst for ridiculous pomp." (Not a wholly inaccurate statement.) Fined and kept among common criminals in a freezing jail, he was reelected handily and became a Republican martyr. The government also indicted Bache (who died before his trial), who by then was editor of the *Philadelphia Aurora* newspaper, and then Bache's successor, William Duane. Callender was prosecuted, convicted, fined, and jailed. Many others followed. As the Quasi-War wound down, the national security argument lost much of its force, and the abusive and unfair nature of the prosecutions became apparent.[15]

While the episode is remembered as a kind of national referendum on the value of freedom of speech, or as the final blunder of the Federalists, it should also be understood as an early skirmish in the battle between the people and the elites. The Federalists made little effort to hide their continuing commitment to elite rule. From this standpoint, the rabble-rousing of the Republican newspapers fed into the age-old narrative about the collapse of republics. People like Bache and Callender were not contributing to public debate but, according to the Federalists, publishing lies—they were issuing propaganda on behalf of Republican demagogues waiting in the wings, propaganda to which ordinary people were alarmingly susceptible. The Sedition Act was a bulwark against mob rule.

To ordinary people, things looked different. All through the country, people protested the laws and marched and clamored for their repeal. A song written by someone who called himself "A Needy War-Worn Soldier" began:

I grub all the day so the well-born can feast
Tho' they can afford the enjoyment
Our rulers may feast on six dollars per day
the Poor must be taxed their extortion to pay
And if we do against them any thing say
They will trump a bill of sedition.

Opposition to the Sedition Act was not just partisan and ideological; it was populist. Freedom of the press was identified with popular freedom, restrictions on freedom of the press with elite rule.[16]

And so it was a kind of populism that defeated John Adams. Adams was a talented man with impeccable revolutionary credentials. Unlike Washington, however, he was too much of an intellectual to ignore the contradiction between elite rule and popular sovereignty that lay at the heart of the new constitutional system. He resolved it in his own mind simply by asserting—incautiously, in his public writings—that the elite must rule. And while his presidency was marked by caution and moderation, his writings, his attitudes, and a few of his policy decisions—notably his support for the Alien and Sedition Acts—allowed his opponents to characterize him as an elitist who sought to restore monarchy. This opened the way for a populist reaction, led improbably by Thomas Jefferson, whose tastes, pedigree, and circumstances were about as far from those of the common farmer or laborer as one could imagine at the time. But Jefferson was an eloquent spokesman for the common man, and at heart he was more of a democrat than Washington, Adams, and their Federalist colleagues. He believed—more than they did—that ordinary people could and should participate in all aspects of self-government.

JEFFERSON TAKES OVER

The hard-fought election of 1800 was a rematch between Adams and Jefferson. This time, Jefferson won. The Republican Party's triumph was decisive. As well as seizing the presidency, it obtained majorities in the House and Senate, which it never again relinquished to the Federalists.

But the election was hardly democratic. The major candidates were experienced politicians selected by the Republican and Federalist congressional caucuses. The caucus system was the device the party leaders used to maintain power: the members of Congress were themselves the highest-ranked party leaders, and they chose among themselves the presidential candidates. The Federalists chose Adams and Charles C. Pinckney for the presidency and vice presidency, respectively; the Republicans chose Jefferson and Aaron Burr. The electors—the leading local politicians—voted next. When Jefferson and Burr tied, the election was sent back to the House, which chose Jefferson. Although the general public followed the campaign closely, its influence on the electoral outcome was only indirect—as required by the constitutional design.

Nor was the election a vindication of the populist ethos that defined the Republican Party. While the Republicans argued that the Federalists were Anglophile elitists, their criticism was not that the Federalists supported rule by the elite. Rather, it was that the Federalists sought to create a corrupt system along the lines of the British monarchy, with an excessively powerful executive controlled by financial interests. Such a system would not serve the interests of the people, but that did not mean that the people themselves were capable of ruling, or that popular rule should replace elite rule.

Jefferson was not a populist; nor did he rule as one. He believed in equal political rights (for adult men), but hardly imagined that ordinary people could or should exercise power. "The mass of individuals composing the society," he thought, were "unqualified for the management of affairs requiring intelligence above the common level."[17] While Jefferson might have believed more people were qualified for government office than Hamilton or Adams did, there was still a limit, based on people's natural or cultivated talents. Madison was even more impatient with populist thinking.

In the arena of policy, Jefferson's presidency did not break with the Federalists, at least not dramatically. Jefferson governed from the center, so much so that his government spawned a renegade faction of Republicans, the Quids, who castigated Jefferson for abandoning Republican ideals. True, Jefferson pardoned or stopped prosecutions of Sedition Act defendants and obtained repeal of the naturalization law from Congress. And he eliminated the whiskey and other taxes that drove so many citizens into the arms of the Republicans in the first place. But Jefferson learned to appreciate the administrative advantages of the Hamiltonian system, and he continued the Federalist practice of appointing well-educated, experienced elites to the top offices.[18] He took forceful actions that were in line with Federalist ideals even if, for narrowly partisan reasons, some Federalists opposed them. Most dramatically, he engineered the Louisiana Purchase (overcoming his scruples in the process), which doubled the size of American territory. And he launched an attack on the Barbary pirates who were harassing American merchants in the Mediterranean.

He enthusiastically advanced the cause of Indian removal to the West, and he continued the Federalist policy of funding internal improvements, establishing a military academy at West Point, for example.

In foreign affairs, Jefferson sought to maintain a policy of neutrality between Britain and France. Here, he blundered by imposing an embargo on trade with the two countries in retaliation for their interference with American shipping as they fought each other on the high seas. The embargo proved disastrous to the United States: The nation rolled into a short depression. Notwithstanding, Jefferson's policies were moderate for the time and mostly popular—boosting the political stock of the Republican Party.[19]

It was in the realm of political theatrics, far more than policy, that President Jefferson attempted to reject the aristocratic vision of the Federalists. His inaugural parade in 1801 was a modest affair. Jefferson walked the short distance from the boardinghouse at which he stayed to the Capitol, surrounded by various officials as well as soldiers, instead of reclining in a fancy horse-drawn coach like Washington and Adams. He also broke from the nascent tradition of wearing a ceremonial sword.

While in office, he governed invisibly. He discontinued the practice of making the State of the Union Address in person before Congress, instead sending a written message, supposedly because he thought that a formal address would smell of monarchy. He gave only two major public speeches—the two inaugural addresses—and otherwise governed through correspondence and meetings, largely hidden from public view. He held dinner parties for government officials and visiting dignitaries in which, in contrast to European royal custom, he presented himself as a social equal. "Our philosophic President chooses to have his singularities as well as European kings—He prefers [common] shoe-strings, when other folks wear [aristocratic] buckles," sniffed a Federalist newspaper. He was known to dress shabbily when he met officials in the White House.[20]

Jefferson's style was not anti-elitist but anti-monarchical. Jefferson sought to distance himself from the Federalists (whom he called "monocrats"), who imitated the courtly practices of the monarchies in Europe because they believed that if the people were not awed by authority, they would not obey it. Jefferson possessed a better sense of the political realities in the United States. He did not believe that Americans wanted to see the president as a king and his subordinates as courtiers. It was Jefferson, after all, who wrote these words:

> But when a long train of abuses and usurpations, pursuing invariably the same Object evinces a design to reduce them under absolute Despotism, it is their right, it is their duty, to throw off such Government, and to provide new Guards for their future security.—Such has been the patient sufferance of these Colonies; and such is now the necessity which constrains them to alter their former Systems of Government. The history of the present King of Great Britain is a history of repeated injuries and usurpations, all having in direct object the establishment of an absolute Tyranny over these States.

The Declaration of Independence attacked the British king above all—not the British people, or even the British Parliament. There was no royal tradition in American politics, and one could not be initiated even if it were desirable. The style Jefferson affected was not, however, populist but republican. He was self-consciously recalling the ideals of the Revolution. He did not present himself as a common man but as an elite uncorrupted by ambition and the temptations of power. The republican ethos was one of simplicity, not ordinariness. To show that he was devoted to the good of the people, rather than to his own ambition, he avoided the pomp and extravagance of the European court. What distinguished the republican from the royal courtier as well as from the common person was his self-discipline, education, and devotion to the public good.

EROSION OF CONSTITUTIONAL BULWARKS AGAINST POPULISM

Jefferson is widely credited for advancing democracy—"Jeffersonian democracy"—against the Federalists' elitist system of governance.[21] While there is some truth to this view, it is also misleading. To see why, let us consider the perspective of the Federalists.

To the Federalists, Jefferson followed the demagogue's playbook, as spelled out by Caesar, Cromwell, and (most recently) Napoleon. A populist *avant la lettre*, Jefferson railed against the elites and establishment institutions and pandered to the masses by claiming to believe that ordinary people could govern themselves. Yet he clearly did not, as his own private correspondence revealed. Like any demagogue, albeit skillfully behind the scenes, Jefferson exploited popular unhappiness with the regime in power and stirred up unrest by giving support to polemicists and political opportunists, including newspapermen who defamed his opponents. Jefferson objected less to Federalist policies, which were badly needed at the time, than to the direction that Federalism seemed to lead. He worried that if the Federalists received credit for their accomplishments, their power would become entrenched.

That is why Jefferson dropped his constitutional objections to executive power, deployed so effectively against the Federalists, once he possessed it. Nor did Jefferson, once in power, take any concrete steps to advance the cause of democracy. He did not use his authority and influence to urge Congress or the states to relax franchise restrictions, for example, though he was personally opposed to them. He did not encourage political participation by the masses. As the historian Daniel Walker Howe observes, the Republican Party "benefited from, rather than fought for, the liberalization of the suffrage." And by destroying the Federalist Party, Jefferson ushered in decades of one-party rule. While Jefferson's reticent style of government could be praised for shunning the spectacle of monarchy, a leader who rarely appeared in person before the masses and sought to exercise influence behind the scenes, in meetings with elites, could hardly be called democratic in spirit.[22]

If this Federalist view is exaggerated, it is because Jefferson was not personally corrupt and, despite tensions with the initially Federalist-dominated judiciary and bureaucracy, did not try to undermine the institutional structure established by the Constitution. Nor did he boast, tell extravagant lies, or make promises he knew he could not keep. He led the country conscientiously and in good faith, in an effort to maintain broad support. If he used some demagogic tactics to gain power, he ruled according to republican principles as he understood them.

Democracy advanced during this period, but not because of Jefferson. The two major trends took place in the states. The first was the erosion of property requirements for suffrage. Under republican ideology, voting was not a right, as it is today. It was a privilege extended to those who possessed the wisdom and virtue that qualified them to exercise political power or a financial stake that they were entitled to defend. James Kent, a distinguished jurist, later made this point bluntly: "The danger in universal suffrage lay in 'active, ambitious, reckless, and unprincipled demagogues, combining, controlling, and abusing the popular voice for their own selfish purposes.'"[23] Only people who owned land, sometimes a substantial quantity of land, would be allowed to vote, as would people who paid taxes.

This view became harder to sustain after the Revolution. Common people served as both soldiers and victims of the war; they joined the crowds that harassed British soldiers. The view spread that these common people should be allowed to vote. A pragmatic consideration also played a role in the thinking of political leaders. If a large number of people were disenfranchised, they might become enemies of law and order. And, indeed, as economic inequality increased after the war, downwardly mobile voters lost the franchise as they fell short of the property or tax qualifications, angering and frustrating people who had become accustomed to exercising political influence. These groups and like-minded people pressured state legislatures to expand the franchise.

Meanwhile, the frontier areas offered the franchise as an incentive for settlement. Frontier governments sought settlers to buy land, pay taxes, and contribute to economic development. The right to vote gave settlers both dignity and political power that they were denied at home. This in turn put pressure on established states to expand the franchise so that they would not lose population to the frontiers. And political parties in both settled and frontier states realized that they could, while in power, entrench their position by offering the franchise to disenfranchised citizens who were likely to support them. These and other ideological and socioeconomic trends drove down property and tax requirements for white adult men in all the states, though the process would not complete itself until the second half of the nineteenth century.[24]

The second trend was the collapse of the Electoral College system. Remember that the Electoral College system ensured that the common people did *not* choose the president. The common people would be allowed to choose *other* people—the electors, who would choose the president. The Founders expected, or hoped anyway, that the people would elect local personages—wise and experienced local leaders—who would then, using their judgment and discretion, cast their votes among the candidates for the presidency. The people might express their preferences among the candidates in an informal way—in speeches in town halls, at rallies, or in letters to newspapers. But the electors were free to disregard the people's opinions.

That's not what happened. Almost immediately, people expected the electors to faithfully vote the people's choice. State governments realized that they could have more influence if they aggregated the votes of all their electors. If a state had, say, five electors, it would be much better if all five electors voted for the same candidate—the candidate preferred by the state as a whole—than if they split their votes among different candidates. Moreover, state governments did not see why they should trust the electors to select the best candidate. Given the prevailing democratic ethos, it was eventually decided that ordinary people should vote for the president. To evade the constitutional restrictions in the original Electoral College system, the states passed laws that required the electors to vote for the candidate who received the highest popular vote in elections conducted by the states.[25]

Yet the Jeffersonian elite maintained control. Jefferson and Madison established a system of one-party rule that would last a quarter century. Jefferson's successors were determined by the party leadership. Madison, Jefferson's secretary of state, succeeded his old friend in 1809. James Monroe, an early loyal supporter of Jefferson and later Madison's secretary of war and secretary of state, succeeded Madison in 1817. John Quincy Adams abandoned the Federalist Party in the early 1800s over its opposition to Jefferson's foreign policy and would later serve various roles in the Madison administration. He served as Monroe's secretary of state and succeeded Monroe to the presidency in 1825. Adams would be the last president of the First Party System. Learned, arrogant, and uncharismatic, he lost the electoral vote to the upstart Andrew Jackson. But Jackson failed to obtain a majority of electoral votes, so the contest was decided in the House, where Adams won after obtaining the support of another presidential candidate, Henry Clay. Jackson later blamed his loss on a "corrupt bargain" between Adams and Clay, a charge that most historians believe was unfair. But the larger truth was that the system was not set up to elect the candidate with the most popular support. Voters could block deeply unpopular candidates but could not select among the others. And so Jackson's loss seemed like a corrupt triumph of the elite political class over the people's candidate.

3

THE FIRST DEMAGOGUE: ANDREW JACKSON

(1824–1837)

He tramples on his personal enemies, whenever they cross his path, with a facility without example.

—ALEXIS DE TOCQUEVILLE, *DEMOCRACY*

IN AMERICA (1835)

Shortly after winning the presidential election, Donald Trump paid homage to Andrew Jackson by visiting his estate, the Hermitage, in Tennessee. The Hermitage, once a great plantation, is more than a thousand acres in size. The Greek Revival mansion where Jackson lived has become a museum. Jackson was not a man of the people, as popular imagination would have you believe, though he did suffer hardships in his childhood. Both of his parents had died by the time he was fourteen, and during the Revolutionary War, he was captured and beaten by British soldiers and nearly starved to death while he was held prisoner. But he benefited from the support of his wealthy extended family and enjoyed a successful career as a lawyer, planter, slave owner, businessman, and politician. He became famous as the military leader who won the Battle of New Orleans in 1815 and defeated Indian tribes and Spanish forces in Florida. He spent years involved in Tennessee politics and was elected to the US House and Senate. Yet he was celebrated as a "man of the people" in the run-up to his election as president in 1828. He was also a demagogue.

Jackson is regarded as one of the great presidents in American history. In presidential rankings by historians, he frequently lands in the top five to ten. Many historians credit Jackson with launching the age of mass democracy. In some history books, the chaos at the inauguration is depicted as a triumph of the common people, who may be rough and disorderly but are collectively wise and entitled to self-rule. However, not all the people who raided the White House at the inauguration were farmers and laborers. Many were office seekers who had come to demand their reward for supporting Jackson during the campaign. "The throng that pressed on the president before he was fairly in office, soliciting rewards in a manner so destitute of decency, and of respect for his character and office [was] among the most disgraceful reproaches to the character of our countrymen," said a Jackson supporter who witnessed the inauguration.[1] These office seekers were shoving the old elite out the doors and windows. Jackson was a beneficiary of the democratizing forces that predated his campaign, rather than their orchestrator. It was his lieutenant Martin Van Buren, a talented politician in his own right and Jackson's successor in the presidency, who perceived these changes and exploited them.

Historians point to other accomplishments, including Jackson's peaceful resolution of the nullification crisis, a dispute between the federal government and South Carolina that might have sparked a civil war three decades before the actual one. But it is the association between Jackson and democracy that has captured the historical imagination. For many historians, Jackson really was a "man of the people" who introduced a new age of popular participation in government. Inevitably, the man of the people becomes a man above the people—larger than life, the Hero of New Orleans. In the hands of the historian Jon Meacham, Jackson's personal defects—his coarseness, his violent temper, his impulsiveness—become both proof of his populist credentials and, paradoxically, proof of his greatness. Even talented historians are vulnerable to the lure of the demagogue.[2]

In many quarters, however, Jackson's reputation has taken a hit as social and political norms have evolved. But for his commitment to states' rights (he was not ideologically consistent), he would be what we call today a white Christian nationalist whose vision of mass democracy excluded Native Americans and African Americans, who were enslaved in the South and being gradually disenfranchised in the North. Before he was president, he had already shown a serious authoritarian and violent streak. He had fought duels and beaten his slaves. As a military leader, he violated his orders as well as constitutional norms—he jailed a federal judge who issued a writ of habeas corpus against him—and slaughtered Indians and foreigners who stood in his way. While his behavior horrified the political class, it thrilled the common people. "What seems to have enchanted people with General Jackson when he became a candidate for President," one historian observed, "was not any principles or policies he advocated but his breaches of decorum, real or alleged."[3] In running for president, Jackson employed the classic populist strategy of claiming that the government was corrupt. Jackson's aides and surrogates arranged the first popular presidential campaign, with songs, marches, and Old Hickory tchotchkes. Popular enthusiasm and popular involvement exceeded all records. Politics became a theater for the masses.

As Jackson was the first and only populist president before Trump, his presidency offers an opportunity to reflect on how populism operates in the arena of presidential politics, taking advantage of the emotional distance offered by the passage of time. Three points will emerge from the discussion. First, Jackson was able to win the presidency because by his time the original constitutional bulwarks against populist demagogues had eroded. Jackson and his aides took advantage of the fluid political atmosphere caused by the decay of the First Party System. Second, Jackson's presidency displays the limits of populism as a governing philosophy. Without any clear program for helping the "common people," the populist is driven to attack elite-dominated institutions, regardless of their value for the public, and falls back on his own resentments and hobbyhorses in lieu of policy. Third, the major effects of Jackson's presidency were to diminish the office and, rather than give power to the common people, to create a new system of elite control.

THE COUNTRY BEFORE JACKSON
The political establishment at the time of Jackson's election was not corrupt, but it was out of touch. The triumphant Republicans had adopted a strategy of welcoming former Federalists into the fold, including John Quincy Adams himself. James Monroe, who was president from 1817 to 1825, faced some significant challenges—including disputes over slavery and an economic crisis—but he managed to remain popular. He was a throwback

to Revolutionary times, one of the few remaining politically active Founders, the last president to wear a powdered wig and breeches. The country was enjoying a period of optimism as national territory expanded and states were carved out of the wilderness. Partisan unity was the order of the day, or so it seemed.

Actually, the country was polarizing along sectional lines. New England, which threw its support to John Quincy Adams in the 1824 election, favored merchant interests, internal improvements supported by the national government, and high tariffs and was beginning to oppose slavery. The West, represented by Henry Clay, favored internal improvements and security against Indians. The South was increasingly defensive about slavery and opposed tariffs. Jackson, with substantial support in the West, the South, and the mid-Atlantic states, did not hold a clear set of political positions but was associated with western and southern interests.

Adams was vulnerable from the start—he was elected by a minority, saddled with the "corrupt bargain" allegation, and beset with suspicion that he was a closet Federalist. It did not help that he declared that internal improvements, the traditional Federalist agenda, would be his major policy goal as president. He failed to win congressional support for most of his program and accomplished little as president. Renowned for his learning (a classicist, he was a professor of rhetoric at Harvard University), intelligence, integrity, and significant accomplishments as a government minister (he was instrumental in developing the Monroe Doctrine), and committed to the public good as he saw it, Adams was a big fat piñata. Even before Jackson's 1828 campaign, he was mocked for being stuffy and aloof. With the misfortune of having been elected at the dawn of mass democracy, he was doomed.

JACKSON'S PRESIDENTIAL CAMPAIGNS

In his presidential campaigns in 1824 and 1828, Jackson, in keeping with the norms of the time, did not personally give speeches or attend rallies—except in 1828, when a commemorative celebration of his New Orleans victory was arranged. The notion that presidential candidates should not be personally involved in a campaign was left over from the founding-era vision of the president as someone above the political fray. The norm would take another half century to fully erode. In other respects, however, Jackson's run-up to the presidency was the first populist campaign. Several features of it stand out.

Jackson's popularity was due to his glorious career as a military leader, rather than his accomplishments as a politician, which were negligible. The political establishment worried that it was Jackson's authoritarian temperament that appealed to the people, in the mold of a classical demagogue. Indeed, Jackson's supporters celebrated his suspension of habeas corpus while military governor of New Orleans as an act of statesmanship. Albert Gallatin, a prominent Republican, made precisely this point while criticizing Jackson for holding himself above the party organization and disregarding the limits on his military commands in New Orleans and Florida. Jackson's violent, Trump-like language—he announced that he would have hanged the leaders of the Hartford Convention of 1814–15, where discontented Federalists grumbled about the direction of government—indicated that he was no friend of the rule of law. (In contrast, Madison, the US president at the time of the Hartford Convention, who might have strengthened his political position by demonizing its leaders, preferred to avoid such demagoguery.)[4]

The 1828 election involved much more significant mass participation than earlier campaigns did, with rallies, marches, and enormous levels of public involvement in the day-to-day operations of the campaign. As the historian Robert Remini describes it:

> An unprecedented number and variety of demonstrations for the candidates occurred during the election of 1828. Much of the ballyhoo was conceived and organized by the new breed of politicians who appeared following the War of 1812. They encouraged the public to feats (hitherto unknown) of organized mayhem. Parades, barbecues, dinners, street rallies, tree plantings (hickory trees for the Democrats) and patriotic displays of every variety occurred throughout the Union—most of them for Jackson.[5]

Scurrilous accusations were also the order of the day (this was not quite as new). Jackson was called a bigamist, Adams a pimp for the czar of Russia, where he had served as US ambassador.

The major theme of Jackson's campaign was the corruption of Washington. Jackson did not have a strong political ideology or policy program. He endorsed Jeffersonian principles in favor of localism, but was also a nationalist with a pronounced hostility toward foreign enemies, Native Americans, and—it would turn out—secession. Localism and nationalism are, of course, opposites. More distinct was his opposition to "corruption." Jackson hated the elites, especially those who had deprived him of the presidency four years earlier. He and his aides and surrogates attacked the Adams administration for its corruption and its aristocratic complexion. As Jackson himself put it, "Look to the city of Washington, . . . and let the virtuous patriots of the country weep at the spectacle. There corruption is springing into existence, and fast flourishing." Adams was, in fact, an honest man, and his administration was honest as well, by the standards of the time. The major evidence of Adams's corruption was his supposed authorization of the purchase of a billiard table for the White House using fifty dollars of public funds. One critic noted the "shock and alarm [of] the religious, the moral, and reflecting part of the community," while Amos Kendall, one of Jackson's great supporters, roared, "If the people tolerate the trifling expense of a billiard table, balls and chessmen, out of the public funds, what may they next expect?" Actually, public funds had not been used, but an incautious defense offered by one of Adams's supporters—that a billiard table was "a common appendage in the houses of the rich and great"—sealed the president's reputation as an out-of-touch elitist.[6]

Corruption was an effective rallying cry. The national government in Washington was powerful, remote, and dominated by an inbred group of established families. Corruption scandals involving some government officials at the state and national levels did occur from time to time, and so fueled a narrative of broad government corruption. Adams's personal connection to the Founders was no longer an advantage; it made him seem like a hereditary aristocrat. To the general public, Jackson was a more appealing person. The Jacksonians did as much as they could to play up Jackson's birth in a log cabin; this would become a trope for future presidential campaigns. The fact that Jackson emerged from the common people meant that he was virtuous, unlike the Washington and eastern elites, and became a reason to vote for him, whatever his other merits. As Jackson put it, "I foresaw the powerful effect, produced by this moneyed aristocracy, upon the purity of elections, and of legislation: that it was daily gaining strength, and by its secret operations, was adding to it."[7]

As he publicly denounced the moneyed aristocracy, Jackson's campaign managers made clear that he would reward his allies with patronage appointments.[8] As we will see, Jackson made good on this promise, introducing the spoils system, a new form of corruption that would damage the federal government for decades to come.

Jackson also made his ongoing conflicts and disputes personal. His public rhetoric—and to a large extent his private conversation—shows a man who interpreted political opposition as a reflection of personal animosity directed at him, his family, and his supporters. To be sure, Jackson was shrewd and careful enough as a politician, and he mended fences when he needed to. His campaign was more disciplined and better led than yet another populist movement, the Anti-Masons, who were also propelled by hatred of the elites. The Anti-Masons believed that the elites conspired against the masses through the secretive Freemasonry organization (to which, ironically, Jackson himself belonged). Jackson also cut deals, made compromises, and, through his adviser Van Buren, who was also his first-term secretary of state and second-term vice president, helped bring about a new system of mass party politics. But the anti-pluralist strain in Jackson's rhetoric would be a theme of populist rhetoric far into the future.

These patterns would be repeated in the 1832 reelection campaign, which was also the first in which a national party convention was held. Jackson decisively defeated Henry Clay, with the major issue turning on the fate of the Second Bank of the United States, discussed below.

JACKSON IN OFFICE

Jackson entered office in 1829 without a clear vision of what he wanted to accomplish, except for one thing—Indian removal. During his military career, Jackson had frequently tangled with the Indians. During the War of 1812, he defeated a renegade band of Creeks who had allied themselves with the British (though in the Battle of New Orleans in 1815, his great victory over the British, friendly Creeks served as many of his troops). After the war, Jackson fought the Seminoles, who were allied with Spain, in Florida. Jackson saw Indian tribes as quasi-foreign nations that posed a military threat to the United States because they could (and did) form alliances with foreign enemies like the hated British. The continued existence of quasi-independent Indian nations within the borders of the settled United States struck him as anomalous.

As president, Jackson got his chance to act on his long-held fears about the Indian question. He drew support mainly from the South and the West. Some Americans saw Indians as a threat to security, and most regarded them as an inferior civilization, but the overwhelming motivation for Indian removal was the desire to grab their land, and America's treaty obligations to the Indians were quickly reinterpreted so that this thirst for land could be quenched. In the lovely words of Georgia's governor, "Treaties were expedients by which ignorant, intractable, and savage people were induced without bloodshed to yield up what civilized peoples had a right to possess by virtue of that command of the Creator delivered to man upon his formation—be fruitful, multiply, and replenish the earth, and subdue it." In Georgia, vast areas were owned by the Cherokees, who had adopted the modern agricultural practices of white people and had developed a peaceful, flourishing society that had partly assimilated to Western ways. Voters in Georgia elected a state government that asserted sovereignty over the Cherokees, in violation of federal law and treaties. White settlers sought to gain possession of Indian lands for themselves, and this pressure was redoubled when gold was discovered on those same lands. Violence broke out, tolerated or instigated by the state government. Various groups—especially Christian and women's groups—argued that the federal government should restrain Georgia and honor its treaty commitments. Others opposed Indian removal because of the expense, as it would require administration by the federal government and enforcement by the US Army.[9]

In his first message to Congress, Jackson advocated firmly for removal. "The emigration should be voluntary, for it would be as cruel as unjust to compel the aborigines to abandon the graves of their fathers and seek a home in a distant land." But with crocodile tears rolling down his cheeks, Jackson also said that the Cherokees "should be distinctly informed that if they remain with the limits of the states they must be subject to their laws," which, as everyone understood, meant being dispossessed. He argued that the federal government was not constitutionally permitted to protect Indian tribes from the states, and that Congress should authorize funds to facilitate the relocation of Indians west of the Mississippi. Jackson's opponents, the remnants of the Republican Party he had defeated in the election, seized on what public outcry there was but were outnumbered and outmaneuvered in Congress, which passed the Indian Removal Act in 1830. That law authorized Jackson to negotiate with the Indians, trading western land for their holdings in the East, and to compensate them and provide financial support for the relocation. The actual execution of the law, which would take many years, was marred by fraud, corruption, and violence.[10]

Jackson's position on the Indians was brutal, anticipating by a century, albeit on a much smaller scale, the Stalinist policy toward Soviet ethnic minorities. But was it demagogic? Both Monroe and Adams held a more enlightened attitude toward the Indians and the accomplishments of Indian civilization, but they recognized that the federal government was powerless to block the advance of white settlers into Indian territory even if it wanted to. Removal had been on the table at least since Jefferson. Indians were not considered a part of the American political community, and political attitudes toward them were largely hostile. Jackson hardly needed to use demagogic rhetoric in order to obtain public support for his position. And the language in his message to Congress was notably gentle. Far from stirring up hate and fear by depicting the Indians as a savage menace, Jackson acknowledged the injustices that Americans had committed against "this much-injured race." Jackson's Indian policy was relatively continuous with the approaches of earlier presidents. In advancing Indian removal, he worked with other political institutions, including Congress, his party, and the state governments.[11]

Opponents complained that Jackson violated the norms of executive power by taking a firm stand on Indian removal and demanding that Congress take action, rather than waiting for Congress to formulate policy. Jackson also disregarded earlier treaties made with Indian tribes, which many people thought was scandalous. In historical memory, Jackson defied the Supreme Court, which in 1831 struck down a Georgia law that prohibited white people from entering Indian territory without the state's permission. But while Jackson did not take positive actions to enforce the Court's ruling, it was also not clear that he was legally required to, and in any event even Jackson's opponents had come to realize that the federal government could not realistically stop Georgia from enforcing its own laws. However offensive Indian removal is to modern eyes (as well as to many of Jackson's contemporaries), it does not seem like an act of demagoguery.[12]

Jackson's most significant accomplishment as president was

his resolution of the nullification crisis. Angry about rising tariffs, South Carolina in 1832 asserted the right to disregard federal laws that it regarded as unconstitutional. Jackson's analysis of the crisis was not very sophisticated. He blamed state politicians, "unprincipled men who would rather rule in hell, than be subordinate in heaven," and ignored the depth of southern discontent with the trajectory of federal policy toward slavery, which was one of increasing skepticism.[13] But he handled the crisis adroitly, obtaining from Congress the authority to use military force against South Carolina if it refused to enforce the tariffs, threatening the nullifiers with charges of treason, isolating them from moderates in South Carolina and elsewhere in the South, and then agreeing to a modification to the tariff law that allowed South Carolina to back down without losing face. Jackson avoided military violence and possibly civil war and helped throw into disrepute the doctrine of nullification, but without making significant concessions on the tariff question. Demagogic? No.

Jackson was a kind of nationalist who sought to strengthen the Union by clearing away Indians and resolving conflict between the sections—though he was also firmly in the camp of states' rights, a position that would soon harden into the dogma of the Democratic Party he led.[14] He put attention and money into internal improvements, too, like ports and canals. In these respects, he was more energetic than his immediate predecessors and successors but not much different from them, and in no way characteristically demagogic. The demagoguery of President Jackson can be seen in other areas of his presidency—above all, the Bank War.

THE BANK WAR

Back in 1790, Alexander Hamilton proposed that Congress create a bank for the United States, to finance the government and help manage the private credit system. Over opposition from Madison and Jefferson, Hamilton persuaded Washington to support the Bank and obtained approval from Congress. The opposition derived from constitutional and policy objections. The Constitution did not authorize Congress to create a bank, and southerners feared that a central bank would serve the interests of northern merchants at the expense of southern planters. Nonetheless, the Bank was approved, and it was operated professionally. After he became president in 1809, Madison abandoned his hostility toward the Bank. Now, with direct understanding of its financial operations and their role in supporting the government, he was persuaded of the Bank's value. The earlier constitutional objections were discreetly placed aside. But agrarian opposition persisted and combined with a new source of opposition—state-chartered banks that resented competition and regulation from the national bank. In 1811, the Bank's charter was allowed to expire.[15]

This turned out to be a serious mistake. During the War of 1812, the absence of a central bank hampered the war effort. Because revenues were so meager, the government needed to borrow money in order to pay the army and navy. But the amount of money the government sought to borrow was enormous—far more than the fledgling state-chartered commercial banks of the time could supply. If the Bank of the United States had still been in existence, the government could have borrowed from it. Since it was not, the government had to make do with small loans and inflationary monetary policy. In 1816, Congress reversed itself, and the Second Bank of the United States was chartered. It was initially mismanaged by poorly chosen leadership but eventually operated smoothly and effectively under the leadership of Nicholas Biddle, who was appointed its president in 1822. The Second

Bank, like the first, was effectively a central bank—like the Federal Reserve today—and far advanced for its time.

Jackson hated the Bank. His hatred was based on a range of mutually reinforcing factors—personal, ideological, and political. As a youth, he had absorbed the agrarian, localist principles of Jefferson, which did not oppose banks per se but did oppose a central bank located in the East, with power over the entire country. As a businessman, he had run up debts with banks and tangled with them over repayment. As a republican, he was suspicious of sources of concentrated power that were outside the control of the people and their representatives. As a politician, he realized his anti-bank stance was popular with agrarian supporters and certain business interests. Biddle was the very embodiment of the East Coast aristocracy. Jackson saw the Bank's hand in his 1824 defeat, and in other political reversals for him and his party. Once he was in office, the Bank became a personal enemy, and Jackson's code of honor was engaged. "The bank, Mr. Van Buren, is trying to kill me, *but I will kill it*."[16]

While his crusade against the Bank began as his own idiosyncratic project, opposed by most of his cabinet, Jackson soon found allies in private banks chartered by the states, which sought the government deposits that were kept with the central bank, and resented the Bank's ability to limit their lending (and hence speculative excess) by returning their notes for specie. His closest allies in the executive branch, and in Congress and elsewhere, were more frequently businessmen (or representatives of business interests) than agrarians. For businessmen, the Bank, a quasi-government agency with quasi-regulatory authority, was an affront to the emerging philosophy of laissez-faire. As Jackson would later shrewdly point out in his veto message, the Bank was a monopoly created by the government; it did not compete on equal footing with other banks. It was soon clear that Jackson would not support the recharter of the Bank at the end of its twenty-year charter in 1836. Pro-Bank forces tried to make the Bank an issue in the 1832 election by proposing a bill to recharter it early. Jackson vetoed the bill. After Jackson won reelection, he removed federal deposits from the Bank, killing it.[17]

The Bank War was one of the great populist contests in American history. The Bank was one of the largest, most successful, most technically sophisticated, and most admired institutions in the country, and it played a profound role in the economy. By global standards, it was far ahead of its time, comparable only to the Bank of England. It was a natural target for populist rage. Yet, as just noted, the Bank's enemies included business interests. Jackson himself, the general of the Bank War, also happened to be the chief executive of the government. What does it mean to say that the president is a "populist"?

At the time, the populist idiom seemed more appropriate for attacking Jackson than supporting him. Jackson's opponents, who were beginning to call themselves Whigs, drew on the anti-monarchial language of the Country, which had been so potent for articulating opposition first to the British and then to the Federalists. "King Andrew" was a demagogue, a successor of Caesar, Cromwell, or Napoleon, who demolished institutions and disregarded political norms. Henry Clay pointed out that Jackson had dismissed or ignored cabinet officials, including treasury secretary William Duane, who had refused to remove government deposits from the Bank; abused the veto power so as to flout the will of Congress; and denigrated the Supreme Court. "He goes for destruction, universal destruction; and it seems to be his greatest ambition to efface and obliterate every trace of the wisdom of his predecessors." Others blamed a secret cabal of advisers rather than Jackson himself, denigrating them as a "kitchen cabinet" that displaced the cabinet of statesmen and manipulated the ill-informed chief executive. Whatever the case, the Country view should have had deep resonance, as it fueled the American Revolutionaries' denunciations of King George and the Jeffersonian Republicans' attacks on the Federalists.[18]

The problem was that the Whigs' constituency was the conservative commercial sector in the East, the merchants and financiers who had lost faith in Jackson or never supported him. This gave Jackson the opening he needed. Jackson drew on the anti-finance element of the Country ideology to portray the Whigs as the defenders of the moneyed aristocracy. As he put it in the Bank veto message:

> It is to be regretted that the rich and powerful too often bend the acts of government to their selfish purposes. Distinctions in society will always exist under every just government. Equality of talents, of education, or of wealth can not be produced by human institutions. In the full enjoyment of the gifts of Heaven and the fruits of superior industry, economy, and virtue, every man is equally entitled to protection by law; but when the laws undertake to add to these natural and just advantages artificial distinctions, to grant titles, gratuities, and exclusive privileges, to make the rich richer and the potent more powerful, the humble members of society—the farmers, mechanics, and laborers—who have neither the time nor the means of securing like favors to themselves, have a right to complain of the injustice of their government.[19]

The Bank was a secretive organization that was beholden to the moneyed aristocracy, which had helped fund the Whig opposition to Jackson. Even worse, many of the Bank's shareholders were foreigners, to whom Americans would be in debt, and it was possible that through transfers of the shares the Bank would become a "foreign bank, to impoverish our people in time of peace, to disseminate a foreign influence through every section of the Republic, and in war to endanger our independence." Jackson thus appealed to the nativism of the public, as so many demagogues would after him. The Bank's ability to pool capital from foreign as well as domestic sources—an enormously beneficial function for a rapidly developing, capital-starved country—thus served as evidence of its disloyalty.

These arguments resonated with millions of Americans, who gave Jackson the political backing he needed to crush the Bank even though they had initially supported it or took no view one way or the other. Jackson's argument was mostly unfair: the Bank was a highly professional institution that was operated in the country's interest. Yet there was also truth to Jackson's argument: the Bank was an enormous and powerful institution at a time when the federal government itself was feeble. Because of its power and independence, the Bank could act against the interest of the public if it wanted to. Bank opponents made much of its loans to members of Congress (albeit to its opponents as well as to its defenders) and its expenditure on publications to defend itself. And when Nicholas Biddle engineered a credit contraction in order to demonstrate what would happen if the Bank were killed, he overplayed his hand. The financial distress that resulted confirmed that the Bank had too much power.

For all their apparent impregnability, elite institutions are vulnerable to the charge of political interference because the act of self-defense against that charge is inherently political. Elite institutions that operate in the general interest are put in a dilemma by populist attacks: they can either surrender or fight back, and if they fight back they are politicized in a way that proves the populist's point.

Thus, the Country ideology, which was originally the language of opposition to executive power, became an idiom that could legitimate a powerful executive who was oriented against the elites. This was the language of "A Farmer," whom we met in chapter 1: "The only remedy the ingenuity of man has discovered for this evil [of aristocracy] is a properly constituted and independent executive." Because those elite interests were thought to be deeply entrenched and frighteningly powerful, the new populist ideology could justify destruction of the institutions, not just reform, including institutions that constrain, or lie outside the power of, the executive. Only the president himself was powerful enough to lead this assault. Thus, the anti-executive component of Country ideology was inverted and became a justification for an unconstrained executive—a leader who derives his power from the people rather than from a set of political institutions, a demagogue.

The Bank's charter expired in 1836. The collapse of the Bank disrupted credit markets, which were further strained by the government's mishandling of its own finances. A full-blown financial panic resulted. The ensuing depression helped destroy the presidency of Van Buren, Jackson's consigliere and successor. Without a central bank, the American economy was subject to increasingly severe cyclical panics and depressions over decades to come. According to one study, the United States suffered through banking crises in 1837, 1839, 1857, 1861, 1873, 1882–84, 1890, 1893, and 1907. The proliferation of bank notes from private banks hampered commerce even in the best of times. The 1907 crisis, followed by a severe depression, finally provided the impetus for a third attempt at a central bank, which was established by the

Federal Reserve Act of 1913. By contrast, Britain, which continued to enjoy the services of the Bank of England, experienced banking crises only in 1825, 1847–48, and possibly 1857. Of course, it is hard to know whether Britain's central bank accounts for the relatively small number of banking crises, or if the United States would have avoided some or all of the crises if the Second Bank had remained in operation. But there is no longer much controversy that an independent central bank is needed to regulate the monetary system of a modern economy. The destruction of the Bank, which set back the government's role in managing the financial system by decades, is the purest expression of the dangers of demagoguery and populism in national politics in all of American history.[20]

THE SPOILS SYSTEM

Another of Jackson's notorious achievements was the introduction of, or one might say the "perfection" of, the spoils system to American politics. The system got its name from the slogan "To the victor go the spoils," and the idea was that a newly elected president was entitled to reward his political allies with positions in government. The supporters could be high-ranking politicians, who might be given a cabinet position, all the way down to party workers who organized meetings, made speeches, and printed ballots, and could be found a place in the postal service or a customs house. Jackson called this system "rotation," a way of ensuring that fresh blood entered the civil service and thus eliminating the stale blood of the old elite. Jackson's campaign made it clear that he would reward his supporters with offices, and once elected Jackson proceeded to do just that. He inaugurated a period of political corruption that would last for decades.

The Declaration of Independence had complained that the

king "erected a multitude of New Offices" in the colonies, which he filled with "swarms of officers to harass our people and eat out their substance." With this memory still fresh, Hamilton wrote in the Federalist Papers that the Constitution would ensure "good administration" by giving the president the power to appoint executive-branch officials subject to the advice and consent of the Senate. The president's ultimate responsibility for executive administration combined with the senatorial check would ensure that appointments would be based on merit rather than on political connections and party interests. George Washington sought to uphold this ideal within the constraints of political realities. A president has a right to expect loyalty from his subordinates, and an understandable inclination to do so as well. Personal connections and previous work on behalf of that president, during a campaign or elsewhere, provide evidence of loyalty. Hamilton and other subordinates made lower-level appointments in a manner that protected the agenda of the nascent Federalist Party. Later, President Adams made last-minute appointments to the judicial branch in order to preserve the influence of Federalists in government after they were defeated in the 1800 election.[21]

Still, the principle was established that the president should appoint officials based on merit, and this meant that when a new president took office, he should retain all officials who were not corrupt or incompetent. Jefferson, Madison, Monroe, and Adams endorsed this principle in public and mostly complied with it in practice. However, some corruption scandals involving public officials—as well as generally lax standards for public integrity at both the federal and state level—gave Jackson an opening. Before and during his 1828 campaign, he railed against public corruption. At the same time, his campaign relied on volunteer workers who were openly promised offices after Jackson was elected. This was where Jackson's innovation lay. While earlier presidents had regarded patronage appointments as a necessary evil, one to be avoided as much as possible, under Jackson the spoils system was open and institutionalized.[22]

The new spoils system was not entirely invidious. The governing class had been replicating itself for decades, relying on its control over political offices and other resources. Many officials had grown too old for the job. A self-serving notion had arisen that men who had faithfully served in a public office were entitled to expect their sons to replace them when they stepped down. Jackson attacked this idea. He cast the old system as a variant of aristocracy in which office was "considered as a species of property, and government rather as a means of promoting individual interests than as an instrument created solely for the service of the people." The spoils system allowed Jackson to mobilize his lower-level supporters for his presidential campaign in 1828. Thus, the spoils system could be seen as democratic, in the sense of increasing public participation and decreasing the power of the governing elites.[23]

But if campaign workers were to be rewarded with public offices, what ensured that the campaign workers would be qualified to serve? Jackson argued that "the duties of all public officers are . . . so plain and simple that men of intelligence may readily qualify themselves for their performance." Here, we see both a classic populist statement and the limits of populism. The logic of populist distrust of elite institutions entails rejection of the commonsense truth that expertise and experience are valuable in government, as they are in all other areas of life. To justify rotation, that truth had to be rejected. To resolve the cognitive dissonance, a new doctrine was formulated: if new, inexperienced people can be assigned to offices, then it must be because the duties of those offices are easy to discharge. Of course, this is not true. Jackson's administration struggled with the problem. One effort involved redefining government jobs so that the tasks were simpler. But Jackson needed to retain competent bureaucrats. For example, the Revenue-Marine, which patrolled coastal waters for smugglers, was not brought under the spoils system. Jackson tried to appoint from the pool of partisans those who were most competent—and that meant middle- and upper-class professionals, rather than farmers, Jackson's most loyal supporters.[24]

As a result of this unpleasant constraint imposed by reality, as well as continuing political opposition to the destruction of the federal bureaucracy, Jackson's own patronage appointments were only modestly more numerous than those of his predecessors. But the change in climate was unmistakable, and the effects were obvious. A House committee complained in 1842 of "the habit of filling the most important clerkships and bureaus with persons who have had no previous experience as to their duties. . . . It very often happens that individuals are brought from a distance, perfect strangers to the duties and details of their offices, installed in bureaus or clerkships with which they never become familiar until in their turn they have to give place to others equally ignorant with themselves." The civil service lost its prestige. Officials were seen as dependent on the whims of political fortune, and as partisans who were not qualified for their office. Opponents mobilized against the spoils system and called out Jackson for spreading corruption. But the Jackson administration ginned up a rhetorical counterattack: it accused existing officeholders of corruption or malfeasance, often based on fabrications or exaggerations. When these persecutions caused an outcry, Jackson relented and, like his predecessors, relied mainly on attrition to empty the ranks of the officeholders.[25]

For all of Jackson's apparently genuine disgust with corruption in previous administrations, his administration was worse. Ignoring the warnings of Van Buren, himself hardly an angel, Jackson appointed an early supporter of his, the politician Samuel Swartwout, to the position of collector of the Port of New York. Swartwout skimmed off more than a million dollars and fled to Europe.[26] This was an enormous amount of money; the federal budget in those days hovered around $30 million per year. More insidiously, corruption played a significant role in Indian removal, diverting federal money from security and compensation for Native Americans to the pockets of soldiers, bureaucrats, settlers, and politicians.

Once in place, the spoils system expanded. Under Jackson, the post office provided the most important patronage opportunities, but so did the agencies that governed Indians, distributed government land, and administered customs. As the lesson of Jackson's victories was absorbed by the political establishment, the parties found themselves trapped in a downward spiral of public corruption. Each party needed to promise offices to its campaign workers, and the parties ended up competing by offering an ever-increasing number of offices to their supporters. This meant that an increasing fraction of the bureaucracy would need to be replaced when one party took over the presidency from the other, and that government officeholders would be enlisted for campaign work by the party in power. The press itself was sucked into the spoils system: newspapers became outlets for party propaganda, and friendly editors and journalists were rewarded with government offices, sometimes while they still worked for their newspapers. The plague of office seekers descending on the newly elected president became a recurring image of popular history. It was supposed to have killed the elderly William Henry Harrison, who succumbed to pneumonia a month after he was inaugurated in 1841. Lincoln, who called the office seekers who swarmed him "Egyptian locusts," said that the spoils system threatened the Union more than the Confederacy did. President James Garfield was assassinated by a disappointed office seeker in 1881. Swollen with unqualified patronage appointments who would be rotated out just as they accumulated experience, the federal bureaucracy was badly degraded. After the Civil War, corruption and related abuses got bad enough to ignite a popular outcry and public support for reform. In 1883, Congress passed the Pendleton Act, which finally set the country back on course to a meritocratic civil service system, correcting the abuses introduced by Jackson more than half a century earlier.[27]

Governments need high-quality bureaucracies to function, and the United States was fortunate before Jackson's presidency to enjoy a relatively good, relatively apolitical federal bureaucracy. It was admired and imitated by foreign countries, including Britain, which was struggling at the time to wrest control of public offices from a decadent aristocracy. But while Britain reformed its civil service by introducing professional standards, the US system collapsed. In attacking or recklessly damaging valuable institutions because they offered a constraint on his power, Jackson acted as a demagogue. While some commentators argue that the spoils system was essential to the advance of democracy, as it was necessary for breaking the hold of the entrenched elites and mobilizing the common people, the ultimate effect of the spoils system was to create a new system of elite rule, along with a degraded bureaucracy.

EXECUTIVE POWER

Jackson's effect on the institution of the presidency was complex. Hamilton had advocated a strong national government led by a strong executive, while Jefferson stood for a weak national government with a weak executive (in principle—once Jefferson took office, he exercised his powers forcefully). Jackson scrambled these categories, advocating a *weak* national government with a *strong* executive. The scrambling might be put down to the complexities of politics. As a matter of principle and political expedience, Jackson sought to act on behalf of ordinary people. Because the federal government was deemed a corrupt nest of elites, the most direct way to benefit the people was to return power to the states. But to break Washington's grip on power, Jackson would need to overcome opposition in Congress. And to do *that*, he would need to assert his own power through the presidency. As we saw, he exploited the powers of the presidency to their fullest in order to push ahead Indian removal, defeat the Bank, and counter nullification.

The paradox was that while Jackson amassed power in his own hands, he badly damaged the presidency. The key to understanding this paradox is that the source of Jackson's power was initially his personal popularity—as Old Hickory, the tough-as-nails hero of New Orleans. He was able to transform his personal popularity into institutional reforms that could be deployed against his opponents. We have discussed some of these institutional reforms—including the party and the spoils system. Others were more subtle. Jackson used the veto more aggressively than earlier presidents, he more aggressively claimed the power to set the policy agenda rather than leaving it to Congress, and he avoided the constraints of cabinet government, which had entangled some of his predecessors and successors. Thus, when Jackson left office, the presidency was transformed.

Jackson had replaced the founding-era conception of the president as an aristocratic leader, properly chosen by the elites, with a democratic ideal: the president was to be a man of the people, selected by acclaim of the public, and duty-bound to represent the interests of the common people in government. But this meant that a president could be effective only as long as he remained popular, and it also meant that future presidents would have to be selected based on popularity rather than merit.[28]

Who is most likely to be popular? The model was not just Jackson but all the demagogues of the past—from Caesar to Napoleon: a glorious military leader. Thus, the new Whig Party, formed by Republicans who had been defeated by Jackson, and others who were unhappy with Jackson's presidency, cast its lot with a war hero, William Henry Harrison. Harrison had defeated a Shawnee military force in a famous battle in 1811, the Battle of Tippecanoe, and served with distinction as a general during the War of 1812. The Whigs ran Harrison in a slate of four candidates in the election of 1836, losing to Van Buren, Jackson's vice president and chosen successor. But in 1840, the fortunes of the Whigs changed. In a supercharged campaign featuring an unprecedented level of popular participation, Van Buren was decisively defeated. Van Buren was hampered by the terrible economy, for which the public held him accountable. The Whigs shamelessly propagandized. They whipped the public into a frenzy with marches, ceremonies, and celebrations that contemporaries likened to religious revivals. They somehow managed to portray Harrison as a Christian symbol to evangelicals, a war hero to the masses, and a man of the people for good measure, claiming that he had been born in a log cabin.[29] (Harrison actually hailed from a wealthy, aristocratic family in Virginia; his father, a planter, signed the Declaration of Independence.) Van Buren lacked Jackson's charisma and inevitably was portrayed as an aristocrat, a new type of political elite, which he was, despite his relatively humble roots.

Harrison may not have been too pleased with the propagandizing on his behalf. In an extraordinary inaugural speech—which stretched for two hours, in the bitter cold, and was studded with classical allusions—Harrison lambasted the Jacksonian legacy of partisan politics and executive primacy. He also warned of the "complicated intrigues of the demagogue" to which the people will fall prey if their "spirit of moderation and forbearance for which our countrymen were once distinguished"—note the past tense—is not revived:

> On the contrary, no care that can be used in the construction of our Government, no division of powers, no distribution of checks in its several departments, will prove effectual to keep us a free people if this spirit is suffered to decay; and decay it will without constant nurture. To the neglect of this duty the best historians agree in attributing the ruin of all the republics with whose existence and fall their writings have made us acquainted. The same causes will ever produce the same effects, and as long as the love of power is a dominant passion of the human bosom, and as long as the understandings of men can be warped and their affections changed by operations upon their passions and prejudices, so long will the liberties of a people depend on their own constant attention to its preservation. The danger to all well-established free governments arises from the unwillingness of the people

to believe in its existence or from the influence of designing men diverting their attention from the quarter whence it approaches to a source from which it can never come. This is the old trick of those who would usurp the government of their country.

And then the historical allusions: "Caesar became the master of the Roman people and the senate under the pretense of supporting the democratic claims of the former against the aristocracy of the latter." And, much later: "But the reign of an intolerant spirit of party amongst a free people seldom fails to result in a dangerous accession to the executive power introduced and established amidst unusual professions of devotion to democracy."[30]

Harrison criticized the sacred Founders for allowing the president to appoint and control the secretary of the treasury, to exercise excessive control over legislation through the veto, and even to serve more than one term. Jackson, of course, had done all these things. Harrison himself swore he would not run for reelection, a promise that was easy to keep thanks to his death thirty-one days later.

Harrison's inaugural speech was instantly forgotten, and the populist ideal that he railed against—that the president should be a "man of the people," self-made, born in a log cabin if possible, and ideally a glorious military leader as well—was now entrenched in the popular imagination. Mass meetings, marches, rallies, and songs would now accompany every campaign, all devices for helping ordinary people identify with a remote candidate they would never meet. Then as now, however, few successful politicians were self-made men. The presidency is an administrative position that requires talents that normally can be obtained only through education, experience, political connections, and demonstrated accomplishments that usually take decades of hard work in the political trenches. Thus, the democratic ideal clashed with the qualifications needed for successfully performing duties of the office, resulting in a string of mediocre presidents through the remainder of the nineteenth century. Polk (1845–49) and Lincoln (1861–65) were the exceptions, but Polk barely so—he was an exceptionally talented politician who was allowed to ascend to the presidency in 1845 only after committing to serve for a single term. Lincoln—whom we will discuss in the next chapter—was a special case.

THE NEW ELITE

Jackson, thanks to his military victories, was a popular presidential candidate who drew his support from the masses. While he was himself a creature of the political establishment, he could credibly claim the role of outsider and reformer. The new party was to be a mass party, one that involved and drew support from ordinary people. Indeed, the name of the party morphed at this time from Republican to Democratic-Republican to Democratic. Jackson's supporters, including historians down to the present day, celebrate this transformation, claiming that the people were finally able to play a role in the selection of national politicians despite the elitist design of the Constitution.

But that was not really the case. While, as we saw, the need to satisfy the people often required presidential candidates who either had or could plausibly claim a populist credential, or some degree of national popularity, a new elite remained firmly in control of the selection of the president. The new elite consisted of the leaders of the new parties—the Democrats, and then the Whigs. As the spoils system expanded, it became necessary for the parties to guarantee an increasing number of offices for campaign workers, which meant that party leaders had to also control the person who would make the appointments—namely, the president. The parties formally selected the presidential candidates at national conventions attended by delegates from all the states, but the candidates for the parties' nomination were winnowed down in backroom deals made by party leaders who controlled the delegates.

Thus, all the major presidential candidates were both members of the country's elite and selected by the elite. In 1840, the Virginia aristocrat William Henry Harrison defeated the incumbent president, Van Buren. In 1844, the Democrats chose James Polk, a former governor and Speaker of the House of Representatives, and a loyal Jacksonian. Polk defeated the Whig candidate, Henry Clay, who was one of the most prominent and experienced politicians in the United States. In 1848, the Whigs chose Zachary Taylor, a military general, who defeated the experienced Democrat, Lewis Cass. In the 1852 election, a long-time Democratic politician, Franklin Pierce, defeated the Whig candidate, Winfield Scott. Scott was a military leader, who had sought the Whig nomination for the presidency twice before. In 1956, James Buchanan—former US senator and member of the House, and former ambassador to the United Kingdom and to Russia—defeated Millard Fillmore (a former president and highly experienced politician) and John C. Frémont (a famous explorer and military leader). Populism may have given a boost to the political prospects of military leaders, but in the new party system, the people chose the president only in the narrow sense of being able to select among the candidates chosen by the party leaders and other elites. That was the limit of popular influence.

The historian Arthur Schlesinger Jr., in an influential book celebrating the democratizing effects of Jackson's presidency, made this point directly, albeit glibly:

> The history of governments has been characterized by the decay of the old ruling classes and the rise of more vigorous and intelligent ones to replace them. This process had already begun in America. The "natural aristocracy" of Richard Hildreth [a contemporary intellectual]—the class composed of merchant, banker, planter, lawyer and clergyman—had started to decline after the War of 1812. The rise of the military hero, a new "natural" aristocrat, hastened the time for a general breaking-up of the old governing elite. In extreme cases one ruling order succeeds another by violent revolution, but a democracy which preserves sufficient equality of opportunity may escape so drastic a solution. The spoils system, whatever its faults, at least destroyed peaceably the monopoly of offices by a class which could not govern, and brought to power a fresh and alert group which had the energy to meet the needs of the day.[31]

In short, the people's president replaced the old elite with a new elite. It might have been said that this new elite was more concerned with the common people than the old elite had been. That seems to be Schlesinger's argument. But it is hard to sustain that view. The period from Jackson to the Civil War is not remembered for the excellence of the national government, or even for an excellent new military aristocracy that Schlesinger, in a strange lapse of judgment, appeared to welcome.

4

THE POPULIST REVOLT

(1865–1897)

You have probably the greatest orator since William Jennings Bryan, coupled with an economic populist message and two political parties that are so owned by the donors that they don't speak to their audience.

—STEVE BANNON, ON DONALD TRUMP (2016)

The late nineteenth century was a period of populism and demagoguery, and yet, while most Americans treasured the memory of their hero Andrew Jackson, they did not elect another populist demagogue to the presidency. By then, the system of mass parties led by political elites was deeply entrenched—so entrenched, and so secure in its power, that party leaders neglected the interests of a vast swath of the population: poor and middling farmers who were losing ground as the country began to industrialize and urbanize. In a remarkable expression of grassroots democracy, these farmers organized and posed a significant threat to the two mainstream parties, the Democrats and the Republicans. They scored some significant victories but were in part beaten back and in part absorbed into the party system, so by the end of the century, the populist revolt was over. Even so, it offers some lessons for the question of demagoguery.

One lesson, as we will see, is that demagoguery can get a hold on the public imagination when the political system freezes out ordinary people in large numbers. Alienated and bitter, they become fodder for a demagogue who sees them as a path to power. Faced with the contradiction between the promise of democracy and the government's failure to address their interests, the people are susceptible to conspiracy theories that divide the population into an evil entrenched elite and the virtuous common folk. This in turn leads to an all-out attack on valuable institutions as well as corrupt ones, and on expertise as well as privilege.

The other lesson, however, offers a glimmer of hope. American political institutions were capable of responding to the interests of people who had been left out, and also of containing the ambitions of the demagogue. At the national level, politicians who avoided demagoguery were more successful than the demagogues were. The demagogues of the populist era never obtained the presidency, while the greatest anti-demagogue of the age was Abraham Lincoln, a man whose origins among the common people were authentic but who appealed to law, reason, and the unifying values of patriotism and religion, rather than to the most destructive emotions, even in time of war.

BEGINNINGS

In 1877, a farmer named F. P. Root met with other farmers and ranchers in upstate New York and created an organization they called the Farmers' Alliance. They were angry with the railroads, which, they believed, gouged them on the price of freight. The New York farmers agreed to lobby the New York state government for relief.[1]

While the New York Farmers' Alliance disbanded after a few years, the idea spread. Farmers in the Midwest and the West began creating Farmers' Alliances or using that name for existing organizations. In Texas, for example, the Knights of Reliance changed their name to Farmers' Alliance.[2] Farmers had always created mutual aid organizations to help them manage the risk of bad harvests and negotiate prices with customers, but these organizations tended to stay out of political matters. Root's goal was political from the start, and the idea that farmers' organizations should act politically, and form political alliances with each other, caught fire. Soon came the realization that farmers could knit together these new political organizations into regional, and then national, operations that, drawing on the enormous numbers of farmers throughout the country, could strike a decisive blow for their interests.

These farmers—who would come to call themselves "populists"—claimed a long list of grievances. In the South, the Civil War had devastated farmland, railroads, the labor force, and trade. Planters, poor white farmers, and newly emancipated black farmers struggled to survive in the chaotic environment. In the West, a mass migration driven by recently opened territory, the advance of the railroad, favorably wet weather in the normally arid climate, and boosterish claims was followed by considerable disappointment and turmoil when it was later discovered that much of the newly occupied land could not be farmed profitably. While not all farmers suffered, and indeed land prices and farm incomes across the country generally rose during the Gilded Age, there was significant regional variation, and short-term fluctuations caused immense hardship. The western land boom was a classic speculative mania. As land prices skyrocketed, people convinced themselves that they could get rich simply by buying land early, often heavily on credit, and then reselling it (akin to the subprime mortgage bubble in the early 2000s, when people "flipped" houses in order to make a fast buck during what seemed like a never-ending rise in housing prices). In the earlier era, the this-time-is-different theory that "rain follows the plow" gained traction—a crackpot theory that agricultural cultivation would itself generate a wetter climate, energetically propounded by a railroad propagandist named Richard Smith Elliott. The railroads, seeking new markets to serve, had hired people like Elliott to encourage migration west. Drought in the 1880s and 1890s ended the mania.[3]

The chaos was driven in part by industrialization. Railroads and telegraphs wove together markets that had once been isolated. The steamship opened access to foreign markets. Farmers who were once self-sufficient or dependent only on a local economy found themselves competing in nationwide and global markets where prices could rise or fall based on rumors of drought in Ukraine or war in Egypt. Farmers relied increasingly not only on railroads for transportation of agricultural products but also on banks for credit, telegraphs for communication, and a range of middleman institutions that sprang up, from warehouses to grain elevators. These businesses would unpredictably change their prices, throwing the farmers' plans into disarray. Farmers also believed—sometimes but not always correctly—that the middlemen were monopolies that gouged them on price and discriminated in favor of their competitors.[4]

Meanwhile, the cities expanded, offering excitement, cultural refinements, and higher-paying jobs, and the children of farmers found such lures difficult to resist. And as people, wealth, culture, and technological innovation concentrated in the cities, so did political power and social status.[5]

The farming life at one time had been lyricized by poets, extolled by politicians, and held out by philosophers as an ideal. Farmers worked the soil, communed with nature, and earned the respect of the community by virtue of their hard-won wisdom and independence. They formed the core of the political community, and governments were overwhelmingly oriented toward their interests and values. Farmers had exerted significant influence on the national government for decades, obtaining relief from tariffs, the opening of lands through Indian removal, the distribution of public lands to settlers, and the creation—during the Civil War—of an entire government bureaucracy, the Department of Agriculture, devoted to their interests. Jefferson and Jackson had founded their political movements on agrarian ideals.[6]

But while the number of people involved in farming increased from 4.5 million in 1850 (including slave labor) to 11.7 million in 1900, the percentage involved in farming declined from 54.8 percent of the labor force to 40.2 percent in that time period. The demographic shift was slow, but the cultural and political change was lightning fast. As they lost their central economic role and political power, farmers developed strong feelings of cultural inferiority. They knew that the "eastern establishment" regarded them with contempt, as rubes, hayseeds, and hicks. The two major political parties—the Democrats and Republicans—ignored them. The farmers had fallen behind in a fast-changing world.[7]

GRIEVANCES

Populist farmers were aware of many of these long-term trends and had no interest in halting modernization. In fact, they wanted to share in the progress. They did not complain about industrialization but believed that the "money power"—the economic elites and their political allies—had rigged the system. Their complaints focused on three areas of economic life.

Monopoly. The late nineteenth century saw the rise of enormous corporations, which came to dominate whole industries—oil, steel, sugar, railroads. These corporations, like today's Silicon Valley titans, sparked a mix of admiration and distrust among the public. By pooling resources and investing in technology, they were able to lower prices and bring new products to market. In doing so, they acquired vast power over the economy and the political system.

Many of these corporations became monopolies, allowing them to manipulate prices and overcharge customers. They also interfered in politics. Their sheer economic weight was impossible to ignore, but they also flagrantly bribed politicians. Americans had never experienced an economic system dominated in this way by vast private monopolies. Public distrust of monopolists spawned an anti-monopoly movement—including the national Anti-Monopoly Party, which was founded in 1884—but serious efforts to counter monopolies through legal enforcement would not occur until the twentieth century.

Farmers hated all monopolists but were mainly concerned with two types of business. Like F. P. Root, they believed that railroads overcharged them, cutting into their profits and preventing them from competing with large agricultural organizations, which they believed the railroads favored. Populist farmers also greatly distrusted banks. Banks charged them interest on loans—at excessive rates, they claimed—and foreclosed on their land when they defaulted. But the populist bestiary contained many other dragons. Telegraph companies, warehouses, grain elevators, and other organizations were also criticized; populists believed that virtually all intermediary institutions that took a cut as crops made their way from farm to customer were out to cheat them.

Populists disagreed about how the government should fix these abuses. Some populists supported national ownership of railroads and national supply of credit, and others argued for more limited forms of regulation. A popular idea known as the "subtreasury" envisioned a vast system of bureaucratic management of markets in farm products—involving both price regulation of farm products and the provision of credit. Farmers believed that the subtreasury would protect them from price fluctuations, cut out middlemen, and strengthen their bargaining power against their customers.

Tariffs. The controversy over tariffs, reaching back to the Washington administration, had never ended. Northern merchants still supported tariffs because they reduced foreign competition, enabling sellers to charge higher prices on their goods. This position could be given a public-spirited spin, as it was by Alexander Hamilton, who argued that tariffs could nurture "infant industries" until they were able to compete on a global stage. But tariffs persisted long after the United States had become an industrial giant.

In the South, plantation owners and small farmers complained that the major effect of tariffs was to redistribute wealth from farmers to merchants. Tariffs increased the cost of imported goods purchased by farmers. Imports were more expensive because importers paid the tariffs, while domestic goods were more expensive because they were protected from foreign competition. Meanwhile, farmers faced the risk of retaliation from foreign countries, which, objecting to American tariffs, could impose their own tariffs on American farm products.

After the Civil War, the debate fell more directly along economic lines than sectional lines. Populist farmers opposed tariffs on manufactured goods, while the business community continued to support them. But as the country expanded, and became less dependent on international trade, the issue faded.

Monetary reform. On July 9, 1896, William Jennings Bryan rose to address the crowd at the Democratic National Convention in Chicago. Only thirty-six years old, he was nonetheless one of the most famous politicians in the country, renowned for his oratory and his populist sympathies. He hoped to secure the Democratic nomination for the presidency. When Bryan sat down ten minutes later, pandemonium broke loose. "The floor of the convention seemed to heave up. . . . Everybody seemed to go mad at once. . . . The whole face of the convention was broken by the tumult—hills and valleys of shrieking men and women." People hugged each other and threw their hats in the air. Hardened political operatives wept helplessly. Bryan was thrown onto the shoulders of his admirers and carried about in a spontaneous procession.[8]

What had set off the crowd? Bryan's speech focused on an issue that might seem esoteric to modern eyes—monetary policy. But his peroration is the most famous in American history:

> If they dare to come out in the open field and defend
> the gold standard as a good thing, we shall fight them
> to the uttermost, having behind us the producing masses
> of the nation and the world. Having behind us the commercial interests and the laboring interests and all the
> toiling masses, we shall answer their demands for a gold
> standard by saying to them, you shall not press down
> upon the brow of labor this crown of thorns. You shall
> not crucify mankind upon a cross of gold.[9]

The hottest topic of the day was whether the United States should depart from the gold standard and allow silver as well as gold to be used as the basis for money. The Republican Party and the business establishment firmly supported the gold standard, while farmers around the country opposed it, arguing that both silver and gold ("bimetallism") should serve as money.

The story begins in 1873, when Congress passed the Coinage Act, later to be known by its critics as "the Crime of '73." Before that year, the United States was on the bimetallic standard. This meant that anyone who owned gold or silver could take it to a national mint, which would convert it into official coinage of the United States. The amount of money that circulated, then, was determined by the amount of gold and silver that had been mined. The cost of mining would put a limit on the money supply, preventing inflation. As the economy expanded and people sought more money in order to buy things, the additional demand for money would raise the price of gold and silver, causing miners to increase production. In theory, then, the money supply would grow steadily with the economy.

The major effect of the Coinage Act was to eliminate the role of silver in the money supply. The supporters of the law would later argue that it was passed for technical reasons, to update old statutes; the better view is that they sought to put the United States on the gold standard. America's trading partners were on the gold standard, and America's participation would enhance international trade. But because of the technical nature of the law, and the high price of silver at the time (which meant that miners sold it on the open market rather than converting it to coin at the statutory rate), it was not immediately clear that the effect of the law would be to eliminate silver as a monetary standard.

Then, in 1873, a panic hit and ripened into the Long Depression, as it came to be known. The price of silver fell. With silver no longer convertible to money, the money supply was drastically limited by the supply of gold, which in turn accelerated the deflation caused by the depression. Deflation hit farmers hard. As money became more valuable and prices declined, farmers were paid less for their crops, which meant that they had less money to pay off their debts. And as money became more scarce, farmers had trouble buying seeds and other inputs. Hoping to reverse these trends, the farmers sought to increase the circulation of money, and they saw in the revival of a bimetallic currency a means for achieving this goal.[10]

THE POPULISTS ORGANIZE

In the aftermath of the Civil War, the major national issue was not economic policy but Reconstruction. The two parties' political support depended on the legacy of the Civil War—with most northerners and southern blacks aligned with the Republicans ("the Bloody Shirt"), while white southerners and ethnic urban northerners aligned with the Democrats ("the Lost Cause"). Business interests expanded their influence over both parties, which as a result became reluctant to interfere with the prevailing laissez-faire organization of the economy.

Meanwhile, farmers focused on their own circumstances. As they struggled to pay off debts, buy seed and equipment, and negotiate with creditors, customers, and railroads, farmers recognized the power of organizing. The Grange movement, which began in 1867, hoped to rescue farmers from their isolation from economic and intellectual trends, emphasizing self-help, self-education, and mutual assistance. It blossomed into a national organization that joined together local chapters with dues-paying members on the

Freemason model. While initially focused on economic matters—especially in establishing farmers' cooperatives—Grange organizations gradually took on a political cast, with the major goal being to regulate railroad rates and the pricing of warehouses and other middlemen.[11]

The Farmers' Alliances, like F. P. Root's, were, from the start, more overtly political. But they were not mere pressure groups. The Farmers' Alliances sought to educate their members and the general public on the plight of the farmers and the need for reform, and for that purpose they sent lecturers around the country. They drew on evangelical language, traditions, and methods, sparking moral and religious fervor among their members, and at the same time were deeply patriotic. As people and ideas circulated, the movement gained enormous strength, involving over a million farm families by 1890.[12]

As cooperation among the Farmers' Alliances advanced, large-scale regional organizations emerged. By the 1880s, Farmers' Alliances from around the country had joined together into three main coalitions. The National Farmers' Alliance, founded in 1880, represented northern Farmers' Alliances. The National Farmers' Alliance and Industrial Union, founded in the 1870s, represented southern groups. The Colored Farmers' National Alliance and Cooperative Union, founded in 1886, represented black farmers. There were other groups as well—organized by region, interest, or demographic—which coordinated with each other in many ways.

THE PEOPLE'S PARTY

In 1890, representatives of these organizations met at conventions in St. Louis, where they negotiated statements of principles and cooperative arrangements, and flexed their political muscle for the nation to see. Leaders of the Farmers' Alliances began to channel the political energy into a full-blown political party. In 1892, the People's Party held a national convention. The setting was Omaha, Nebraska, the heart of farm country in the West. There, they hammered out a platform, which they called the Second Declaration of Independence. They saw their movement as a second founding, a renewal of the commitments at the core of the nation's identity.

The preamble of the Omaha Platform was written by the populist leader Ignatius Donnelly. Donnelly was one of those crank intellectuals that America's fertile soil produced in abundance. He wrote numerous bestselling books, including *Caesar's Column*, a science fiction novel that extrapolated Gilded Age politics and economics into a dystopian future; *Atlantis: The Antediluvian World*, which described a glittering ancient civilization that was destroyed by a comet; and *The Great Cryptogram*, which argued that Francis Bacon wrote Shakespeare's plays. Donnelly was also a professional politician, a Republican member of Congress from Minnesota in the 1860s, and a holder of various state offices thereafter. He joined the populists in the 1890s.

Donnelly immediately hit the central theme of populism—the corruption of the elites, seen as so pervasive and fundamental as to reach apocalyptic dimensions:

> The conditions which surround us best justify our co-operation; we meet in the midst of a nation brought to the verge of moral, political, and material ruin. Corruption dominates the ballot-box, the Legislatures, the Congress, and touches even the ermine of the bench.

Donnelly then zoomed in on the institutional and moral damage that corruption had produced:

> The people are demoralized; most of the States have been compelled to isolate the voters at the polling places to prevent universal intimidation and bribery. The newspapers are largely subsidized or muzzled, public opinion silenced, business prostrated, homes covered with mortgages, labor impoverished, and the land concentrating in the hands of capitalists. . . . The fruits of the toil of millions are boldly stolen to build up colossal fortunes for a few, unprecedented in the history of mankind; and the possessors of those, in turn, despise the republic and endanger liberty. From the same prolific womb of governmental injustice we breed the two great classes—tramps and millionaires.[13]

Here we see the basic duality of populism: the *people* versus the *elites*. Each group is presented as internally unified, even undifferentiated, but the two groups are separated by a moral chasm. As the platform later declares: "The interests of rural and civic labor are the same; their enemies are identical." The preamble continues:

> We have witnessed for more than a quarter of a century the struggles of the two great political parties for power and plunder, while grievous wrongs have been inflicted upon the suffering people. We charge that the controlling influences dominating both these parties have permitted the existing dreadful conditions to develop without serious effort to prevent or restrain them. Neither do they now promise us any substantial reform.

Hence the necessity to create a third party, a party for the people, the People's Party.

The platform included reforms that the populists had long sought: nationalization of the railroads, Free Silver (a monetary system based on silver as well as gold), an income tax, nationalized credit (issued by postal savings banks), and prohibition on land ownership by foreigners.

From a modern perspective, the politics and ideology of the People's Party may be difficult to understand. We tend to think of liberals and conservatives, Democrats and Republicans. And yet the People's Party does anticipate some themes of the coalition that elected Donald Trump. A large group of working-class people have lost economic and political status and social prestige. Their personal values are fundamentally conservative—religious, rural, traditional, suspicious of change—but they seek, or at least are open to, policy changes that may well be radical. Thus, some of Trump's advisers and supporters—notably Steve Bannon— supported policies, including anti-monopoly policies, that would advance the interests of working-class people at the expense of the business elite. Trump himself did not choose this program once he became president but at times embraced the rhetoric.

The People's Party nominated James B. Weaver, a former Union general, for the presidency in 1892. Weaver made a good showing for a third-party candidate, winning 8.5 percent of the national popular vote, five states, and twenty-two electoral votes. At the national level, the populists never gained more than a handful of seats in the House and Senate. But they did better in their home states. Populists won numerous seats in state legislatures and were elected governor in Kansas (1893, 1897), Colorado (1893), Nebraska (1895), Nevada (1895), South Dakota (1897), and Washington (1897).

But then the populist movement lost momentum. The farmers who formed the core of the movement did not compose a large and influential enough part of the national population to prevail at the national level. Rather than risk losing another election, party leaders decided to fuse the People's Party with the Democratic Party, which adopted the Free Silver platform but little else of the populist agenda. Bryan, the hero of the 1896 convention, was a loyal Democrat. After delivering his Cross of Gold speech, he was nominated by Democrats for the presidency but lost to Republican William McKinley in the general election. In 1897, economic good times returned for farmers, partially driven by the discovery of gold in Canada, which halted the deflation and reduced the burden of farm debt. For the time being, the push for agrarian reform was halted, and the parties turned their attention to other issues.

WHAT IS POPULISM?

Historical research has opened a wide gap between the historical populists and "populism" in modern usage. The nineteenth-century populists were a diverse group of people who held different views on all kinds of things. Most were not well educated and put their grievances in a language that drew on American myths and traditions, which may have appeared simple-minded but nonetheless expressed legitimate complaints of unfair practices they identified. Like most other mass political movements, populists trafficked in exaggerations, platitudes, and conspiracy theories, and they harbored outlandish hopes and fears. Sarah E. V. Emery's book *Seven Financial Conspiracies Which Have Enslaved the American People* (1887), which detailed the sinister efforts of the "money kings of Wall Street" and English capitalists to enslave working Americans, was one of the most widely read populist tracts of its day.[14] For many populists, the "money power" was a sinister unseen force, at work everywhere and the explanation for everything. But there were populist intellectuals as well, who made sophisticated arguments that stood well against the false-hoods, exaggerations, and fantasies flung back at them by many establishment figures.

The concept of populism, as it is now used by political sci-entists and public commentators alike, does not do justice to the populist movement of the nineteenth century, but it does pick out some important elements of their worldview—or at least the worldviews of many of them, including many of their most influ-ential members.[15] And since the term "populist demagogue" also plays a big role in American political history, we need to think about what populism means in order to understand what a dem-agogue is.

SUPERIORITY OF FARMERS

The modern understanding of populism owes a great deal to the historian Richard Hofstadter, who himself trafficked in exagger-ations but nonetheless brilliantly captured—or maybe invented—the populist ideology. Hofstadter was a sophisticated East Coast liberal: he found the populists' wacky ideas amusing, their extremist tendencies unsettling, and their cultural prejudices alarming. Writing during the McCarthy era, Hofstadter hoped to undermine the witch hunts by tracing McCarthy's rhetoric to the paranoid conspiracy theorists of a movement that had gone down in flames. Thus, Hofstadter took a sledgehammer to the farmers.

Hoftstadter's version of populism downgraded the economic deprivation suffered by farmers and stressed their loss of cultural status in an age in which the economy was moving decisively from agrarian to industrial. Many farmers faced hard times, were taken advantage of by banks and railroads, and were ignored by politicians. But farmers were hardly in a worse position than the masses of Irish, Italian, and Jewish immigrants who inhabited the filthy slums of the big cities, the canal diggers and miners, the factory workers and soldiers. As Hofstadter shrewdly noted, farmers were not proletarians but mostly small businessmen with middle-class values and aspirations.

The farmers' ideology drew deeply on history, myth, and politics. The Romans idealized rural landscapes and the virtue of the farmer. The Roman general Cincinnatus, George Washington's model, gave up political power and retired to his farm. Virgil rhapsodized about the farmers of Arcadia, which, by the Renaissance, stood for utopian pastoral simplicity. As cities grew and developed reputations for political corruption, vice, violence, disease, and pollution, the farm became an ever more idealized place, its hardships forgotten. Jefferson's paeans to a farmers' republic were vastly more appealing than Hamilton's hard-nosed focus on finance, trade, and manufacturing. The connection between farming and political virtue would persist well into the twentieth century. Hofstadter observes sardonically that the agrarian ideal had its origin among aristocrats and intellectuals who imbibed the classical poets, and he mocks a photograph of Calvin Coolidge, which shows the well-tailored president sitting stiffly on a hay rig. Farmers did not cavort with nymphs and fawns, or reside in the executive mansion, but lived rough lives to which the ideological inheritance from the aristocrats gave some dignity. "Although farmers may not have been much impressed by what was said about the merits of a non-commercial way of life," Hofstadter wrote, "they could only enjoy learning about their special virtues and their unique services to the nation, could hardly mind hearing that their life was intrinsically more virtuous and closer to God than the lives of many people who seemed better off."[16]

Populist ideology, then, begins with the superiority—on economic and moral grounds—of the life of the farmer. Farmers live at one with nature, avoid the moral and physical filth of the city, and provide the sustenance on which civilization thrives. In William Jennings Bryan's words, "I tell you that the great cities rest upon these broad and fertile prairies. Burn down your cities and leave our farms, and your cities will spring up again as if by magic. But destroy our farms and the grass will grow in the streets of every city in the country."[17] Yet farmers turn out to be poor, politically powerless, and the object of contempt. Populist ideology seeks to explain this puzzle.

The answer is, inevitably, a conspiracy theory. A shadowy elite consisting of merchants, industrialists, bankers, and politicians has seized power, both political and economic, and steered policy toward its own interest, at the expense of the "people."[18] This was the "money power" to which populists often referred. But this move already required some complicated intellectual footwork. Who exactly were the "people" and who was the elite?

THE UNIFIED PEOPLE

Who were the "people"? Populist intellectuals faced a conundrum. The "people" could be just the farmers, those identified by history, literature, and economic theory as the vital class of virtuous producers. But the farmers were not numerous enough by the 1870s to force national change. The farmers' organizations that made up the bulk of the populist movement tried to attract labor organizations and urban workers to their cause, and in many cases succeeded. They also attracted middle-class reformers, professionals, and intellectuals. If this diverse crowd constituted the populist movement, then farmers alone could not be the "people." But if the "people" actually consisted of nearly everyone aside from the (undefined) elite, then what to make of all those who did not farm?

To square the circle, the populists insisted that the members of their movement were the "producers," the entire range of people who engage in productive work—farmers, factory workers, small business people. In some appealingly ecumenical theories of populism, African Americans, ethnic immigrants, and women were also included. But this definition of the "people" was not politically sustainable. Farmers and factory workers agreed on some things but disagreed about many others. The farmers' preoccupation with farm credit and railroad regulation meant nothing to urban workers, while the workers' focus on fair wages and hours was of little interest to farmers, many of whom employed people, and in this respect were more closely allied with the capitalist class than with the swelling urban proletariat. And the cities were diverse multiethnic places, teeming with immigrants, many of them Catholics and Jews, who were unmoved by the oratorical flights of evangelical moralism employed by the rural Protestant farmers.[19]

Even the focus on the farmer required some fancy maneuvers. It simply wasn't true that farmers, as a class, were united. The populist movement was centered in two locations: the South and the near West. The southern farmers were cotton planters; the western farmers—in Kansas, Nebraska, South Dakota, and North Dakota—grew wheat. Farmers who grew different crops in different regions of the country did not share the same enthusiasm for the populist movement. In Wisconsin, for example, wealthy dairy farmers sought to collaborate with government officials and business leaders whose help they needed for entering new markets.

They had no interest in the noisy protests of the populists. Indeed, many farmers in the Midwest and South were quite prosperous and wanted nothing to do with the populists, preferring to work with commercial and industrial interests. Meanwhile, once the populists attached their grievances to the gold standard, and therefore advocated Free Silver, they obtained additional allies—silver miners in Colorado and other states in the Rockies. The owners of the mines supplied funds to the populist movement, giving them outsized influence despite their indifference to agrarian ideals.[20]

The Farmers' Alliances and the other agrarian organizations shared an interest in promoting the economic and political power of farmers, but they differed in many ways as well. The northern alliance allowed black farmers to join; the southern alliance did not. And cooperation among the separate organizations faltered. The black farmers of the Colored Farmers' Alliance did not share the wealthier white landowners' concerns about farm credit and railroad rates. And as the ideology and institutions of white supremacy advanced in the South, black farmers faced lynching and other forms of violence when they attempted to engage in collective action, increasingly at the hands of the white populists themselves. The agrarian movement was tied up with the evangelical movement, and some of the leading issues of the day—temperance, for example—further divided rural and urban areas, Protestants and Catholics. By 1896, about the only thing that the populists could unify around (possibly with a push from the silver mines) was Free Silver, and that was not enough.[21]

ANTI-PLURALISM

Political scientists use the bland term "pluralism" to describe the normal, unromantic, day-to-day politics in a democracy. Pluralism refers to the plurality of groups that contend for political influence. A group is a cluster of people who share certain moral or political attitudes and goals, and attempt to achieve them by organizing. The organized groups, or interest groups, combine people's money, energy, and influence, enabling them to exert a greater impact on the government than they would if they acted alone. Some interest groups are relatively narrow, focused on a single issue like abortion rights or Israel; others are broader, offering a means of political influence for a class of people, like women or evangelicals or the elderly.

In the United States today, interest groups exist for every imaginable interest or value—reproductive rights, guns, libertarians, Christian Scientists, vegetarians, residents of the Mississippi Delta, transhumanists, cosmetologists, peanut farmers in Alabama. These groups cooperate in shifting alliances with like-minded groups to support politicians, referenda, legislative projects, or appointments to the government that serve their common interest. When groups achieve their goals, they might take on new goals or break apart. People frequently belong to multiple groups or switch allegiances; they disband old groups and create new ones. Laws, regulations, and other political projects emerge from the often mysterious, frequently hidden, and extremely complicated interactions of all these groups as they exert influence on the various politicians and appointed officials who control the levers of government. This system seems workable, consistent with democratic stability, maybe even as good as or better than the alternatives, but opaque and uninspiring because the constant need to compromise with ideological enemies interferes with devotion to clear and exciting principles and convictions.

Populism rejects this style of politics and reaches for inspiration. Its premise is that interest-group politics—pluralism—is corrupt. In the populist view, a group of vaguely defined "elites"—politicians, lobbyists, business leaders, lawyers, financiers—control the government and use their control to enrich themselves at the expense of the "people." Thus, the complex mass of interest groups, with their ever-shifting alliances, is replaced with a single dichotomy: the good people versus the corrupt elites. To protect themselves, the people need to organize—not into thousands of different interest groups but into a single righteous cause. The goal is to overthrow the elites and put into place a government that obeys the people's will.

Ironically, the populists were themselves excellent organizers, and they worked hard to form a coalition by knitting together different interest groups—wheat farmers and cotton farmers, silver miners and factory workers, and so on. As Hofstadter notes, the farmers were able to make real progress politically when they stopped thinking of themselves as the "people" and started thinking of themselves as, or at least acting as, an independent interest group. They gained further political influence when they abandoned their efforts to forge a mass movement and fused with the Democrats in 1896—and even more in the twentieth century, when they simply took their place as government lobbyists at the public trough. Their tough-minded leaders saw fusion in tactical terms: it gave them influence on one of the two major parties. For the romantics, including many historians, fusion was a betrayal. It destroyed the moral high ground from which the populists insisted that they were different, that they reflected the people rather than just one more interest. As one historian observed, "Having identified itself as a Pentecost of Politics, [populism] had no language with which to articulate a sense of itself in the brokered world of partisanship."[22]

THE ENEMY ELITES; ANTI-PARTYISM

The great diversity of the populists helps explain their obsession with the elites. Every demagogue knows that people will unify against a common enemy. As long as populists could convince themselves that the "money power" threatened them all alike—midwestern farmers, urban workers, Protestants and Catholics, blacks and whites, middle-class reformers, utopian dreamers—they could unite.

But identifying the elite also caused problems for populist ideology. It was one thing to blame bankers, industrialists, lawyers, and politicians for the farmers' problems. However, the logic of us versus them—the masses versus the elites—led the populists to distrust anyone with power, and that, of course, meant distrust of government itself. Anti-elitism means anti-government, and, building on the anti-government ethos of the Jefferson-Jackson tradition, the populists made the government a target. At the same time, the populists demanded government action—new legislation that would make markets fairer and give farmers a chance. Indeed, the populists extolled the post office—the largest organization in the government—and sought to use it as a model for further bureaucratic growth across the rest of government. But if the government was run by the elites, why trust it with reform?

This paradox cropped up in many places. In the Omaha Platform, for example, the demand for the nationalization of the railroads was accompanied by the following notable qualification:

> Should the government enter upon the work of owning and managing all railroads, we should favor an amendment to the Constitution by which all persons engaged in the government service shall be placed under a civil-service

regulation of the most rigid character, so as to prevent the
increase of the power of the national administration by
the use of such additional government employes [*sic*].[23]

The problem is that nationalization of the railroads (or even a
weaker remedy like rate regulation, which was later adopted) requires massive government involvement. Government officials
would manage and operate railroads all around the country. But
if government officials belong to the elite, and the elite are corrupt, this just means that the private corruption of the monopolists is replaced by the public corruption of the government.

As we saw in Donnelly's preamble to the Omaha Platform,
the populist response was that the government was not inherently
corrupt; it was corrupted by the parties—by the spoils system
invented by their hero, Andrew Jackson. They believed, correctly,
that national politics were controlled by the elites in each party,
who made policy or chose candidates in caucuses and backroom
deals. Civil service reform would help eliminate the parties' influence, allowing a nonpartisan "government-as-business vision of
politics." Surprisingly, in light of the reputation of populism for
rural nostalgia, many populists held a technocratic view of government, seeing it as a managerial science that involved applying
scientific principles to economic problems rather than the pluralistic making of deals embodied by the party system.[24]

GOVERNMENT AS BUSINESS

What exactly would this entail? The populists were never very
clear about how their ideal government would work, but both
their reform proposals and discussions pushed toward a central-
ized bureaucracy managed by experts and headed by a strong
leader. Tom Watson, a leading populist, saw in Napoleon a model

for American politics. He was not alone—many Americans at the time longed for a great leader who would unify the nation—but he took his admiration to extremes, writing two vast books about France and the emperor. Watson admired Napoleon's bureaucratic innovations and claimed that Napoleon's dictatorship actually reflected "the democratic impulse of the nation," under "intelligent direction."[25]

The two great literary expressions of populism—Edward Bellamy's *Looking Backward* (1888) and Donnelly's *Caesar's Column*—also offered fantasies of bureaucratic perfection. Bellamy's futuristic utopia emerges from the ashes of nineteenth-century capitalism after the corrupt plutocratic elite is defeated, but is itself governed by—a bureaucratic elite. Donnelly's America collapses into a nightmarish dystopia, but Uganda, the peaceful and prosperous country that shelters the hero, is governed by a virtuous intellectual elite. Neither place seems much like a democracy.

This is not to say that the populists opposed democracy. They saw themselves as democrats who opposed the corrupt, elite-dominated party politics of the late nineteenth century. Moreover, their reform proposals were not always unreasonable, and, contrary to myth, they were not averse to ideas. Their concerns about deflation, monopoly, the distribution of farming products, and agrarian poverty were legitimate. They were correct that the major political parties did little for farmers. Many of their remedies—monetary reform, nationalization or regulation, and rural credit systems—were eventually adopted in the United States and other countries, in one form or another. And they were deeply committed to educating themselves, going so far as to fund lecture circuits and reform schooling. But their concerns and remedies would all have been consistent with the pluralistic understanding of politics. The populists were at their best when they simply made arguments that farmers had interests, too, and the political system should address them. The problem was that these reasonable diagnoses and remedies were organically intertwined with a great foundation of politically potent fantasy—that the "people" were pure and undivided, and the elites were corrupt.[26]

NATIVISM

Other elements of populist thinking sat on these foundations. Because the populists were pro-rural, they were anti-urban. And because they found virtue and simplicity in the heartland, they were anti-foreigner, which also meant anti-immigrant. And if, as Hofstadter emphasizes, populist rhetoric sometimes had an anti-Semitic tinge (inevitably, Jewish bankers were invoked),[27] and populists supported exclusion of Chinese workers who had immigrated to the West Coast, their positions on these matters were mainstream. Andrew Jackson had already helped popularize the notion that America was a white, Protestant nation, and many populists, like other Americans, found it difficult to accommodate themselves to Asian, Irish and Italian Catholic, and Jewish immigrants, not to mention African Americans. If they did so at all it was with great reluctance.

Nativism is infertile ground for ideological consistency. The populists, Hofstadter observes, were both isolationists and jingoists. They were suspicious of foreigners, suspecting them of collaborating with the elites in pushing the gold standard on America. They accused the American elites of preferring foreign countries to the heartland. Bryan, who as we will see avoided the worst of populist rhetoric, couldn't resist voicing this point of view in an early speech:

Are we an English colony or an independent people? If there be some living along the Eastern coast—better acquainted with the beauties of the Alps than with the grandeur of the Rockies, more accustomed to the sunny skies of Italy than to the invigorating breezes of the Mississippi Valley—who are not willing to trust their fortunes and their destinies to American citizens, let them learn that the people living between the Alleghanies [*sic*] and the Golden Gate are not afraid to cast their all upon the Republic and rise or fall with it.[28]

The populists opposed a large military establishment and imperialism, which they saw (in the first case) as an instrument for elite oppression and (in the second) as a style of elite exploitation. But they were not pacifists. As Hofstadter put it, "What the nativist mind most resolutely opposed was not so much war itself as co-operation with European governments for any ends at all."[29] Populists later gave their support to the war against Spain in 1898, one of many American wars that started out as support for the oppressed and ended as an exercise in imperialism.

THE POPULIST AND THE DEMAGOGUE

So much for the populists; what of the "populist demagogue"? Strikingly, while people in the late nineteenth century frequently referred to demagogues, as they had throughout American history, and also referred to the populists, and often accused populist leaders of being demagogues, they rarely used the term "populist demagogue." The conjunction of the two words did not appear with any frequency until the 1950s, when commentators began to use "populist demagogue" to refer to Joseph McCarthy and to various racist southern politicians.

The populist leaders were not indigenous to the populist movement. They were not farmers but mostly journalists or professional politicians who had fallen out with establishment Republicans or Democrats or had dabbled with other third parties.[30] Like nearly all other political leaders, they used demagogic tactics from time to time. But while it seems doubtful that there was much more demagoguery in the populist movement than in other political movements, populist leaders helped establish the image of the populist demagogue in our political culture.

One such demagogue was Tom Watson. Watson, who was born in Georgia in 1856, was elected as a Democrat to the state legislature in 1882 and to the US House in 1890. As a Democrat, he caucused with the emerging People's Party, then helped found the People's Party in Georgia. From the start, he advocated on behalf of poor farmers and opposed the railroads. Like other southern populists early in the movement, he saw the possibilities of a coalition between poor white farmers and blacks to oppose a political establishment that was controlled by planters and merchants. He supported voting rights for the emancipated slaves and condemned lynching. He helped promote the national populist movement as well, which he portrayed in his *The People's Party Campaign Book* (1892) as the only hope for a society that was divided into extremes of rich and poor.

But then the populist movement collapsed. Democratic politicians in Georgia and elsewhere in the South beat back populism by disenfranchising African Americans, destroying any possibility of a coalition with poor whites. Watson's principles turned out to be flexible. While he retained his populist ideals as an advocate for poor farmers, his craving for political power now put him on the path to white supremacy. The enemies were now blacks, Catholics, Jews, and foreigners. He filled his newspaper with lurid and violent assaults on all these groups: blacks were savages who sought to dominate white farmers and rape white women; Catholic priests used the secrets of the confessional to seduce young women; Jews had organized a financial conspiracy.[31]

In 1913, Watson saw his chance. Leo Frank, the Jewish manager of a pencil factory located in Atlanta, was accused of raping and murdering Mary Phagan, a thirteen-year-old girl who worked in the factory. Locals assumed Frank's guilt, and the courthouse where his trial was held was swarmed by mobs howling for his execution. Frank was found guilty by a jury despite the absence of evidence that he committed the crime, and he was sentenced to death. The presiding judge and various reviewing courts expressed doubt about his guilt, and ultimately the governor of Georgia commuted the sentence.

Public outrage at the governor, and at others who defended Frank or expressed doubt about his guilt, was intense. Watson poured fuel on the conflagration, attacking the political establishment and the press ("If the Atlanta politicians and editors are crazy enough to make war on [the prosecutor], because he did his duty in the Frank case, LET THE WAR BEGIN"), the governor ("Our grand old Empire State HAS BEEN RAPED!"), Frank's lawyers ("You have blown the breath of life into the monster of Race Hatred; AND THIS FRANKENSTEIN . . . WILL HUNT YOU DOWN"), and Frank himself (who "belonged to the Jewish aristocracy, and it was determined by the rich Jews that no aristocrat of their race should die for the death of a working class Gentile"). In a later issue, he wrote, "THE NEXT JEW WHO DOES WHAT FRANK DID, IS GOING TO GET EXACTLY THE SAME THING WE GIVE TO NEGRO RAPISTS." When Frank was later dragged from the prison by a mob and lynched, Watson wrote, "THE VOICE OF THE PEOPLE IS THE VOICE OF GOD." Or as he put it another

time, "WHEN MOBS ARE NO LONGER POSSIBLE, LIBERTY WILL
BE DEAD." A new Ku Klux Klan was formed at the height of
the controversy, causing the historian C. Vann Woodward to
observe, "Yet if any mortal man may be credited (as no one may
rightly be) with releasing the forces of human malice and ignorance and prejudice, which the Klan merely mobilized, that
man was Thomas E. Watson."[32]

The Frank episode merely brought into sharp relief Watson's standard operating procedure. He whipped up the public
by playing on its most primal emotions. Watson's newspaper
emphasized, in the most lurid terms possible, Mary Phagan's
virginal purity, the superior status and wealth of the Jews, the
lofty attitude and supposed hypocrisy of northern public opinion,
which embraced Frank's cause, the low status of Georgia's white
citizens, and the indifference of the governing elite. Watson, who
wrote more than half a dozen books—on Jefferson and Jackson as
well as his beloved Napoleon—knew what he was doing.

Anger, hatred, resentment, disgust—these emotions play a
large role in people's lives and can protect and motivate them in
positive ways. But they are immensely destructive when they become the basis for political action, as they can feed on each other,
deepening divisions, hardening positions, and preventing compromise, without which collective life is impossible. Of these
emotions, anger can be justified when it is directed against a
legitimate threat, including oppressive conditions; it helps motivate people, and dissipates when the source of threat is removed.
But once anger is widespread, reconciliation may be difficult. Far
more troublesome than anger is hatred, which motivates people to
destroy rather than live with each other, and can be satisfied only
with elimination of the enemy. A group can alleviate anger by

making amends or concessions but will fight to the death against hatred. The whole institutional structure of the state is devoted to managing and channeling these emotions. The judicial system, with its chilly insistence on procedural regularity, proportionality, and—ideally—dignity for the accused, channels these emotions into socially productive forms of conflict resolution.[33]

The demagogue attacks institutions because those institutions curb his power. And he stirs up the negative emotions because only those emotions are powerful enough, when collectively deployed, to break the hold of institutional power. Watson attacked virtually all institutions—the press (though he ran a newspaper himself), the parties, the courts, the government—by promoting the mob. The lynch mob is the purest metaphor of demagogic power because the mob is unconstrained by institutions and beholden only to itself. The demagogue becomes the mouthpiece of the mob—in ideology, if not in actuality, a mere servant. As Watson said, "The people need spokesmen—not leaders—men in the front who will obey, not command."[34] This from the man who idealized Napoleon. The logical consequence of the opposition to institutions and glorification of the mob is Caesarism.

The South, in the wake of Reconstruction, was prone to mob rule. The wounds of the Civil War were still raw. The national government had forced institutional change on the South— through constitutional amendments, federal regulation, and military occupation—and the most effective way to strike back was to undermine those institutions through mob rule. Watson realized this, as did many other southern politicians, including conventional Democrats who lacked Watson's populist sympathies for impoverished farmers. Eventually, having undermined the institutional

structures imposed by the national governments, southern demagogues were able to reinstitutionalize white supremacy through
Jim Crow. In doing so, they were no longer demagogues but defenders of the establishment.

Watson was a transitional figure in populism, one who joined
its earlier left-wing reformist anti-capitalist position and its later
right-wing nativism. There were many others like him; indeed,
many establishment Democratic politicians in the South, like Ben
Tillman ("Lynch law is all we have left"), turned populist rhetoric
against the populists by claiming to speak for poor farmers and at
the same time rallying them with racist appeals. These populist-
style Democrats argued that the elites cared more about African
Americans, and moralistic crusades like temperance, than about
the interests of white farmers. In the North, this rhetoric appealed to white ethnic immigrants as well. And with the advance
of industrialization and the new threat of vast corporations, the
populist Democrat could wed these racist and cultural appeals to
reform legislation aimed at banks and railroads. In the populism
of today, the echoes of left-wing anti-capitalism and right-wing
nativism reverberate.[35]

THE GREAT COMMONER

Yet for all that, the most important populist leaders were not demagogues. James B. Weaver, the populist candidate for the presidency in 1892, had served successfully as an officer in the Union
army, worked in the political trenches for decades, mostly for the
Republicans, and had been elected to Congress twice after switch-
ing to the Greenback Party. He was a lawyer and professional politician through and through, and in his speeches and writings
made reasonable arguments that appealed to theory and evidence.

While Weaver's views were advanced for the time, he was a tactician, not a visionary.

By far the most famous populist leader was William Jennings Bryan—though he did not belong to the People's Party. Bryan was born in 1860 in the small town of Salem, Illinois. His father, Silas Bryan, was a prosperous lawyer, farmer, and town leader. From an early age, Bryan was exposed to the two major influences that would define his political career: religion and agrarianism ("Jesus and Jefferson," in the happy phrase of the historian Michael Kazin, which would have made Jefferson squirm). His parents were devout—his father a Baptist, and his mother, Mariah, a Methodist. The atmosphere of his hometown, and indeed of most of America, was intensely Christian. Many of the great social movements of the nineteenth century—anti-slavery, anti-poverty, temperance—were led by evangelical organizations, which enjoyed great authority among masses and elites alike.[36]

Bryan's hometown was also a farming town, and Bryan would spend his life among farmers in the Midwest—first in Illinois and then later in Nebraska, where his political career began in earnest. A brief residence in Chicago confirmed his distaste for urban areas, which, like many agrarians, he associated (not without reason) with corruption. Like his idol Thomas Jefferson, Bryan believed that the farming life was virtuous and the foundation of democracy, and that ordinary people possessed the wisdom to govern themselves.

While Bryan studied law and briefly practiced as a lawyer, he was drawn to politics from an early age. And it turned out that he possessed an extraordinary gift for oratory, which would be the key to his political career. The closing lines of his Cross of Gold speech, quoted above, would be memorized by generations of schoolchildren. But his genius was not so much his choice of words as his ability to speak with extraordinary conviction that listeners found riveting. A Republican who disagreed with Bryan's policies nonetheless admitted, "I listened to his speech as if every word and every gesture were a revelation. . . . I felt that Bryan was the first politician I had ever heard speak the truth and nothing but the truth," though the spell was broken when he read a transcript of the speech the next day.[37] Unlike in our own age, oratory was an essential feature of American life. People orated every chance they got, and they took seriously the demands of the discipline. Highly skilled orators were frequently sought for civic and personal events. And Bryan seems to have been the best. Stories abound of Bryan's oratorical genius, which was able to reduce hardened political operatives, including his rivals and enemies, to puddles of tears. Later in his career, he made immense sums of money by giving speeches for pay.

While the Great Commoner took on many populist causes—including Free Silver and anti-monopoly—he rarely made demagogic appeals. The oratorical style of the day made him prone to vivid images and exaggerations, but they were leavened by an essential decency and reasonableness, and a religious piety that inclined him toward generosity toward others, as well as a politician's instinct for maximizing his appeal. Demagogy when it occurred came off as a mild remonstrance: "I fear the plutocracy of wealth, I respect the aristocracy of learning, but I thank God for the democracy of the heart."[38] He did not demonize his opponents or attack courts, the party system, or the press; he did not glorify mob rule. He appealed to the emotions, but mainly in a positive vein, with heavy religious content. He was, in fact, a conventional professional politician in all respects except for his rhetorical gifts.

ANTI-DEMAGOGUES FROM LINCOLN TO McKINLEY

The Gilded Age was a period of political and economic turmoil, as the country recovered from the Civil War, absorbed millions of immigrants, and industrialized. Politics at the national level was far from inspiring, but not one of the presidents was a demagogue. They were colorless professional politicians who tried to keep coalitions together, mostly avoided invective, and ruled cautiously.

The Gilded Age is usually dated from the 1870s, but we begin with Lincoln. Although revered by the populists as one of their own, the Great Emancipator was the great Anti-Demagogue of the American presidency, rivaled only by Washington. Lincoln started off as a canny, hard-nosed political operative. But despite presiding over the collapse of the Union and a savage Civil War, he refused to appeal to the negative emotions—anger, resentment, greed—and to indulge the conspiracy theories that bubbled up among his followers, preferring to honor the truth to the extent possible. The toolkit of the demagogue was left unused.

Lincoln invoked the Constitution and the laws, the wisdom of the Framers, the strength of American institutions, and the common bond between North and South. In his 1860 campaign, he mildly countered the South's demagogic attacks against the Republicans with lawyerly logic:

> You say we are sectional. We deny it. That makes an issue; and the burden of proof is upon you. You produce your proof; and what is it? Why, that our party has no existence in your section—gets no votes in your section. The fact is substantially true; but does it prove the issue? If it

does, then in case we should, without change of principle, begin to get votes in your section, we should thereby cease to be sectional. You cannot escape this conclusion; and yet, are you willing to abide by it? If you are, you will probably soon find that we have ceased to be sectional, for we shall get votes in your section this very year. You will then begin to discover, as the truth plainly is, that your proof does not touch the issue.[39]

In his first inaugural address, he counseled reason and moderation: "My countrymen, one and all, think calmly and *well* upon this whole subject. Nothing valuable can be lost by taking time. If there be an object to *hurry* any of you, in hot haste, to a step which you would never take *deliberately*, that object will be frustrated by taking time; but no good object can be frustrated by it." In the famous peroration:

> We are not enemies, but friends. We must not be enemies. Though passion may have strained, it must not break our bonds of affection. The mystic chords of memory, stretching from every battle-field, and patriot grave, to every living heart and hearth-stone, all over this broad land, will yet swell the chorus of the Union, when again touched, as surely they will be, by the better angels of our nature.[40]

Even in the heat of war, after the carnage of Gettysburg, Lincoln refused to appeal to hatred. He tried to unite the North in grief and gratitude toward the fallen soldiers. He continued to refuse to vilify the South ("and malice toward none"), or to blame the South for the war, even to mention that region of the country.[41]

Lincoln did take actions that were thought inconsistent with the Constitution, including suspension of habeas corpus and the imposition of martial law. But he was commander in chief at a time of war, the Constitution itself granted him extraordinary powers, and he obtained congressional authorization when he could. Liberals in Europe called him a demagogue at the start of the war, but by the end they recognized him as one of the great statesmen of the era. While lawyers and historians continue to debate the propriety of some of Lincoln's actions, no one thinks anymore that Lincoln sought to damage institutions in order to amass personal power. Even if he is justly criticized for using improper means to protect the Union, he did not use demagogic means. After the Civil War, both Congress and the judiciary reasserted themselves, the party establishment revived, and the military retreated. As wartime censorship was lifted, the press flourished. If damage was done, it was temporary.

Lincoln's vice president and successor, Andrew Johnson (whose candidacy for the vice presidency Lincoln accepted for reasons of political expediency), presents a different situation. While he sought reconciliation with the South, he lacked Lincoln's moral authority, political talent, and judgment. Johnson and the Republican-dominated Congress came to loggerheads on Reconstruction policy, and Johnson appealed to the public in a speaking tour in which he used demagogic language—accusing members of Congress of seeking "despotism or monarch."[42] But Johnson failed to move the public and ultimately abandoned his demagogic efforts. He simply got himself impeached in the House, and while the Senate failed by one vote to remove him, he was rendered politically impotent for the remainder of his term. Subsequent presidents of the Gilded Age—Ulysses S. Grant, Rutherford B. Hayes, James Garfield, Chester Arthur, Grover Cleveland, Benjamin Harrison, and William McKinley—were temperamentally bureaucrats and professional politicians and (other than Grant, thanks to his military accomplishments during the Civil War) today are mostly forgotten.

For all the turbulence of the era's politics, the American public never elected a demagogue to the presidency during the Gilded Age. The reason has less to do with the popular temper than with the institutional setting. Demagogues were popular in the South, where they could channel mob violence against the hated northern order and give voice to ruined farmers who chafed under the corrupt governments of planter and merchant aristocracies. In cities in the North, machine politicians, commentators, and many other people spouted demagogic rhetoric as well. But at the national level, the political establishment was extremely powerful. The Republicans and Democrats dominated. The parties were vast and complex institutions that were coalitions of diverse interests, and the politicians who ascended to the top of the parties were skilled bureaucrats who sought to avoid alienating people. In the normal manner of the cautious politician, they sought compromise and incremental gains for their supporters. The candidates whom the parties made available for public election had to survive a careful screening process through which no demagogue could pass.

5

THE TRIUMPH OF ELITE TECHNOCRACY: THEODORE ROOSEVELT TO FRANKLIN ROOSEVELT

(1901–1945)

A perfect democracy can come close to looking like a dictator-ship, a democracy in which the people are so satisfied they have no complaint.

—HUEY LONG

The reformist energies of populism flowed into different channels as the century turned. The country was rapidly urbanizing; farmers were losing political power. A movement known as Progressivism materialized. The Progressives, who took their name from the book *Progress and Poverty,* by the great economist and reformer Henry George, in turn gave their name to the self-described progressives of our day. The original Progressives, like the populists, objected to the concentration of capital in big business, as well as corruption in government exemplified by the machine politics in cities. The Progressives also were heavily influenced by evangelical Christianity. But the Progressives, who were more oriented toward the urban masses than toward farmers, were less radical than the populists, more academic and sophisticated—their leaders included professors, lawyers, and other educated urbanites—and more adept at gaining power. Under Theodore Roosevelt and Woodrow Wilson, Progressivism focused on using law and administrative regulation to break up or regulate monopolies. As Progressives set up and improved regulatory agencies, they relied increasingly on academic experts. Government management of the economy during World War I helped create and legitimize vast bureaucracies that populists like Watson might have vaguely imagined but did not actually experience. These bureaucracies, however, might have given him pause: the experts who populated them seemed increasingly like a new type of aristocracy.[1]

A major difference between the Progressives and the populists is that the Progressives distrusted the ordinary people whom the populists celebrated. Looking around at their fellow citizens, the Progressives recognized that vast numbers of Americans were uneducated, even illiterate or semiliterate, ignorant about the world, mired in poverty, and often drunk, drug-addled, and violent. The crime-ridden slums of the cities teemed with recent immigrants who often could not speak English and did not trust, understand, or appreciate American institutions. Terrified by the rapidly growing numbers of people they regarded as beyond hope, many Progressives supported eugenics. More benignly, the Progressives sought to educate the common people and improve their characters. Hence their crusade against alcohol and their support for Prohibition. This also led them to distrust popular democracy. As early as the 1920s, Progressive intellectuals like Walter Lippmann (in his 1922 book *Public Opinion*) were arguing that the masses must accommodate themselves to rule by experts. Lippmann, whose views reflected a new skepticism about democracy in intellectual circles, was simply updating the Founders' view for the age of technology: the elite—now consisting of social scientists, area experts, and professional politicians—must rule because the masses cannot.[2]

But populism never went away. During the Great Depression, hardship among the farmers and the urban masses gave it a boost. It was also in this period that populism took on its distinctively modern right-wing and left-wing variations. The older populism was a jumble of both ideologies—celebrating traditional rural ways of life, often racist or xenophobic, and advocating for government regulation that would redistribute wealth. By the 1930s, right-wing populism would be personified by the priest Charles Coughlin, who blamed America's woes on foreigners and Jews in his immensely popular radio broadcasts. The left-wing version would be represented by Huey Long, who gained the governorship of Louisiana by presenting himself as a tribune of the neglected and suffering common man. Long's program was to redistribute wealth from rich to poor—make "every man a king," in his slogan—and to invest resources in education and infrastructure. As is always the case with left-wing populism, it was both popular among poor people and energetically resisted by the established political class and business interests. To overcome political resistance, Long consolidated power in extralegal ways, becoming a kind of quasi-dictator until he was assassinated in 1935. Before his death, Long achieved national prominence and deeply worried President Franklin Roosevelt, who moved to the left in order to steal away political support from Long.

But Roosevelt's New Deal would ultimately be very different from Longian populism, owing more to the vision presented by Lippmann. The legacy of the New Deal, building on Progressivism, was the rise of the national government as a regulator of business. The theory was that the free market, left to itself, resulted in numerous pathologies—monopoly, financial crisis, depression, unfair distribution of wealth—that needed to be corrected by government regulation. A bureaucracy was required to supply regulation, and a university-educated elite was needed to staff the bureaucracy.

The irony of the New Deal system was that while it shared the populist goal of helping ordinary people by protecting them from big business, and was immensely popular for just that reason, the critics of the New Deal would eventually hit upon populist themes and rhetoric to attack it. The problem was the bureaucracy. Once government took over running the national economy, economic problems—which were unavoidable but not always understood to be so—could be blamed on the failures of the bureaucracy. Indeed, it was easy to argue that the bureaucracy was just a new elite, and as corrupt as the elites of the nineteenth century. Moreover, bureaucracy was experienced by ordinary people as disempowering and alienating. If policy was determined by appointed bureaucrats, then the realm of politics shrank. One's vote counted less. And the national bureaucracy was soon to be dominated by liberals, whose views about the world—secular, cosmopolitan, egalitarian, individualistic—conflicted with the values of many ordinary people. The victory of elite rule—which was a kind of vindication of the Founders' vision—rested on unstable ground.

Another major development of this period was the growth of the president's position as the leader of the massive federal bureaucracy. The Progressives and their successors, the New Dealers, believed in a strong national government, and it turned out that a strong national government required the leadership of a strong president. Institutional reform created just such a figure. This meant that if a demagogue ever took the presidency, he would have far more power than the type of president imagined by the Founders. And elite rule expanded through its occupation of the federal bureaucracy, which reached deep into everyone's daily lives. As people came to expect the federal government to solve problems, and to be disappointed by the results, the historical suspicion of elites became a more explosive threat to governance. Meanwhile, populism germinated at the local and state level, where it offered opportunities for local demagogues to hone their craft.

THEODORE ROOSEVELT

With Theodore Roosevelt, we encounter a new leadership style. Roosevelt, born in 1858, was an upper-class reformer with a strong sense of public duty. He might have been a demagogue if he had chosen to, and in some instances he came close. He certainly possessed the talents that a demagogue needs: a craving for power, energy, charisma. And he was the first president who self-consciously tried to develop an image—we might say a "brand"—that would appeal to the public and serve as an engine to carry him to power. George Washington and Andrew Jackson also made strong impressions on the public prior to their elevation to the presidency, but neither of them created his image in the studied way that Roosevelt created his.

Roosevelt worked his way up the political ranks. He was a thoroughly professional politician: member of the State Assembly of New York; member of the United States Civil Service Commission; president of the New York Police Commissioners Board; assistant secretary of the navy; New York governor; vice president. But he did not act like a normal politician, at least not the type who aspired to the presidency. He cultivated a tough-guy image as a rancher, hunter, and soldier. Roosevelt overcame his childhood shyness and his weak physical constitution by aggressively testing himself in difficult situations. Throughout his life, he loudly advocated the manly virtues of courage, self-discipline, ambition, and toughness.

Roosevelt approached his presidency in a similar spirit. The Republican Party in the late nineteenth century had been dominated by big business, but liberals and other reformers created a progressive wing that Roosevelt helmed. Roosevelt used the antitrust laws, which had been enacted in 1890 but had lain mostly dormant since, to attack some of the great monopolies of the time, supported food regulation to protect consumers, championed a law authorizing the government to regulate railroad rates, and advanced the cause of conservation by protecting federal lands from development. In foreign policy, he trumpeted American power by sending a fleet around the world, and orchestrated a revolution in Colombia that would eventually lead to the construction of the Panama Canal. He was an aggressive and popular president.

But was he a demagogue? The populist demagogue "Pitchfork Ben" Tillman, now a senator, accused him of being one. Tillman complained that Roosevelt "owes more to newspapers than any man of his time, or possibly of any other time." Tillman was right. Roosevelt had manipulated the press by playing favorites, punishing detractors, leaking confidential information, bottling up cabinet members so as to ensure a consistent message, and staging publicity stunts, like riding a submarine to the bottom of Long Island Sound and shooting a bear. Roosevelt was the first president to employ PR flacks and devoted more energy to cultivating journalists than any of his predecessors did. He was the first president to understand the importance of the mass media and how to use it to create a popular image.[3]

Roosevelt also made speeches like no other president before him. In 1906, he took a nine-week tour through the West, traveling 14,000 miles and delivering 265 speeches. In his speeches, he frequently denounced his critics, on both left and right, calling the former demagogues and the latter reactionaries. Nor were his speeches models of rigor. His first message to Congress used the violent death of President McKinley as an excuse to demand restrictions on immigration. (The assassin, Leon Czolgosz, was American born.) In one of the most shameful episodes of his presidency, he defended his controversial decision to order the dishonorable discharge of 167 African American soldiers who had been falsely accused of committing and covering up crimes—in a speech full of falsehoods and exaggerations. But this was an exception. Roosevelt did not gain or try to maintain power by race-baiting—quite the contrary. He was one of the first presidents to reach out to black leaders; he invited Booker T. Washington to dinner at the White House, a small gesture that produced a politically damaging outpouring of condemnation from southern politicians. Few people other than Tillman accused Roosevelt of demagoguery, probably because his policies were decidedly middle-of-the-road, and the tenor of his claims was optimistic and unifying. He cooperated with Congress and other government institutions and was generally honest.[4]

As president, Roosevelt confronted the chasm between his reformist ambitions and an obstinate Congress. Like Andrew Jackson, Roosevelt claimed that Congress was captured by interest groups, and only the president was capable of advancing the public good. Drawing on Jackson and Lincoln, Roosevelt articulated a "stewardship" theory of the presidency. He rejected the old idea that the president was the "servant" of Congress and argued that the president—as the representative of the public at large— was responsible for advancing the public interest in any way he could, except when Congress or the Constitution blocked him. Roosevelt relied on existing legislation and his constitutional powers to advance his conservation policies and battle monopolies. While Roosevelt never violated a statute, he seized opportunities to act on his own that earlier presidents had assumed were foreclosed.

Roosevelt, who liked to accuse left-wing reformers of demagoguery, knew that his stewardship theory opened him up to the charge of demagoguery as well. Intent on amassing power, the demagogue sees the legislature as a barrier and seeks to undermine it. But the stewardship theory acknowledged that the legislature could block the president if it wanted to. Roosevelt also argued that he would appeal to the public over the heads of the legislators only "as a last resort," after exhausting the traditional path through congressional leadership. A demagogue would show no such scruples.[5]

While Roosevelt clashed with Congress, he did not in fact push it aside. Congress acquiesced to some of his reforms but retained its central policymaking role. Still, as we will see, Roosevelt began to hollow out one of the major bulwarks against presidential power: the separation of powers, and in particular the primacy of Congress in the creation of policy. This process would be pushed forward by subsequent presidents, above all Franklin Roosevelt.

To appeal to the public, Theodore Roosevelt needed a means to communicate. Like his predecessors, and in an era before radio and television broadcasts, he relied on newspapers and magazines to take his message to the public. Roosevelt worked hard to cultivate journalists. He largely succeeded, though he fought battles with the hostile Hearst chain of papers, even asking the Justice Department to investigate whether it engaged in seditious libel.

Roosevelt was a Progressive, but to a striking degree the form of government that emerged during his presidency resembled Tom Watson's populist fever dream. The key resemblance involved the apparently odd conjunction of national bureaucracy—meritocratic, routinized, colorless, mechanical—headed by a Napoleon rather than a functionary. What was it about America (or France, for that matter) that required a marriage of bureaucracy and one-man charismatic leadership? This is certainly not what the Founders had in mind. But in the end Roosevelt wasn't a demagogue—either he couldn't be, because he was too heavily constrained by institutions, or he wouldn't be, because demagoguery would have violated his patrician sense of honor.[6]

THE RISE OF TECHNOCRACY: THE BUREAUCRACY AND SOCIAL SCIENCE AS THE NEW BULWARK

Roosevelt's stewardship vision was one in which the president took center stage in making policy. Congress would be reactive rather than the primary policymaking body. It was not entirely clear how this would work. From where exactly would the president get his authority to act, or the funds? Roosevelt did not think the president could tax people; that remained a congressional power, firmly established in the Constitution. As we will see, the answer would be . . . from Congress itself. It would create new agencies and give the president authority over them, while supplying funds without much question.

Before we get to these developments, we should pause and ask, What constrains presidential power if Congress is shoved to the side? The answer was supplied by the Progressives: science.

In the late nineteenth and early twentieth centuries, the American educational establishment began to mature. Influenced by the more advanced German university system, American scholars began to push for the professionalization of research. The American Economic Association was founded in 1885, for example. Richard Ely, one of its founders, had been trained in Germany and would become one of the great Progressive reformers, who characteristically married his aspirations for reform with a commitment to scientific rigor. Science had earned immeasurable prestige through its demolition of religious dogmas and contributions to the engineering feats of the Industrial Revolution, including the railroad, the telegraph, and the electric lightbulb. Economists and other scholars applied (or tried to apply) proven scientific methods to the study of society. These new "social scientists" persuaded government (and business as well) that their techniques could be used to put policymaking on a scientific basis. As the government began to regulate food and drug purity, for example, it could use both scientific and social-scientific techniques to ensure that industry did not poison consumers.

The Progressives argued that science promised not only

technical accuracy but also political neutrality. The policy that emerged from science would not favor Democrats or Republicans, farmers or urbanites, business or proletarians. It would simply be right, the best for the public. And if policy could be determined scientifically, there was really no need for Congress. Congress did not do things scientifically—far from it. In Congress, policy emerged from deal-making, which is about as unscientific as you could get.

As the twentieth century rolled on, a consensus developed that policymaking thus should be transferred, at least in part, from Congress to federal agencies. The agencies would be organized along scientific lines. They would be staffed with experts— scientists, economists, lawyers—who were charged with the task of solving social problems using expert techniques. The staff would be hired under meritocratic principles established by the Pendleton Act back in 1883. The agencies wouldn't be entirely independent of politics, of course. They would obtain funds from Congress and would be subject to some kind of ambiguous supervision by or influence from the president. This model began to emerge as early as 1887, when Congress created the Interstate Commerce Commission to regulate railroad rates. It was perfected throughout the twentieth century, in such agencies as the Food and Drug Administration (which regulated the purity of food and the safety and efficacy of drugs), the Securities and Exchange Commission (which regulated capital markets), the Federal Communications Commission (which regulated radio, and later television); the Environmental Protection Agency, the Federal Energy Regulatory Commission, and so on.

But where does that leave the public? Lippmann argued in a pair of books written in the 1920s that the public is (and should be) left out. The "bewildered herd" on the farms and in the cities could not comprehend the enormous complexity of society.

> The individual man does not have opinions on all public affairs. He does not know how to direct public affairs. He does not know what is happening, why it is happening, what ought to happen.[7]

Lippmann and many other Progressives believed that the complexity of modern life brought about by enormous advances in technology and economic organization in the late nineteenth century placed policy far beyond the grasp of ordinary people. Policy decisions needed to be made by experts and sold to the public by political leaders. Thus, the notion that the experts would choose policies that benefit the public underwent a subtle transformation: if the public itself didn't know what benefited it, then those policies would reflect expert judgment about what was in the public's interest. On this view, the problem with Congress was not so much that it advanced special interests but that it could not reflect the interests of the public even if it wanted to—because neither the public nor members of Congress, who are not experts, have any idea what the public's interest is.

As the technocratic view expanded, the notion of the demagogue—at least, among the elites—did as well. A demagogue was someone who shunned science and bureaucracy, appealed to the public for the answers, and promised to carry through whatever answers the public supplied. Think of Donald Trump's technique of determining policy according to the volume of the response when he flung out a proposal to a stadium audience. Lippmann was, however, far from clear about what would keep the elites in line—serving the public rather than themselves—and why a "bewildered herd" would obey them. As the philosopher John Dewey pointed out:

> If the masses are as intellectually irredeemable as [Lippmann's] premise implies, they at all events have both too many desires and too much power to permit rule by experts to obtain. The very ignorance, bias, frivolity, jealousy, instability, which are alleged to incapacitate them from share in political affairs, unfit them still more for passive submission to rule by intellectuals.[8]

However, Dewey, who sought to advance democracy in the form of more open and fairer public debate with greater reliance on facts, never adequately justified his claim that the public was actually capable of open and fair debate and willing to accept the policies, if any, that public debate led to.

THE RISE OF THE IMPERIAL PRESIDENT

At the same time technocracy advanced, so did a concept that seems to conflict with it: the imperial president. Recall Tom Watson's vision of government. The farmers' problems would be addressed through an expert bureaucracy—technocracy—and yet a Napoleonic leader would occupy the presidency.

While Watson, by this time a professional racist and nativist, had little use for the progressive Theodore Roosevelt, Roosevelt was the first president to advance Watson's vision of government. Roosevelt both promoted the large activist government-by-bureaucracy that Watson envisioned and—was this a coincidence?—began the process of enlarging the presidency, both its image and its power. Young, energetic, fearless, martial, and decisive, Roosevelt embodied the romantic spirit of Napoleon, but a cowboy version suitable for the New World.

Roosevelt believed that while bureaucracy was necessary for the humdrum business of governing, resolving disputes between clashing interests, and developing expertise to bring to bear on public problems, the public wanted an inspiring, unifying figure, someone who would elevate everyday life and embody the masses' values and ambitions. That inspiration could no longer be found in local politicians in a nationalizing era, nor in the great orators of the Senate, who also seemed provincial. The Constitution supplied only one national leader, and that was the president.

As Congress pulled aside to make room for the bureaucracy, a major constraint on presidential power—and hence rule by demagogue—began to erode. The nineteenth-century idea that Congress makes policy and the president implements it, always under pressure in times of crisis, could no longer be sustained.

What would this mean? Most of Roosevelt's immediate successors were not ambitious enough to test the new powers of the presidency. Only Woodrow Wilson was. Earlier in his life, as an academic, Wilson gained fame by criticizing the cumbersome structure of the US Constitution and urging America to move toward a parliamentary-style system where the executive and legislature would be more closely bound together. In the British system, which he admired, the prime minister and a small group of advisers made policy that would be rubber-stamped by Parliament as long as they maintained its confidence. After Wilson entered office in 1913, he successfully pushed forward the bureaucratic expansion of the US government and then led America into World War I, where the national government's role as economic manager opened up new possibilities of bureaucratic supremacy.

We can see in Roosevelt and Wilson a model for the resolution of the later debate between Lippmann and Dewey. Messy deal-making politics led by professional politicians who engaged the loyalty of their constituents—traditional democracy as it was idealized—would be replaced by technocratic bureaucracy above which stood a single charismatic figure with whom the public could identify. The bureaucracy performed the Lippmannesque function of bringing expert opinion to bear on matters of public policy, generating policy outcomes that would advance the public good. The charismatic leader would satisfy the public that their values and interests were being taken into account, thus keeping a kind of democracy in place, even if not at all the participatory type of democracy that Dewey championed. But how exactly was the charismatic leader supposed to act? And what ensured that he would act in the public interest?

FRANKLIN ROOSEVELT: A DEMAGOGUE?

Franklin Delano Roosevelt, a distant relation of Theodore, was born in 1882. Graced with a superb temperament, brilliant political instincts, wealth, and excellent family connections, he enjoyed a meteoric political career. After attending Columbia Law School and working for a few years, he won a seat in the New York State Senate, where he pursued a Progressive agenda. An early supporter of Woodrow Wilson, he was rewarded with an appointment as assistant secretary of the navy. He served with distinction through World War I and its aftermath. In the 1920s, he became seriously ill and was left a paraplegic, but he nonetheless was elected governor of New York in 1928. Roosevelt was a popular governor, and he distinguished himself with an energetic response to the economic collapse that would become the Great Depression.

The misery of the 1930s was biblical in its intensity. Factories shut down, producing armies of unemployed workers who flooded soup kitchens and threw up shantytowns called Hoovervilles after the sitting president. Banks foreclosed on houses and farms, then collapsed themselves, wiping away the savings of ordinary people. Droughts led to dust storms and the destruction of farmland, producing mass migrations and depopulating parts of the country. The populism of the 1890s made a comeback, and so did radical ideas on the left and right.

President Herbert Hoover flailed helplessly at the disaster. The economic orthodoxy of the time held that downturns were inevitable and that there was nothing to do but ride them out. Some commentators even celebrated them as a just punishment for those who had invested recklessly. Hoover was not so heartless—he was a great humanitarian and brilliant man who had earned fame, gratitude, and admiration for his coordination of food relief to famine-stricken Europe after World War I. But he did not know what to do; nor did the experts on whom he relied. He also lacked the foresight, temperament, and political support to engage in radical action. While, contrary to popular belief, Hoover did not sit on his hands, his efforts to address the national emergency were limited and fruitless.

Hoover's defeat in the 1932 election was foreordained. The Democrats united under Franklin Roosevelt. Roosevelt knew he would win the election unless he made a serious error, and so he waged a cautious campaign, which was heavily criticized for its blandness. No one understood what caused the Depression or how to address it; Roosevelt did not want to commit himself to a particular economic prescription. Under pressure from journalists and commentators, he gave one speech in which he denounced Wall Street executives as "selfish and opportunistic" and called for "bold persistent experimentation," which alarmed conservatives.[9]

At the start of his first inaugural address, Roosevelt firmly rejects the greatest tool of the demagogue: fear. "So, first of all, let me assert my firm belief that the only thing we have to fear is fear itself—nameless, unreasoning, unjustified terror which paralyzes needed efforts to convert retreat into advance." The speech proceeds with a frank acknowledgment of the country's difficulties (which Trump's "American carnage" inaugural address vaguely echoes but with far less justification), along with optimism about its prospects now that the "unscrupulous money changers," who have brought the country nearly to ruin, "have fled from their high seats in the temple of our civilization"—an oblique anti-Semitic reference that recalls the populists. Then, after a brief homily on the "falsity of material wealth as the standard of success," Roosevelt promises "action now." Then follow several proposals. And a warning:

> It is to be hoped that the normal balance of executive and legislative authority may be wholly adequate to meet the unprecedented task before us. But it may be that an un- precedented demand and need for undelayed action may call for temporary departure from that normal balance of public procedure.

This veiled threat is followed by the suggestion that Congress may need to grant the president "the one remaining instrument to meet the crisis—broad Executive power to wage a war against the emergency, as great as the power that would be given to me if we were in fact invaded by a foreign foe." Roosevelt never made good on this threat, as Congress—overwhelmingly Democratic—passed more than a dozen new laws he proposed within the first one hundred days of his presidency. These laws, and others that would follow, set up new federal agencies under Roosevelt's control, which would allow him to regulate and give relief without requiring additional congressional participation.[10]

The major institutional challenge to Roosevelt's rule came not from Congress but from the Supreme Court. The Court had long shown skepticism toward progressive legislation—laws that attempted to constrain the power of corporations, including minimum wage laws. Progressives had furiously criticized the Court since Theodore Roosevelt's administration, arguing that its judicial philosophy favored the rich. The progressive economist Richard Ely, for example, wrote in 1907 that the majority of justices legislated the "economic individualism of the eighteenth century." Roosevelt himself worried that the Court would block the New Deal. While the Court initially showed some flexibility toward government action in light of the emergency economic conditions, it struck down several New Deal laws in the mid-1930s, notably the National Industrial Recovery Act, which gave the president the power to regulate wage and price competition.[11]

While the Court's rulings are often blamed on a conservative commitment to laissez-faire, this criticism is a bit unjust. They also reflected uneasiness with presidential authority. The Court worried that if Congress could give the president the power to regulate wages and prices, and other industrial conditions, without any constraint, it was abdicating its role as policymaker to the president. Even the more progressive justices on the Court joined the libertarian majority in *Schechter Poultry Corp. v. United States*,

the 1935 case in which the Court struck down the National Industrial Recovery Act because it was "an unconstitutional dele-
gation of legislative power" to the president.[12] FDR believed that
emergency conditions, and the failure of economic orthodoxy,
justified such a transfer of power. A few months after his massive
reelection triumph in 1936, Roosevelt proposed the innocuously
named Judicial Procedures Reform Bill. He meant to bring the
Court to heel by packing it with his supporters.

There is no doubt that Roosevelt's goal was simply to stop the
Court from blocking New Deal laws. However, he claimed that the
law was addressed to a separate problem—the aging of the judiciary. Hence the bill applied to the federal judiciary as a whole,
not just the Supreme Court, and authorized the president to appoint new judges (and justices) to courts where existing judges
reached the age of seventy and failed to resign, subject to a limit
of two judges for each lower federal court and six justices for the
Supreme Court. But given the demographics of the Supreme
Court, this would have allowed Roosevelt to engineer a pro–New
Deal majority through appointments easily confirmed by the
Democratically controlled Senate.

FDR proposed the bill in early February 1937. As opposition mounted, he abandoned this deception and made an explicit
case for packing the Court. On March 9, he delivered a fireside
chat over the radio in which he forthrightly accused the Court's
majority of implementing its "personal economic predilections"
(as asserted by one of the minority in a dissenting opinion) and
acting as a "super-legislature." FDR also explained that a constitutional amendment to increase the size of the Court would
be blocked by opponents of the New Deal and noted that the
number of justices had been changed before. The plan divided
the public and was blocked by Congress in July, after the Court's

majority seemed with surprising alacrity to drop its objections to New Deal laws. While no other New Deal law would be struck down, the fallout badly damaged FDR's political standing and the Court itself.[13]

Meanwhile, war between Japan and China broke out in that same month. Adolf Hitler had consolidated his power over Germany and was preparing to assert it against Europe. By the time Germany invaded Poland in 1939, Roosevelt realized that both Japan and Germany posed serious threats to American security, and that the United States might need to go to war. But isolationist sentiment in the United States was extremely powerful. Congress had passed neutrality legislation in 1935, 1936, and 1937, which severely hampered Roosevelt's ability to provide military aid to the countries embroiled in the conflict. And with an election to win in the fall of 1940, Roosevelt could not afford to appear bellicose, or even willing to consider American military participation or aid to the beleaguered Allies. The Republican candidate, Wendell Willkie, sensing Roosevelt's vulnerability, accused him of hiding his intentions to enter the war. Roosevelt denied the charge: "I have said this before, but I shall say it again and again and again: Your boys are not going to be sent into any foreign wars." And Roosevelt darkly warned of "certain forces within our own national community, composed of men who call themselves American but who would destroy America." He was not above implying that his political opponents were traitors.[14]

Some scholars argue that Roosevelt all this time, and especially after the surrender of France in June 1940, sought to engineer an "incident" that would provide him with the public support he needed to enter the war. In fact, Roosevelt had told Churchill that he hoped to do exactly that. The opportunity arrived in the summer of 1941. The USS *Greer*, a destroyer, skirmished with a German submarine in the North Atlantic. In a radio speech, Roosevelt claimed that the submarine provoked the attack knowing that the US ship belonged to a neutral nation and that the United States did not seek a "shooting war with Hitler." All these claims were lies: the destroyer had joined an attack initiated by a British military plane, and the submarine commander could not know from the depths that the *Greer* was an American ship. The political scientist John Mearsheimer sees Roosevelt's lies as "fearmongering," necessary to rally the public by dramatizing the risks posed by a foreign adversary whose dangerousness is not understood. Fearmongering is often seen as a kind of demagogy; indeed, Mearsheimer, while sympathetic to Roosevelt's predicament, calls fearmongering "antidemocratic at its core."[15]

But that view is too simple. Modern democracy is representative democracy, and the theory of representative democracy assumes that ordinary people will not be continuously consulted by political leaders. With better information, the advice of experts, and the time to deliberate and debate about policy, elected officials are expected to disregard rather than to track the day-to-day fluctuations of popular opinion, and to make decisions on behalf of the public that the voters will ratify during the next election cycle. The Founders themselves expected the president to act in secret when events so required, an expectation that was vindicated in the first administration of George Washington. It follows that the president cannot always be candid about his intentions, and may at times be justified in using the tools of indirection and even deception.

Roosevelt used some demagogic tactics, but he is exonerated

in this instance for several reasons. First, he acted during a serious emergency—actually two emergencies, the Great Depression and the start of World War II. The creaky American constitutional system inhibits executive action, and while that may be tolerable in normal times, in a national emergency a timid executive may spell doom. The Great Depression was already three years old when Roosevelt took office, and a new banking crisis had begun just months earlier. Hoover was not up to the task. Roosevelt also faced an extraordinarily complex situation in the run-up to World War II, when he sought to signal to Germany that America would come to the aid of the Western alliance while avoiding a domestic political backlash that could have hamstrung the eventual war effort.

Second, he calibrated his rhetoric and actions to the task at hand, avoiding excessive deception and maintaining a degree of respect for his institutional opponents. His threat to Congress was veiled, not explicit, and he chose his words with care. His threat to the Supreme Court was, in the end, ill advised, but he backed down, and his plan, while convoluted, was contrived to give him the minimum necessary control over the Court. The extent of his deception of the public and Congress prior to the 1940 election remains contested by scholars; he seems to have been feeling his way rather than following a conspiratorial design. And certainly some of his statements crossed a line—like his claim about a Nazi plan to create an International Nazi Church with *Mein Kampf* replacing the Bible.[16]

Third, Roosevelt largely avoided the negative emotions and the vilification of opponents, to an extent surprising for the times. The rich were widely hated, and while Roosevelt indulged the public with his attacks on Wall Street, his language was always vague. His complaints about Congress were institutional, not personal; his criticisms of the Supreme Court were measured and reasonable. Even in his speeches and messages about the war with Germany and Japan, he avoided the paranoid, bombastic, incendiary language of the demagogue. The mildness of his language, in fact, almost recalls Lincoln (in 1945: "We have learned the simple truth, as Emerson said, that 'The only way to have a friend is to be one'"). His speech seeking a declaration of war against Japan on December 8, 1941, was a short legalistic address that merely insisted that the Japanese had acted wrongfully by launching a premeditated surprise attack on the United States. (Roosevelt did, however, authorize the internment of Japanese Americans and Japanese aliens after war was declared, and took other harsh war measures, including censorship of anti-war activists, which have been heavily criticized.) Overall, his rhetoric was optimistic, pragmatic, and unifying.[17]

Fourth, when events allowed, Roosevelt proceeded deliberately, and with support from a range of institutions and persons. The Supreme Court really was an ideologically rigid and geriatric institution, wholly out of date and unable to appreciate the challenges of the Depression and the inadequacies of the national administrative structure. Legal scholars, journalists, politicians, and reformers had urged Roosevelt to address the problem years before he finally acted. Leaders in Congress supported reform. The Justice Department explored many different avenues for reform, and worked for years on a constitutional amendment before abandoning the effort as too vulnerable to an eviscerating interpretation by the Court's majority. Roosevelt tolerated numerous reverses on the Court, hoping that he would get a chance to appoint justices through natural attrition.[18]

Fifth, Roosevelt was vindicated by events, as much as history ever allows. While the New Deal was a hodgepodge of measures, some bad and others good, it was a political stroke of genius that got America through the long Depression without the extremism, polarization, and political violence that occurred in many other countries at the time. The New Deal finally pushed the US government into the modern era, after Theodore Roosevelt's and Wilson's baby steps, with the creation of a bureaucracy capable of addressing a national economy. Roosevelt correctly diagnosed the threat posed by Nazi Germany and understood the inevitability of American involvement in the world war. Roosevelt sought power and enjoyed wielding it, but he used his power for the public good.

Still, with Roosevelt, the line between demagogue and statesman was an ambiguous one. The demagogue claims to know the public will and brooks no dissent. Roosevelt did not go that far, but popular sovereignty was a flimsy thing in his conception. As he said:

> Government includes the art of formulating a policy, and using the political technique to attain so much of that policy as will receive general support; persuading, leading, sacrificing, teaching always, because the greatest duty of a statesman is to educate.[19]

Here is a softened (or merely diplomatic?) version of Lippmann. If the public must be educated, then its views must be inaccurate. Roosevelt allows that the public must be persuaded if the president wants to act—and he was painfully aware of this constraint in the years leading up to the war—but if he cannot persuade the public, then the problem lies with the people, not with the president.

THE LURE OF THE DEMAGOGUE

Hardly anyone called Franklin Roosevelt a demagogue. A class traitor, yes. Even at the height of the debate about the Court-packing plan, he was accused of seeking excessive power or disregarding the Constitution, but not of demagoguery. And this was not because the word was out of fashion in the 1930s. One of the most prominent political figures of the Depression—Louisiana governor Huey Long—was widely regarded as a demagogue.

Southern soil was a fertile source of demagoguery after Reconstruction, so much so that the "southern demagogue" or "Dixie demagogue" became a stock character in American politics. Tom Watson of Georgia was a demagogue, and so was one-eyed "Pitchfork Ben" Tillman, the governor of South Carolina before he was elected US senator in 1894, who called Theodore Roosevelt a demagogue. So were Jeff Davis, governor of Arkansas from 1901 to 1907 and US senator from 1907 to 1913; James Vardaman, governor of Mississippi from 1904 to 1908 and US senator from 1913 to 1919; Coleman Blease, governor of South Carolina from 1911 to 1915 and US senator from 1925 to 1931; Theodore Bilbo, governor of Mississippi from 1916 to 1920 and from 1928 to 1932 and US senator from 1935 to 1947; and many others.

It's hard to generalize about these men, but certain features stand out. Many of them were talented people—brilliant speakers who brought their audiences to their feet by spraying colorful insults at their opponents, but also by presenting complex issues in simple, which is to say simplistic, terms. Anticipating Trump, Davis invented effeminate nicknames for his (male) opponents—Aunt Puss, Sister Hinemon, Aunt Jennie. The demagogues portrayed themselves as tough guys, attacked intellectuals, and engaged in clownish antics that mocked the solemn rituals of establishment politics. Bilbo used "delightfully shocking profanity and Biblical

allusions" and linked his opponents to "lumber, utility, and manufacturing interests" and Wall Street. He promised to redistribute wealth, build roads, raise the price of cotton, and much else,
which he never accomplished in office. The demagogues were
charismatic and energetic campaigners. They were amoral and
opportunistic. They made outlandish promises that they never
kept. They attacked the courts, the press, and other established
institutions and celebrated the mob. Governor Blease, for example, praised lynchers for acting "like men. . . . You defended
your neighbors and put black bodies under the ground." They
presented their constituents—farmers and working people—as
victims of the "money power," of northern politicians, of blacks,
and of trusts, and themselves as martyrs to their cause, always
under threat from these same hated enemies. They came to power
as a voice of rural farmers who had been left behind and were ignored by the political establishment, and they all either advanced
or took for granted white supremacy.[20]

In many cases, southern demagoguery was more a matter of
style than substance. The southern political system was frozen by
one-party rule and tremendously corrupt. The railroads, the oil
industry, and other interests financed both the more polished
and educated establishment politicians and the rough-hewn
demagogues, and as a result could expect either type of politician
to do their bidding. Poor whites as well as African Americans were
disenfranchised. Some observers have argued that southern voters
did not expect much from their politicians, and so demagogues
could obtain support because of their entertainment value and
because they would give voice to the people's resentment toward
business interests.[21] Many of the demagogues simply joined the
line at the trough of corruption once they achieved power—they
were co-opted by the governing and business establishment—

while others were ultimately thwarted by their opponents. On this view, the demagogue hardly deserves to be singled out as a constitutional problem. If the political system as a whole is not democratic, and power lies behind the scenes, it hardly matters whether a demagogue or a nondemagogue is elected.

Huey Long resembled the other southern demagogues in some respects but stands out from the crowd. He seems to have been genuinely concerned about the poor and, while personally racist and willing to engage in race-baiting when circumstances called for it, did not advocate white supremacy in the relentless, vicious style that was so common in the South at the time—although more likely because of the complex racial politics in Louisiana than because of any personal scruples. Also, because he amassed far more political power than the other southern demagogues did, he could point to some political accomplishments, such as educational improvements and road construction—though the extent of those accomplishments has been debated by historians. Long was also less willing to traffic in southern myths, nostalgia for the antebellum South, and the Lost Cause—though no doubt because these ideas played less well in Louisiana than in places like South Carolina, and in the 1920s than in an earlier era. In all these ways, Long was a more appealing and significant figure than the other southern demagogues. However, Long dominated Louisiana politics through crafty opportunism, his personal magnetism, and his contempt for the law. For a brief period, he was feared by Franklin Roosevelt and the rest of the national political establishment, who saw him as an American Mussolini or Hitler.

Long was born in 1893 in Winn Parish, Louisiana. Winn Parish was a poor area with a long history of political dissent—resisting secession in 1861, supporting the populists in the 1890s, and even giving significant support to the presidential campaigns of the socialist Eugene V. Debs. Long was highly intelligent, with a superb memory, and after some early setbacks he established himself as a talented lawyer in his early twenties.[22]

Demagogues throughout the South drew their strength from the common features of the region. The Civil War had demolished the antebellum political systems as well as the economy, and in the turmoil that followed, various oligarchies reestablished themselves, dominated by wealthy farmers, professionals, and rising commercial interests, including giant corporations like Standard Oil. Because the Republican Party was tainted by its association with the North, the Democratic Party was able to establish one-party rule in every state. Meanwhile, the mass of citizens—mostly impoverished farmers, and some industrial workers—remained poorly educated and often politically passive. The theory of white supremacy, mingled with nostalgia for the slave era, was a potent political weapon, which the Democratic establishment, in order to maintain power, skillfully exploited to divide poor blacks and whites. The racist principles enforced by mob rule in the Reconstruction era were gradually institutionalized as Jim Crow.

By the 1920s, the system favored professional politicians who kowtowed to the oligarchy, along with the occasional demagogue who gave voice to the oppressed without actually challenging the establishment or doing much for them. Louisiana was a particularly backward state, with complex politics and an effective machine in New Orleans. The governor was selected behind closed doors by political bosses and business leaders who manipulated the elections. Reformers made little impact against entrenched interests. Long saw a different path to power. He was far too impatient to work his way up through the established political hierarchy. He realized that many people resented the local political boss and other members of the establishment, and that he could obtain supporters by attacking them, while making any promises that might resonate. He would gain power by challenging the oligarchy, and to do this he mobilized poor white farmers whom the oligarchy neglected but who enjoyed the advantage of numbers. To be sure, he also received financial backing from wealthy businessmen who sought state contracts.[23]

Long's dazzling rise to power began with his election to the Railroad Commission in 1918, a moribund utility regulator that Long revived and used to harass the railroads and other corporations. In 1924, at the age of thirty, Long ran for governor, lost, and then almost immediately began campaigning again, winning in 1928. He consolidated power by exploiting the already considerable patronage system. He gave posts to legislators who supported him; he forced appointees to sign undated resignation letters so that he could easily fire them if they showed any disloyalty; and he deducted a portion of the salary of state employees to finance his political organization, which also took kickbacks from state contractors. After beating back an impeachment attempt, Long instituted virtual one-man rule over a compliant legislature, the judiciary, the bureaucracy, and local governments. Meanwhile, he taxed and attacked the press, even relying on censorship when possible.[24]

Louisiana limited the governor to one term, but so powerful was Long's hold on the state that he continued to rule Louisiana after he was elected to the US Senate in 1932. He engineered the election of Oscar K. Allen, a childhood friend, to the position of lieutenant governor; Allen then ascended to the governorship when Long moved to the Senate. O. K. was a puppet; he did Long's bidding thereafter, as did the legislature. Long's policies were progressive by the standards of Louisiana politics. He established programs for the free distribution of textbooks to schoolchildren, launched a building program that both employed the poor and produced much-needed infrastructure for Louisiana, improved public health, and gave modest tax relief to lower-income people at the expense of modest tax hikes on corporations. Critics then and now argue that Long's accomplishments were meager and simply served to consolidate his hold over the public. But, like his soon-to-be archenemy Franklin Roosevelt, he boosted the morale of farmers and working people who had been neglected by the oligarchy and now felt that they had an advocate. The poor farmers of Louisiana adored him. A contemporary journalist wrote, "They do not merely vote for him, they worship the ground he walks on. . . . He is part of their religion."[25]

Long helped Roosevelt win the Democratic nomination by delivering Louisiana to him at the national convention and bringing into line delegates from other states. But the two men soon fell out of each other's favor. Long moved to Roosevelt's left, advocating a more radical New Deal than Roosevelt believed was politically feasible. In his first year in the Senate, Long became a disruptive force, filibustering New Deal bills that he deemed too moderate, and attracting press and popular attention with his antics. In 1934, he seized national attention by proposing his Share Our Wealth Plan. The plan envisioned steep taxes on wealth of more than $1 million and on income of more than $1 million per year. The revenues would be redistributed to families in the form of a "household estate" of $5,000 plus a minimum income of $2,000 to $2,500 per year, plus other benefits like educational assistance. The math did not quite work out—there weren't enough millionaires to fund such a generous social welfare system—but the plan was immensely popular and spawned Share Our Wealth Clubs that Long saw as an organizational stepping-stone to a third party.[26]

By this point, the national Democratic establishment was getting the jitters. Along with Charles Coughlin, the radio priest whose increasingly fascistic radio broadcasts drew audiences in the tens of millions, Long posed a threat to Roosevelt's power. The New Deal had generated great popular excitement, but the Depression remained stubbornly in place. Long planned to run for president in 1936, and while he didn't think he could beat Roosevelt, he hoped to divide the Democrats, allowing a Republican to win, destroying Roosevelt politically, and opening a path for Long to obtain the presidency in 1940. However, in 1935, at the age of forty-two, Long was assassinated by Carl Weiss, a member of a prominent Louisiana political family with which Long had feuded.

Franklin Roosevelt called Long "one of the two most dangerous men in the country" (the other was Douglas MacArthur), and ever since, historians have debated whether Long was a demagogue. His defenders say that while Long used unorthodox and sometimes troublesome tactics, those tactics were necessary to defeat an oppressive aristocratic system of rule in Louisiana and bring some measure of relief to the masses. Textbooks for children, roads and bridges, better medical care, an improved state university, and a (small) tax on oil companies are hard to argue with—though these accomplishments were marred by patronage, debt, significant corruption, and various forms of political abuse. At the national level, Long pushed the New Deal to the left in ways that may have been necessary and that, from the standpoint of today, no longer seem radical. Even the Share Our Wealth Plan, while wildly unrealistic at the time, anticipated the more progressive national tax and welfare system that would be developed after Long's death. The historian Alan Brinkley, in his book *Voices of Protest*, defends the Share Our Wealth Plan against the charge of demagoguery because it was not "an attempt to divert attention away from real problems; it did not focus resentment on irrelevant scapegoats or phony villains."[27] No one denies that Long was an opportunist and a power-maximizer, but he did maintain a consistent ideological core and refused, unlike other southern demagogues who obtained power, to sell out to the establishment.

Was Long dangerous to the country because he was a demagogue, or was he dangerous to Roosevelt because he was an effective tribune for the impoverished masses whom the New Deal failed to rescue from the Depression? Whatever one's final judgment on Long, he was widely denounced as a demagogue at the time, unlike most other politicians, including Roosevelt himself. Thus, it takes more than political popularity and a mass following to earn the label. What does it take, then?

Long's style of politics is part of the explanation. He attacked his political opponents with as much viciousness as he could summon ("thieves, bugs, and lice"). In the words of one biographer, "He took a savage delight not merely in beating opponents but in humiliating them." He exploited every angle to gain power. As governor, he searched through the statute book for powers that others had forgotten about. He frequently lied—to the public, to his opponents, to his supporters—and broke promises. Long did not take seriously his duties in the Senate, from which he was usually absent; when he was present, his disruptions brought him national attention but interfered with legislation at a time of national peril. He attacked the money interest on behalf of the virtuous masses, inflaming divisions throughout the country.

While most of Long's most famous addresses—like his Share Our Wealth speeches—are argued in a logical, reasonable way, he was also a master manipulator. Long appealed to the public's envy, greed, anger, and fear at a delicate time in the nation's political history.[28]

He also exploited every angle to obtain attention from the press. Violation of political norms got coverage, and Long realized that he could attract attention by playing the clown. He donned outrageous garb, affected an exaggerated backwoods accent, carried on public debates on the merits of cornpone (a cheap kind of cornbread popular in the South, which had become a byword of southern rural backwardness), and greeted ambassadors while wearing pajamas. Of Long's first day in the Senate, one author writes:

> It had been a debut, however, that the capital was still talking about. There is a well-established rule that not only are freshman senators supposed to be silent, they are supposed to be invisible. But on his first day in the Senate, Huey bounced onto the Senate floor, slapped one distinguished senator on the back, poked an Old Guard Republican in the ribs, and ran around the chamber telling everyone the Kingfish had arrived—all the while puffing on a big cigar, in violation of Senate rules. By the end of the week, Long had attracted more attention than had been accorded a freshman senator in many, many years.[29]

The clownlike antics served other purposes as well: they generated publicity and endeared him to the mass public while causing the elites to underestimate him—at first.

Long also attacked the political and civic institutions that stood in his way. In Louisiana, his favored instrument was patronage.

He demanded loyalty from all public officials—legislators, judges, low-level bureaucrats, janitors. He bought loyalty with graft or public projects. Independent agencies lost their independence; they became stockpiles of his cronies and did his bidding. Civic organizations, like the state bar association, were disbanded. Businesses were subject to arbitrary taxation and regulation. Long ordered the firing of a professor at Louisiana State University, which he treated as a pet project; the professor was rehired after a national controversy erupted, but in other instances Long bullied professors and the school's administration, forcing them to toe his line. Anticipating the debate over Trump's violation of political norms, Long disregarded the norms that kept the Louisiana legislature at the center of power. He disrupted committee meetings, issued threats, publicly ordered legislators how to vote. "I'd rather violate every one of the damned conventions and see my bills passed, than sit back in my office, all nice and proper, and watch 'em die," he said. At the height of his power, he dictated legislation, which the legislature rubber-stamped.

> Despite having no technical authority, Huey packed the membership of government boards, courts, and parish councils with his own majority, gerrymandered political divisions to remove enemies from office, stripped opposing public officials of their power to hire and fire and to make and spend money, and, without warning, revised the dates for elections and length of time in office to oust his enemies and open the door for his loyalists. When his cronies broke the law, he engineered their pardons.

At the national level, he attacked the party system—its norms, hierarchies, and organizational imperatives. Back in Louisiana, he tried to smash the independent press, which he called "the lying newspapers," by taxing hostile newspapers out of existence but was thwarted by the courts. So he established his own newspaper, which spewed forth propaganda like Watson's before him, and gave speeches over the radio. And Long resorted to thuggery on occasion, once ordering his guards to kidnap a troublesome whistle-blower and hold him until he recanted his opposition.[30]

Huey Long helped some people, but he also damaged Louisiana's political institutions. The Louisiana government had always been corrupt and dysfunctional, but Long made it worse.[31]

LOUISIANAN DEMAGOGUE

Long was the most successful American demagogue of the twentieth century. Highly intelligent, astonishingly energetic, charismatic, and cynical, he owed his success to the terrible economic times and to his ability to entrance a mass audience and navigate around the institutional barriers to power. He demonstrates better than any other historical figure American democracy's vulnerability to the demagogue. As a matter of theory, democracy means rule by a majority, but in normal times, the majority of voters are content with the status quo and cannot be organized and mobilized to support a plan of radical redistribution. In bad times, however, they can be. Then it is a matter of identifying an underlying cleavage between a majority and a minority. For the left-wing Long, that cleavage divided the rich and the poor, creating a rare chance to mobilize the more numerous poor to support expropriation of property from the wealthy. For rightwing demagogues like Coughlin, the cleavage divided whites and nonwhite minorities. Most southern demagogues targeted a narrower but still majority group of poor white voters, hoping to expropriate from the rich and from African Americans. To mobilize supporters, the demagogue circumvents established arbiters of opinion and appeals directly to the masses, using whatever advances in communication are ready at hand, and draws on emotionally resonant images, ideas, and arguments to stir up tribal emotions—anger, greed, envy, resentment. The truth is pushed to the side to make room for conspiracy theories that explain all that is wrong. The final step is the use of graft and patronage to destroy institutions that stand in the way of power, and to organize new institutions—one's own political party if possible—to replace them.

But while Long elevated demagoguery to an art form, it seems unlikely that he could have been elected president in 1940 as he planned. Long prospered in backward Louisiana, but his style was otherwise inconsistent with the spirit of the times. The Progressives had earlier targeted government corruption, machine politics, and the tribal aspects of party competition. Many of their innovations—including the introduction of the secret ballot, voter registration, and government regulation of the party primaries—were contrary to Long's no-holds-barred style of political warfare. The Progressives' commitment, bequeathed to the New Dealers, to administrative regularity, nonpartisan expertise, and academic specialization could not have been further from Long's backslapping, deal-making, pajama-wearing tactics. Long could not gain control of the national Democratic Party in such an environment. And a Share Our Wealth Party would have petered out, as the People's Party did in the 1890s. The two-party system had not seen a significant challenge since 1912, when Theodore Roosevelt, head of the short-lived Progressive Party, received eighty-eight electoral votes. And Theodore Roosevelt's cousin Franklin Roosevelt was a far cannier politician than any of Long's opponents in Louisiana were. Long's demagoguery was a game for keeps; if he attracted attention and support by attacking entrenched interests, he also made powerful enemies of those same interests. Long spent the last years of his life ringed by bodyguards.

But if Long could not obtain the presidency for himself, he did show that demagogy could carve a path to power at the national level. His lessons would be quickly absorbed.

6

THE ANTI-TECHNOCRAT BACKLASH
FROM THE NEW RIGHT

(1945–1989)

One of the least passionate demagogues I ever encountered.
—JAMES A. WECHSLER, ON JOSEPH
MCCARTHY (1953)

The populist became the favorite bogeyman of establishment liberals in the 1950s. Indeed, the term has been used in public commentary much more frequently since that decade than it was before. Thanks to Richard Hofstadter, the populist now stood for someone who was in favor of economic centralization and extreme egalitarianism, allowing liberals, who preferred technocratic market regulation, to distance themselves from the economic far (socialist) left. The populist was prejudiced and culturally backward, allowing liberals, who had recently recognized the claims of minorities, to distance themselves from the cultural right. And the populist was inclined toward a type of mass-based authoritarianism, or Caesarism, by contrast to which the rights-protection and managerial bureaucratic instincts of liberals could seem democratic. Most of all, the populist was consumed by resentment toward the elites rather than motivated by legitimate values and interests. Thus, the image of populism that emerged flattered the liberal self-image and could be used to hammer away at Joseph McCarthy and to create a détente with establishment conservatives, who strongly rejected economic centralization and egalitarianism, disliked authoritarianism, and were moving away from racism.[1]

The détente did not last. It depended not so much on a false interpretation of populism as on a false understanding of the American public. Hofstadter tried to delegitimize the nativist, racist, nostalgic, and also radical and utopian strains of American thinking—both extremes of the political spectrum—but practical politicians knew that these sentiments remained popular and could be harnessed to challenge the liberal consensus. What kept demagoguery in check was not the essential moderation and good sense of the American public, as Hofstadter believed, or anyway hoped, but the array of political institutions that constrained the public's influence on the selection of the president and other major politicians.

These institutions would continue to erode through the second half of the twentieth century. We will examine this erosion through a series of vignettes that show the normalization of demagoguery at the national level. We start with Joseph McCarthy, the red-baiting senator from Wisconsin, who in the 1950s became the most famous politician in the country while paralyzing the political establishment. Next, we discuss George Wallace, the most successful of the southern demagogues, whose popularity rested on his effective attacks on the national liberal establishment elites. Richard Nixon and Ronald Reagan refrained from using the worst tactics of McCarthy and Wallace but adopted their populist anti-establishment rhetoric and—with Reagan—began to turn the government against itself. They were helped to power by the errors of the establishment—above all, Vietnam—which in the 1960s and early 1970s led to populist efforts to democratize the party system, which in turn loosened the establishment's hold on the selection of presidential candidates.

McCARTHY AND THE INTELLECTUALS

Joseph McCarthy was one of the great demagogues of American history. Unusually, he was a legislator rather than a president or governor, which greatly circumscribed his freedom of action. Yet he drew on the demagogue's playbook as effectively as Huey Long or Andrew Jackson.

After brief service as a state judge (undistinguished) and an officer in the military during World War II (also undistinguished, but which he subsequently embellished), McCarthy won election to the Senate in 1946. After several years in the Senate (also undistinguished), and casting about for an issue that could make his name, the junior senator from Wisconsin seized on a suggestion from an associate that that issue should be communism. President Harry Truman and the Democratic Party were vulnerable on this issue. As in earlier historical episodes, this one reflected the classic scenario of elite failure and public reaction. The elites—now the liberal technocrats in government, academics, journalists, and Democratic politicians—had been riding high. The Roosevelt administration was credited with maintaining public morale during the Great Depression and winning World War II. Yet the Roosevelt administration also had normalized relations with the Soviet Union in 1933, allied with it against the Axis during World

War II, and ceded control over Eastern Europe to it at Yalta in 1945. The Roosevelt administration also enjoyed the support of the left, including the extreme left once the United States and the Soviet Union made common cause. Many members of the left supported or participated in the administration; some of these members belonged to the American Communist Party, considered themselves communists, or wrote articles or books broadly sympathetic to communism or the Soviet Union. A few of them lent support to the Soviet Union in morally questionable ways, and a tiny number engaged in espionage.[2]

Seen from our point in history, none of this might seem particularly troubling. But most Americans at the time feared radicalism, and the radicalism of the Soviet Union—atheistic, hostile to capitalism—was particularly horrifying, especially after the Soviet Union emerged as a superpower and America's great enemy after the war. Working-class support for communism and the anarchism of immigrants from Italy and Eastern Europe were forgotten as Americans realized that many of communism's supporters were intellectuals—university professors, journalists, politicians, and government officials. In 1948, the House Un-American Activities Committee had exposed Alger Hiss as a spy, making the reputation of Richard Nixon, then a young congressman. Hiss, a Harvard-educated lawyer and card-carrying member of the eastern establishment, had served in the Roosevelt and Truman administrations, where he worked in the State Department. Cosmopolitan, liberal, and festooned with university degrees, he was a perfect embodiment of the hated elite.

The red menace became an extraordinarily potent weapon against Roosevelt's memory, the Truman administration, and the Democratic Party. Leading Republicans accused the Truman administration, despite its aggressive actions against the Soviet

Union and the Korean War, of coddling the communists. The idea took hold, thanks in part to the Hiss affair, that the Truman administration was soft on communism because some government officials *were* communists, and even Soviet agents.

McCarthy was not the first Republican politician to make this connection. But other Republicans were hampered by a problem—the facts. As Soviet espionage was discovered, the FBI and other government agencies lurched into gear, conducted investigations, cleaned house. By 1950, most former communists had recanted or left government and other positions of prominence, and there was little evidence of continuing espionage or subversion by American government officials. The ferreting out of foreign spies and disloyal government officials was the responsibility of the executive branch, and to all appearances it had discharged it. Republicans in Congress could harangue Truman and the Democrats for being soft on communism all they wanted, but the charges did not stick because Truman's foreign policy was so truculently anti-communist.

In 1950, McCarthy gave a routine speech at an obscure forum in Wheeling, West Virginia, in which, according to audience members, he claimed:

> I have here in my hand a list of 205 . . . a list of names that were made known to the secretary of state as being members of the Communist Party and who nevertheless are still working and shaping policy in the State Department.[3]

McCarthy possessed no such list and apparently made up the number 205, which changed with further iterations. But no matter. McCarthy had struck a match in a political climate that was saturated with the fumes of suspicion and fear, and in the media explosion that followed he became the most famous man in the country. Over the next several years, he falsely accused numerous people—government officials, journalists, Hollywood writers, lawyers, professors—of espionage and communist associations. McCarthy did not possess any solid information that any of them were communists, just rumor and innuendo that had long ago been checked out by the FBI and other government agencies. In a series of committee hearings, he and his colleagues bullied, smeared, and humiliated a long line of witnesses—none of whom was ever convicted of a crime in a court, but many of whom lost their jobs because of skittish employers. Hollywood screenwriters drawn into the net were blacklisted.

No one doubted that communism was a foreign policy problem for the United States. McCarthy's contribution in the annals of demagoguery was not to draw attention to this problem, which had long been acknowledged, but to blame communism on the elites—in government, in civil society. Those elites, according to McCarthy, were communists or sympathized with communism or tolerated communist subversion, and for that reason the public could not trust them to protect America from the red menace. Once McCarthy made headway with the public, his claims were virtually impossible to refute. Elites who criticized McCarthy were— according to McCarthy—communists or communist stooges. Their opposition to McCarthy was proof!

A small honorable group of Republicans opposed McCarthy, but most of them feared McCarthy's hold on public opinion. They also appreciated the damage McCarthy did to the Democrats and to Truman. Thus, Republicans were divided in how to deal with McCarthy and took years to muster the courage to stop him. McCarthy's reign finally came to an end in 1954. He had overreached by attacking the Republican administration of Dwight Eisenhower, and his lies and corruption had caught up with him. The turning point came during hearings on communist infiltration of the army, in which the army counterattacked by claiming that McCarthy and his aides had pressured the army to give special treatment to McCarthy's ex-aide G. David Schine. The hearing was broadcast on ABC and reached its climax when McCarthy tried to discredit the army's special counsel, the lawyer Joseph Welch (a partner at the Boston law firm Hale & Dorr), by insinuating that Welch had "foisted" one of his assistants, Fred Fisher, on the committee even though Fisher had belonged to a communist organization.

In fact, Welch had earlier sent Fisher home when Fisher told him that he had belonged to the National Lawyers Guild when he was in law school and shortly afterward. The Guild was a leftish lawyers' organization, whose members had included some communists or communist sympathizers back in the 1930s. By the 1950s, it was by and large respectable; still, a cloud hung over it because of the communist hysteria, so McCarthy's exposure of Fisher's membership on national TV was a national humiliation. McCarthy either did not know or care that Fisher was no longer on Welch's team—probably the latter, as McCarthy earlier had used a doctored photo and a forged letter to press his case against the army. Welch reacted angrily:

> Little did I dream you could be so reckless and cruel as to do an injury to that lad. It is true he is still with Hale & Dorr. It is true that he will continue to be with Hale & Dorr. It is, I regret to say, equally true that I fear he shall always bear a scar needlessly inflicted by you. If it were in

my power to forgive you for your reckless cruelty, I will
do so. I like to think I am a gentleman, but your forgive-
ness will have to come from someone other than me.

After some more back-and-forth, Welch uttered words that still
thrill the hearts of liberals:

Let us not assassinate this lad further, Senator. You have
done enough. Have you no sense of decency, sir, at long
last? Have you left no sense of decency?[4]

Six months later, the Senate censured McCarthy, and popular
opinion turned against him.

What was the nature of McCarthy's demagoguery, and why
did he succeed so well? Like Long, McCarthy realized that he
could get attention for himself, and advance his career, by violating norms. The Senate was not a place where someone impatient
for power could achieve it quickly. It was a collective body that
gave influence to the most senior members and those who mas-
tered the intricacies of parliamentary procedure. But it could be
used as a platform for gaining attention. McCarthy, like Long before him, broke the rules of the Senate with great frequency and
attacked fellow senators personally, vindictively, and ferociously.
He made a sport of tormenting expert witnesses at committee
hearings by bombarding them with phony calculations and spu-
rious analyses, and insulting his senior colleagues who tried to
rein him in. While he made enemies, he also gained power. The
Senate depends on cooperation, which in turn is possible only
when all or most members respect a complicated web of norms,
customs, and folkways. Most senators respect these rules because
only through collective action can they pass laws that please their

constituents. But McCarthy, like Long, wasn't interested in passing laws. He wanted to use the Senate to advance his career.[5]

Also, like Long, McCarthy played the country bumpkin. He dressed poorly, bragged about his sexual exploits, gambled and drank, and expressed contempt for the upper-class tastes and activities of his colleagues in the Senate. As the historian David Oshinsky observed, "McCarthy was a man who loved his vices and saw how they could be used for political advantage. They were, he believed, the vices common to rugged American males, the very things that set him apart from his colleagues."[6]

And, like Long, McCarthy manipulated the press. He did it so ingeniously that the journalists who were his victims gasped with reluctant admiration. News broadcasters and most newspapers were anxious to appear objective, so they were reluctant to editorialize. If a major politician made a controversial statement, the newspaper would report it. If the politician provided no evidence, the newspaper would report that as well, but the overall impression for readers was that the politician's statement should be taken seriously because it was in the news. The headline would report McCarthy's accusations, and then doubts and countercharges would be buried in the story. McCarthy took advantage of this norm by making sensational accusations he knew to be false, reaping the publicity, and then attacking journalists or editorialists who contradicted him. He threatened them with lawsuits; he defamed them on the Senate floor, where he enjoyed immunity from legal action; he hired private investigators to dig up dirt on them; he even physically assaulted a newspaper columnist, Drew Pearson. He encouraged corporations to withdraw ads from "pro-communist" media that criticized him. Many reporters were intimidated, but even those who weren't felt themselves compelled to report McCarthy's slander in a straight way that ended up giving it credence to the public. And even when McCarthy failed to intimidate the press, he saw the benefits of publicly upbraiding it: "If you show a newspaper as unfriendly and having a reason for being antagonistic, you can take the sting out of what it says about you." Trump, asked by a journalist why he kept attacking the media, would later make the same point: "I do it to discredit you all and demean you all, so when you write negative stories about me no one will believe you." As Oshinsky described this strategy in McCarthy's hands:

> He portrayed the differences between the critic and himself as ideological (pro-Communist versus anti-Communist); he attempted to maximize the critic's discomfort; and he never backed away from a fight. It didn't matter if the critic was a liberal or a conservative, a Democrat or a Republican, a powerhouse or a non-entity. Anyone who attacked Joe McCarthy could expect some trouble.

Despite all that, reporters regarded him as a "dream story": "The press flocked to McCarthy because he was bizarre, unpredictable, entertaining, and always newsworthy," Oshinsky wrote. Meanwhile, to avoid being accused of communism in the headlines of the nation's newspapers, politicians tried to avoid crossing McCarthy, however much they disapproved of him and his methods. The parallels with Trump are hard to miss.[7]

The final piece of the puzzle was the atmosphere of hysteria, which had already arisen naturally in response to world events and then been whipped up by responsible as well as irresponsible politicians who believed that it was necessary "to scare hell out of the country," as Senator Arthur Vandenberg put it to Truman, to achieve public support for the fight against communism.[8] We might pause to consider whether Truman's effort to scare the country was itself demagogic or simply reasonable. The country really had something to fear from a nuclear-armed expansionist state that rejected many values prized by Americans, but ordinary people would not give their support to a reasonable policy of containing the Soviet Union unless the threat was exaggerated. Whatever the case, McCarthy took this idea to its logical extreme. He argued that the public should fear not only the nuclear weapons of the Soviet Union but American government officials, university professors, journalists, Hollywood screenwriters, educators, and politicians. He manipulated the rational fear of the Soviet threat, so that this fear ballooned into something grossly out of proportion to the magnitude of that threat. He did so in a way that initially created public confidence in himself and damaged public confidence in government institutions. It was this that marked him as a demagogue.

While McCarthyism was one of the most significant episodes of demagoguery in American history, and caused significant human carnage, there was never a chance that McCarthy himself would be elected president, let alone become a dictator. McCarthy was hampered by his position as just one member of the Senate. He made many enemies, and his methods were thwarted, albeit slowly, by the contending institutions of the US government. Two presidents resisted his requests for information and refused to prosecute people he claimed to have exposed as communists. The bureaucracy, while terrified of him, was protected by civil service laws, political patrons, and its employment in the executive branch. Courts, despite the unceasing efforts by Congress and the executive branch to harass and silence radicals and people with communist associations, however slight, were largely unsympathetic to perjury cases against witnesses at the McCarthy hearings, defamation suits brought by McCarthy against his enemies, and terminations of government employees tarred by McCarthy. The press and opposing politicians slowly organized, exchanged information, and launched the movement to censure him. Eisenhower, who finally saw McCarthy as a challenge to his authority, contributed as well. And while McCarthy's hold on public opinion gave him his power, or at least appeared to, that hold weakened as he overplayed his hand and failed to follow through on his promise to expose communists, opposition mounted and organized, and the Cold War hysteria ended.[9]

In his persecutions of suspected communist subversives, McCarthy relied heavily on the talents of the fantastically repulsive New York lawyer Roy Cohn, who became his chief counsel at the age of twenty-four. Cohn helped McCarthy persecute gay people and popularize the notion that they were security threats, although Cohn himself was gay. Back in New York, Cohn practiced law for several decades; hobnobbed with Mafiosi, politicians, and celebrities; evaded taxes and very likely committed other crimes; and was finally disbarred for unethical conduct shortly before dying from AIDS-related complications in 1986. The legendary ruthlessness of his approach to law, a kind of privatized McCarthyism, earned him many admirers, including his most famous client, a young real estate developer named Donald Trump.

GEORGE WALLACE

It was McCarthyism Richard Hofstadter had in mind when he defined populism as the political vehicle through which resentment against elites is mobilized. McCarthy's target was communism, but his method was populist, based as it was on the theory that intellectual elites were communists, sympathetic to communism, or "soft" and unmanly—unable to make the hard choices necessary to eliminate subversion from the US government and civil society. With Hofstadter's definition, McCarthyism could be linked to another unwholesome development in American politics—revival of the southern populist demagogue.

Its most gifted practitioner was the Alabama segregationist George Wallace. When he began his political career in the 1940s, he was not, by the extremely low standards of the time and place, particularly hostile to African Americans. From 1953 to 1959, he was a state judge who developed a reputation for fairness to black defendants. Unlike the other judges, he addressed black lawyers in a respectful manner rather than calling them by their first names. One black lawyer, later a civil rights leader who condemned him as a "dangerous and unprincipled opportunist," nevertheless recalled that "George Wallace was the first judge to call me 'mister' in the courtroom" and treated him fairly in a case in which he sued white-owned companies on behalf of poor black farmers and prevailed.[10] Like Watson and Long, Wallace ran for office as a populist voice for the common man, advocating a traditional liberal agenda in favor of better schools and more spending on social programs. But after he lost the Democratic primary for governor in 1958 to an outspoken racist, Wallace—like Watson before him—built his political identity on his opposition to civil rights and defense of segregation. He won the race for the governorship in 1962, and in his inaugural speech famously proclaimed "segregation now, segregation tomorrow, segregation forever!" He ran for president in the Democratic primary in 1964 before dropping out, and then in 1968 as the head of a third party called the American Independent Party. In the 1968 elections he was crushed, able to win only five southern states. He tried again in

1972, but his campaign was cut short by an assassination attempt that gravely injured him and ended his influence in national politics.

Wallace campaigned to the right of Richard Nixon, blaming the crime and disorder of the 1960s on integration, Supreme Court rulings in favor of criminal defendants, and—in a somewhat veiled way, since he sought to appeal to audiences outside the South—civil rights. He used the now-familiar demagogue's bag of tricks: name-calling (he frequently called people liars); exaggeration ("the Supreme Court of our country has made it almost impossible to convict a criminal"); hints of violence ("You elect me the President, and I go to California or I come to Tennessee, and if a group of anarchists lay down in front of my automobile, it's gonna be the last one they ever gonna want to lay down in front of!"); lying ("I've never made a racist speech in my life"). He attacked the press ("I want to say that anarchists—and I am talking about newsmen sometimes") and castigated his opponents as "pin-head socialists." The unifying theme was also the (now familiar) attack on the elites at the behest of the common man. In an interview on *Meet the Press*, he declared a "backlash against big government in this country":

> This is a movement of the people, and it doesn't make any difference whether top, leading politicians endorse this movement or not. And I think that if the politicians get in the way . . . a lot of them are going to get run over by this average man in the street—this man in the textile mill, this man in the steel mill, this barber, the beautician, the policeman on the beat . . . the little businessman. . . . They are the ones . . . Those are the mass of people that are going to support a change on the domestic scene in this country.

Stephan Lesher, Wallace's biographer, calls the national reaction "stunning." Wallace's words electrified masses of people, even outside the South, who believed that politicians ignored them.[11]

While Wallace was a failure at national politics, his version of right-wing populism would prove influential. Wallace realized that there was a white working-class constituency for a combination of social conservatism, welfare-state liberalism, and anti-internationalism. Despite the success of the civil rights movement, many whites resented aspects of it that unsettled their lives or seemed to grant privileges to African Americans—including forced busing, affirmative action, and constraints on policing at a time of rising crime. They also were uneasy with gains made by women, abortion rights, and the denigration of their religious convictions. But they were not opposed to the New Deal, supported unions, and valued entitlements like Social Security and Medicare. Wallace also tapped into a long tradition of isolationist sentiment, which had recently given way to the challenges of Nazi Germany and the Soviet Union but remained powerful in many parts of society.

NIXON, REAGAN, AND THE NEW RIGHT

Richard Nixon was another president who often crossed the line into demagoguery. He was not McCarthy, though he was, as a member of the House Un-American Activities Committee, instrumental in exposing Alger Hiss as a spy. But Hiss really was a spy (or very likely was), and Nixon's involvement was more lawyerly than demagogic. In his subsequent campaign for Senate, he attacked his opponent—Helen Gahagan Douglas—by claiming that she had communist sympathies ("EVERY COMMUNIST WHO GOES TO THE POLLS WILL VOTE AGAINST NIXON AND FOR MRS. DOUGLAS," read Nixon's campaign literature),[12] but the campaign was full of name-calling on both sides. Mostly, Nixon was a professional politician who labored diligently as representative, senator, and vice president under Eisenhower.

In his 1968 campaign for the presidency, however, Nixon showed a dark side. Journalists observed that from campaign stop to campaign stop, he would change his positions to please the local audience. While reporters duly reported Nixon's flexible relationship with the truth, their stories did not hurt him. And both in that campaign and, especially, his 1972 campaign, Nixon and his aides engaged in dirty tricks and illegal activities, including burglarizing the Democratic National Committee's office in the Watergate complex to obtain information about the DNC's plans, misusing campaign funds, and covering up these crimes.

All these activities were troubling, but they are not Nixon's chief contribution to the legacy of demagoguery. No doubt influenced by Wallace, Nixon innovated by attacking the elites, including the universities, the press, and the courts; championing ordinary people, whom he called "the silent majority"; and exploiting racist and nativist sentiment, albeit in veiled terms. Like many demagogues, Nixon realized the possibilities of a new technology before anyone else and exploited it more effectively than anyone before—in his case, television. In his famous Checkers speech in 1952, Nixon rescued his political career from charges of corruption with a long accounting of his finances and a sentimental story about the family's cocker spaniel. The speech was ridiculed by intellectuals, who proclaimed Nixon finished. It was watched by 60 million Americans—the largest audience ever for a TV program—and was a smashing success.

Nixon obtained power by taking several positions, and

engaging in activities, that would have lasting significance for Trumpism. First, he attacked the courts. He opposed the turmoil of the '60s, including the counterculture, by running on a law and order platform. He blamed the rising crime rate and other elements of disorder on the Supreme Court, which in a series of decisions under Chief Justice Earl Warren had granted rights to criminal defendants, dissenters, and people who were prosecuted for obscenity.

Second, Nixon attacked the press. Nixon had become convinced the major press organs—like *The New York Times*, *The Washington Post*, and the TV network news programs—were biased against him. Thanks to the Vietnam War and Johnson's many lies, the press lost its historic trust in the government and became significantly more aggressive than it had been in the previous few decades. Moreover, a new generation of journalists had absorbed the left-wing ethos of the '60s. Journalists distrusted Nixon because of his red-baiting history, and possibly because of his awkwardness and strangeness. Nixon was also a devious and unapologetic liar, as journalists well knew. As president, he never directly attacked the press but instead used his vice president, Spiro Agnew, as an attack dog. Agnew famously called the press "nattering nabobs of negativism."[13]

Third, Nixon attacked the intellectuals. Nixon harbored deep animosity toward the world of the academy. Intellectuals at the time were mostly liberals, and they, along with the press and leading Democratic figures, formed a like-minded community, which Nixon called the eastern establishment. Many of them were intellectual and even social snobs, while Nixon's roots were humble. Nixon also believed that ordinary people resented intellectuals—the liberal establishment as well—for their airs and condescension. Agnew, taking the cue, complained that "a spirit of national masochism prevails, encouraged by an effete core of impudent snobs who characterize themselves as intellectuals."[14]

Fourth, while Nixon did not openly attack the government bureaucracy, he worked hard to maneuver around it—mainly by keeping secrets from it—and he manipulated and abused it on occasion. He directed the FBI to spy on his political opponents, and at the same time tried to block the FBI and the Justice Department from investigating the criminal activities of his subordinates. Nixon did not trust civil servants, or even his own political appointees, who he believed were often disloyal.

But it seems wrong to reduce Nixon to a simple demagogue. He was not Joseph McCarthy or Huey Long. The major distinguishing feature is that—Watergate aside—he was a reasonably successful politician, who took policy seriously, took pains to understand it, and tried to govern in the public interest as he saw it. The opening to China and the initiation of détente with the Soviet Union were major foreign policy accomplishments—which he achieved despite the legacy of his own earlier right-wing demagoguery on these topics in the 1950s. His domestic policies were centrist, pragmatic, and for the most part reasonable if not always successful. He was not a unifying figure, but politics were extremely polarized in the late 1960s, and he made concessions to the left and right while trying to present himself as a tribune of long-suffering middle-class and working-class Americans. In the end, he was defeated by the institutions he had challenged. The press exposed Watergate, his own bureaucracy investigated it, the courts compelled him to release the Watergate tapes, and Congress forced him to resign.

Nixon's attacks on the courts, press, intellectuals, and bureaucracy are less well remembered than Watergate, but they are more important for our story. Hardly anyone defended Watergate, once the truth came out. No respectable politicians defended dirty tricks, espionage against political opponents, and the president's covering up of serious crimes, which involved a great deal of public deceit. Nixon was a popular president until the truth of Watergate became known, whereupon his poll numbers plunged and his Republican allies in Congress abandoned him. In contrast, Nixon's attacks on civic and political institutions as centers of elite power set the stage for subsequent presidents, above all, Ronald Reagan.

Reagan, at the time considered by elite opinion a scary right-winger, had enjoyed two successful terms as governor of California from 1967 to 1975. He governed mostly in a pragmatic centrist manner, but he was an outspoken conservative and gained popularity for his attacks on the welfare system and his approval of harsh police tactics against the student protesters who provoked unrest at Berkeley and other campuses.

In the 1970s, the US economy faltered, and an intellectual movement arose that blamed sluggish economic growth and inflation on liberal economic theories and, particularly, excessive regulation of the economy. The movement came to be known as the "deregulation" movement, though of course its supporters did not advocate the elimination of all regulation. The argument was rather that certain sectors of the economy had been subject to excessive or unwise regulation. Thus, the movement was not opposed to regulation per se, and many of its major legislative victories took place during Jimmy Carter's administration, with the support of the Democratic president and Democratic members of Congress.

While the movement was bipartisan, Reagan was its most enthusiastic proponent among major politicians. And in attacking regulation, Reagan made an important rhetorical shift. Rather than arguing that *some* regulation was excessive or unwise, he attacked regulation in general and, significantly, the federal bureaucracy, or government itself. As he joked, "The most terrifying words in the English language are: I'm from the government and I'm here to help." Or as he said on Inauguration Day: "Government is not the solution to our problem. Government is the problem." Even more important, Reagan charged that the government bureaucracy was controlled by an elite. As he put it in a speech during Barry Goldwater's election campaign in 1964:

> This is the issue of this election: Whether we believe in our capacity for self-government or whether we abandon the American revolution and confess that a little intellectual elite in a far-distant capital can plan our lives for us better than we can plan them ourselves.

And on another occasion:

> Extreme taxation, excessive controls, oppressive government competition with business, galloping inflation, frustrated minorities, and forgotten Americans are not the products of free enterprise. They are the residue of centralized bureaucracy, of government by a self-anointed elite.[15]

This charge resonated with many ordinary people who understood nothing about economic regulation but resented the government bureaucrats who seemed to have too much power over their lives.

But while Nixon and Reagan sounded populist themes, and resorted to deceit on occasion (for Nixon, *frequent* occasions; for Reagan, mainly in connection with the Iran-Contra scandal), they mostly avoided the language of the demagogue for the day-to-day business of governing. Both of them reached for inspiration and unity, as so many presidents had before them. Their attacks on the judiciary were made in constitutional terms. Nixon's most contemptuous remarks—about liberals, Jews, Democrats, civil rights leaders, just about everyone—were made in private. And even when Reagan attacked the bureaucracy, he usually couched the attacks in general terms—complaining about waste, overspending, and excesses—rather than directly attacking the integrity of civil servants.

That said, Nixon and Reagan, two professional politicians who owed their presidencies to the elites who financed and staffed their campaigns, saw that they could gain power by attacking elite rule. One, the other, or both successfully attacked elite-dominated institutions—the press, the courts, the intelligentsia, and the bureaucracy—which both constrained the presidency and made it difficult for outsiders to obtain the office. And in doing so, they stirred up the masses, encouraging them to feel that the elites regarded them with contempt and deprived them of their political power.[16] Starting with Nixon, public confidence in many government institutions began a long slide from which it has never recovered.

THE PARTIES DEMOCRATIZE: THE LAST OF THE BULWARKS

The Founders expected that the president would be selected by local elites chosen by (mostly) propertied voters. Acting in the Electoral College, those elites would draw on their wisdom to choose among candidates for the presidency, rather than on popular opinion. The Federalist Party correctly saw this system as one that ensured an elite-run government. Unhappy at their second-class status, ordinary people rushed to Jefferson's Republican Party, which promised to expand the influence of the masses but instead created a system of quasi-dynastic one-party rule by the Virginia planter aristocracy supported by a quasi-oligarchy of political leaders in Congress. When, in 1824, the presidential election was thrown into the House, and leading political figures chose John Quincy Adams for president over the more popular Andrew Jackson, the elitist nature of the national political system could no longer be denied. Van Buren's development of a mass-based political party, the new Democratic Party, was supposed to give people the voice that they had been denied. But the new party system created a new system of elite-dominated rule, one that gave power to state and local political elites—governors, state legislators, mayors, city councilmen, ward leaders, aldermen, and their various advisers, donors, and hangers-on.

These local elites chose the delegates who traveled to national conventions to select the party's presidential candidate. The people were allowed to choose the president in the general election, but their choice was limited to (usually) two candidates previously chosen by the elites. During the Progressive Era, a new effort to give political influence back to the masses resulted in the invention of primaries. But the party elites disliked primaries and eliminated them in some states while maneuvering around them in others. As late as 1968, Hubert Humphrey received the Democratic presidential nomination at the riot-marred Chicago convention without having run in, let alone won, any state primary. Humphrey was selected because he seemed electable to the party elders, but the selection process was attacked by enraged members of the party's anti-war left wing. Reforms by both parties in the wake of this controversy firmly established that candidates for the presidency must first win the support of the voting public in primaries in each state. Federal legislation that attempted to limit the influence of party leaders was also enacted. State primaries regained their importance for the selection of the candidates, and it seemed likely that they would weaken the power of the elites, leading some observers to warn that inexperienced people would be elected to the presidency.[17]

The effect of primaries on elite control, however, was complex. The primaries did not simply transfer power to the masses. To win a state party primary, a candidate could not just put his or her name on the ballot and expect to receive votes. One needed thousands of people to sign petitions in every state, and that cost millions of dollars. One needed public recognition, money for advertising and campaigning, and support—from party officials and other prominent people, like union leaders or business executives, from whom the public would take their cue. To obtain the support of party elites and other prominent people, not-yet-declared candidates would spend years during the so-called invisible primary traveling around the country, meeting with countless elected officials, former elected officials, party officials, journalists, and (above all) donors—all to obtain name recognition, support, cash, and informal commitments. Thus, as recently as, oh, 2016, it was possible to believe that only someone with broad support among the elites of each party could become a candidate and win the presidency. This meant that the parties retained their screening function: they would not permit someone to run for office unless he or she was sober, experienced, and qualified, someone who had been put to the proof by winning earlier elections and governing successfully—the Hillary Clintons, the John McCains, the Mitt Romneys.[18]

The problem with this story is that the whole system could

be gamed—by someone with a lot of money, a lot of name recognition, and the ability to appeal to a broad audience. The people with a lot of money figured this out quickly. In 1996, and then in 2000, the publishing tycoon Steve Forbes ran in the Republican primaries. He won only a few primary elections in the first contest and none in the second; what is notable is that he possessed no prior experience in office and yet was still taken seriously by the public. The weakening of the party organizations also made room for third-party candidates like H. Ross Perot, a billionaire who ran as an independent in 1992 and 1996. He received 19 percent of the popular vote in 1992 and 8 percent in 1996. Forbes was an incompetent campaigner, Perot more skillful, but neither Forbes nor Perot could have gotten as far as they did in an earlier era, where party control ensured that only experienced politicians (or exceptional leaders like Dwight Eisenhower) could be candidates in the general election. They also benefited from a changing media environment, which could deliver name recognition to anyone willing and able to pay for it.[19]

The parties hardly disappeared, but they lost some of their ability to screen out candidates for president who were unfit for the office—who lacked experience, judgment, or temperament, as proven by prior political experience. Another bulwark against demagoguery had eroded.[20]

THE NATIONAL POPULISTS: PEROT AND BUCHANAN

The Soviet Union collapsed in 1991. America had won the Cold War and should have been riding high. But a recession in 1990 and 1991 dampened the public spirit; the giddy excitement of being the sole "hyperpower" would need to wait a few years. The president at the time, George H. W. Bush, was in trouble.

The election campaign of 1992 pitted Bush against a moderate Democrat, Bill Clinton, but the most interesting part of the election for our story involved two other candidates: Patrick Buchanan and Perot. Buchanan, a conservative columnist and former speechwriter for Richard Nixon, challenged Bush in the Republican primaries and made a respectable showing in the New Hampshire primary before fading out. Buchanan ran again for the Republican presidential nomination in 1996 but lost to Bob Dole, then ran as a third-party candidate in 2000 and lost again.

Buchanan and Perot stood out from the crowd because they rejected the prevailing internationalism of both the Democratic and Republican Parties. Perot made the centerpiece of his campaigns his attack on the North American Free Trade Agreement. NAFTA, which became effective in 1994, had been in the works for more than a decade and was supported by both parties. Perot argued that NAFTA would send American jobs to Mexico (the "giant sucking sound going south," as he memorably put it), where labor costs were significantly lower. Buchanan agreed, but placed his opposition to NAFTA within a broader and more far-reaching agenda for the white working class. Buchanan (unlike Perot) was a religious conservative who sought to appeal to working-class whites by celebrating traditional values.

In Buchanan, one sees a proto-Trumpian right-wing populism. Buchanan attacked immigration—both legal and illegal—and many of America's traditional international commitments. He expressed sympathy for the working class, and he took religiously informed conservative positions on virtually every social issue, from abortion to prayer in schools. In his 2002 book *The Death of the West*, Buchanan lamented the rise of multiculturalism, secularism, and hedonism and the loss of America's identity

as a white Christian nation. Buchanan delighted in attacking the
elites. In 1996, he claimed the populist mantle:

> We shocked them in Alaska. Stunned them in Louisiana.
> Stunned them in Iowa. They are in a terminal panic. They
> hear the shouts of the peasants from over the hill. All the
> knights and barons will be riding into the castle pulling
> up the drawbridge in a minute. All the peasants are com-
> ing with pitchforks. We're going to take this over the top.[21]

But Buchanan pulled back in a crucial way. The accepted
wisdom among conservatives in the 1990s was that the Republican Party, and the conservative movement in general, should
try to attract, or at least not repel, minorities—including African
Americans and, even more so, Hispanics, many of whom were
conservative Catholics who had much in common with the Republicans' white working-class constituency. Most Republicans,
including those of the Christian Right, shied away from the
immigration issue because they did not want to offend Hispanics. Buchanan accepted this view, and even while attacking illegal
immigration made clear that he was attacking the "rotten regime"
of Mexico rather than "hardworking" Mexicans.[22]

For Republican leaders, Perot's and Buchanan's defeats confirmed the conventional wisdom that the party should not attack
immigration. The failure of the two candidates also seemed to
confirm the stability of the two-party system and the domination
of the establishment politicians who ran it. Yet, with the benefit
of hindsight, we can see in Perot's and Buchanan's remarkable
successes hints of the public's openness to populist attacks on the
political system.

THE PRESS AND COMMUNICATIONS
TECHNOLOGY

The demagogue's enemy is the press. This is not because journalists are pure, objective, and disinterested friends of democracy. The news media in this country was intensely partisan—indeed, often controlled by the parties or politicians—until the early twentieth century. Early in the nineteenth century, most newspapers were actually party organs, and long after the Civil War newspapers declared their affiliation to one party or the other and in return received patronage, government contracts, and other benefits from party officials.[23] Predictably, reporting was extremely biased, and a demagogue could always expect the partisan press on the other side to score points against him. As the twentieth century advanced, a norm of, or at least aspiration toward, objectivity set in, but journalists have always harbored political biases, and the norm of objectivity was always vulnerable to forms of manipulation; even if facts were not invented, stories could be written, placed, or suppressed to advance an ideology or the interest of a party. But journalists, whatever their political views, have usually been intensely skeptical of demagogues. Journalists who follow politicians on the stump, talk with their advisers, and enjoy various forms of access become attuned to the tension between the image and the reality, and resent being manipulated to promote the image at the expense of that reality. Of course, legitimate politicians also distrust the press and attempt to manipulate it. But while a normal politician can live with even a skeptical press, demagogues cannot, so they see the press—or at least the mainstream press—as an existential threat.

Demagogues—and, as we will see, legitimate politicians as well—have tried to address the problem of the press by circumventing it. Some demagogues, like Tom Watson, sponsored their own newspapers, which presented their point of view unadulterated by critical commentary or scrupulous accounting of the facts. Others, like Huey Long and Charles Coughlin, exploited a new technology. With the invention of radio broadcasting, a demagogue could reach a far greater audience than ever before. The key thing about the radio was that it allowed *unmediated* access to the national public. Before radio, a politician could reach a national audience only by giving a speech that a newspaper might reproduce (but more likely would ignore or quote snippets from) or publishing a book (that would reach only those willing to buy it). Newspapers would pay attention only to established politicians who had worked their way up through the political elite.

Thus, the radio was—like the internet today—first celebrated for its democratic potential and then almost immediately condemned for its demagogic power. John Dewey saw it as a powerful tool for educating the masses in the spirit of democracy, but soon Huey Long and Charles Coughlin discovered its merits for spreading conspiracy theories and attacking the establishment. Franklin Roosevelt, while using radio effectively in his fireside chats for explaining and justifying New Deal policies, also worried about its demagogic potential (even as his critics argued that *his* radio broadcasts were demagogic), and by the late 1940s and 1950s, the federal government, acting through the Federal Communications Commission, was trying to regulate it, in order to ensure that radio waves were used only in a "fair" way.[24]

For television, the great innovator was Richard Nixon. His Checkers speech in 1952 rescued his political career. He and his advisers realized that political advertisements on television, soon to be attack ads, could get his message to a national audience, circumventing the hostile press. In the internet era, it was Barack Obama whose advisers realized that social media could be used to reach young supporters. Donald Trump perfected the medium with the tweet. A short, snappy, poorly spelled insult could get far more attention than a speech, and because the press felt compelled to report Trump's tweets, he got double mileage out of them. Commentators reacted to Trump's tweets the way they did to Nixon's Checkers speech, wondering how anyone could believe them or take them seriously. But people did.

THE BIG LIE

Barry Goldwater called Nixon "the most dishonest individual I have ever met in my life."[25] There is a tendency these days to call all politicians dishonest, but this is lazy thinking. Politicians often tell lies, but they do so to different degrees, and in different contexts. Most presidents tend not to lie in their public pronouncements. Moreover, when they do lie, their lies are not always unjustified, and some lies, even if unjustified, are not demagogic. Not all lies are the lies of a demagogue, and it is important to make some distinctions.

POLICY LIES

In 1960, the Eisenhower administration denied that a plane that had gone missing was a U-2 spy plane that was snooping in Soviet airspace. This lie was exposed by Soviet premier Nikita Khrushchev, who revealed that the Russians had shot down the plane and captured the pilot. Eisenhower had hoped to keep the espionage secret ahead of a summit with Khrushchev. In 1962, the Kennedy administration told the press that Kennedy had to return to Washington, DC, from a campaign trip because of a cold; in fact, Kennedy returned to the White House in order to manage a crisis in Cuba. More to the point, the Kennedy administration concealed from the public the concession that ended the Cuban missile crisis: the promised removal of American missiles from Turkey. In wartime, US presidential administrations have always told lies—to deceive the enemy, to maintain secrecy, to boost morale. This type of behavior seems to be acceptable to the public as long as the lies advance the war effort. Thus, Franklin Roosevelt remains one of the greatest presidents in American memory despite his many subterfuges. However, Roosevelt benefited from the hot war of World War II, in which government use of deception could be tolerated as long as it was confined to a military emergency. During the long Cold War, the line between emergency and normalcy disappeared. White House deception reached a new low point as Lyndon Johnson sent troops to Vietnam, using a number of subterfuges to initially conceal the troop buildup and then to justify it. Johnson's lies, which were exposed by journalists and in the Pentagon Papers leak, were not forgiven. The Vietnam War was unpopular and a policy disaster, and the administration's wholesale resort to deception destroyed its credibility. History would repeat itself in 2003, when George W. Bush and top officials in his administration claimed that they had evidence that Iraq possessed weapons of mass destruction when they did not, and used this claim to justify a military invasion of that country.[26]

Policy lies can even be unavoidable in extreme cases. During financial crises, for example, presidents and their top officials often realize that honesty may undermine the policy goal of reviving confidence in the financial system. In some cases, the statement "the banks are sound" is a self-fulfilling prophecy: even if they are not sound, they may become sound if people return their deposits to them in reliance on the official statement.

SIMPLIFIED MESSAGES AND ATMOSPHERICS

A politician who tries to explain complicated ideas to the public can't resort to the methods of a university professor, who opts for precision and clarity while students doze. In political life as in everyday life, communication takes shortcuts that emphasize vivid metaphors, memorable images, slogans, or homely analogies. Taken out of context, these messages might be considered deceptive; in context, they are the most effective means to communicate. Thus, Truman's secretary of state Dean Acheson insisted that the Soviet threat must be made "clearer than the truth"—a dry recital of facts and figures would not convey its seriousness.[27] In his enjoyable romp through presidential politics *Republic of Spin*, David Greenberg shows the many ways that presidents and their teams have used Madison Avenue methods to project comforting or impressive images of a president or a presidential candidate: Eisenhower, the decent and avuncular war leader; Kennedy, the glamorous boy genius; Carter, the honest peanut farmer; Reagan, the patriotic cowboy.

BIOGRAPHICAL SPIN

Hardly any president seems able to tell the unvarnished truth about his past. Even Jimmy Carter, who presented himself as an honest, ethically pure alternative to Nixon and Johnson in the wake of Watergate, exaggerated his credentials (he was not a nuclear physicist as he claimed), burnished his image (he was not really a humble peanut farmer), and concealed his rough edges (including, it has been argued, some questionable race-baiting in his campaign for governor of Georgia and exaggeration of his record). In his 1988 presidential campaign, Joe Biden plagiarized speeches and lied about his academic record. Barack Obama couldn't resist calling himself a professor at the University of Chicago Law School, though he wasn't one. At least since Andrew Jackson, presidents have exaggerated the modesty

of their roots and the excellence of their accomplishments, or
have allowed surrogates to do so for them.[28]

INSTITUTIONAL LIES

Presidents operate within a complex world of institutional loyal-
ties. They lead their party, their administration, and the executive branch. While candidates, they must make deals in order to
secure the support of other politicians, interest groups, and donors. Once in power, they must maintain this support in order to
govern. The web of alliances necessary to achieve power always
entangles presidential candidates as they try to offer a consistent
vision or message to the public. The contradictory pressures sometimes lead to direct deception but more often result in vagueness,
inconsistent promises, and rapid policy changes. When presidents
appoint important allies to high-level positions to repay them for
political support while publicly claiming them the best for the
job, they engage in deception, but a kind of easy-to-see-through
type that seems necessary to the office.

SCANDAL LIES

As the Watergate scandal unfolded, Nixon resorted to a continuous stream of deception in order to ward off investigations by the
press, Congress, and his own Justice Department, denying that
he and his subordinates had engaged in political espionage and
misused campaign funds. During the Iran-Contra scandal, Reagan told the public, "In spite of the wildly speculative and false
stories of arms for hostages and alleged ransom payments, we
did not, repeat, did not, trade weapons or anything else for hostages. Nor will we." In fact, he did, though there is some doubt
about how much he knew about his subordinates' activities. His
vice president, George H. W. Bush, lied about his involvement

as well. In 1998, Bill Clinton famously uttered, "I did not have sexual relations with that woman, Miss Lewinsky." Of course, he did.[29]

ADMINISTRATIVE LIES

During the Watergate investigation, Nixon lied frequently to his subordinates, including his lawyers. During the Lewinsky investigation, Clinton lied frequently to his subordinates, including his lawyers. But these were hardly special cases. Franklin Roosevelt was widely regarded as duplicitous by his subordinates. Presidents frequently manipulate their staff—cajoling, bullying, lying to them—to get them to follow their will.

CAMPAIGN LIES

We saw that Franklin Roosevelt promised that "your boys are not going to be sent into any foreign wars," even as he planned war with Germany because he feared that isolationist sentiment would otherwise prevent him from being elected in 1940. Nixon, on the campaign trail in 1968, touted a "secret plan" to end the Vietnam War while having no such plan. But there is a more general phenomenon, linked to the institutional lie, which is the need for a kind of comforting blather so that the president can inspire enthusiasm and present a unifying message. Simple-minded claims that do not withstand expert scrutiny—that tax cuts will eliminate the deficit by stimulating the economy, or that new government programs will solve entrenched social problems— seem to be a normal price of democratic governance.

And that brings us to the demagogic lie. It is tempting to think that if presidents lie so often, they are all demagogues, and so it makes little sense to classify some presidents as demagogues and others as ordinary politicians or statesmen. That temptation

should be resisted. If there is a little demagoguery in every president, as Plato might have predicted, it remains the case that only
a few really are, or have been, demagogues.

The key distinction between run-of-the-mill lies and demagogic lies comes back to the idea of divisive manipulation for
the sake of power, and at the expense of the public good. The
policy lies were intended to advance the public good, and many
of them (arguably) did so.[30] Biographical spin rarely amounts to
serious deception because the press and the rival campaign provide a check, and so many of the exaggerations are mild and of
limited importance—a type of puffery that is largely understood.
Same with simplified messages: they are not really lies but efforts
to penetrate the noise of public debate, relying on mood, emo-
tion, metaphor, and vivid images. Institutional lies are ubiquitous
outside politics as well as inside: a familiar example is the legal
system, where lawyers make the best cases for their clients—cases
the lawyers themselves might not believe—because the judge and
jury are given responsibility for sorting out the truth. Administrative lies may be objectionable or not, but they are not demagogic
because they are not directed at the public. Campaign lies are
sometimes demagogic, but they are unavoidable because an effective president cannot always be bound to promises and statements
he made before he was given access to classified information
and the levers of power. The reality is that lying in politics, as in
business and social life, is ubiquitous and unavoidable, but most
political deception does not undermine democratic rule because
the competitive structure of democracy puts a check on lying—
most of the time. This is because norms and conventions arise
that manage political competition, and those norms and conventions permit certain types of lying that seem to be in the public
good, or necessary to lubricate the complex process of organizing

groups—much as in ordinary social life, where white lies and social lies seem necessary for human coexistence.

Indeed, some public lies appear to be necessary and not just an unfortunate by-product of the struggle for power. During the Democratic primary in 2008, Barack Obama remarked of working-class Americans in depressed areas, "They get bitter, they cling to guns or religion or antipathy to people who aren't like them or anti-immigrant sentiment or anti-trade sentiment as a way to explain their frustrations." Hillary Clinton, his opponent, called these remarks "elitist and out of touch." Eight years later, in her campaign against Donald Trump, she called "half of Trump's supporters . . . deplorables. . . . The racist, sexist, homophobic, xenophobic, Islamophobic—you name it. And unfortunately there are people like that. And he has lifted them up." Trump's spokesman criticized her for her "true contempt for everyday Americans."[31]

Obama and Clinton committed the famous Kinsley gaffe: "when a politician tells the truth—some obvious truth he isn't supposed to say."[32] Or, in this case, both Obama and Clinton clearly said what they believed (whether true or not), but in fact their truth-telling was a species of demagoguery because it was divisive in an emotionally resonant way, rather than unifying or empathetic. The unifying lie—made famous when Jefferson in his inaugural address claimed to bury the differences between Federalists and Republicans—is analogous to the social lie, here a form of political lubrication that helps to allow cooperation among people who disagree with each other. But neither Obama nor Clinton was a demagogue—their statements were slips that they later regretted, and were inconsistent with the unifying messages that they were otherwise trying to send.

So the difference between the demagogue and the statesman

is not entirely that the first lies and the second tells the truth. The demagogue has a tendency toward deception, and a politician toward the truth, but the larger difference involves the path to power. The demagogue uses lies to divide the public and is indifferent to the damage he might do to the public good, civic institutions, and public confidence in government. The demagogue violates the conventions that keep political lying in check or broadly consistent with the public good. The demagogue's major technique is to blame a group of people for the nation's problems, and he uses lies to inflame public opinion against that group. For right-wing southern demagogues like Tom Watson, the groups in question were African Americans, Jews, and Catholics, and the big lie was the claim that black men wanted nothing more than to rape white women, and that if they obtained political power they would use it to dominate white people. A range of subsidiary lies—reckless or false accusations—bolstered the master idea. For left-wing demagogues from Andrew Jackson to Huey Long, the big lie was the shadowy conspiracy of money interests who colluded in order to control politics. For Joseph McCarthy, the big lie was communist subversion of the national government, and the little lies were the individual accusations, false or reckless, that damaged so many people. Not that there was never a core of truth somewhere. There really were corporations that colluded and bribed legislatures, and government employees who spied for the Soviets. The falsehoods and exaggerations were used to transmute a manageable problem into an existential threat to the health of the nation, the result of the irresponsible behavior of the elites—and calling for the intervention of one man who had not been tainted by corruption and scandal.

7

THE SECOND DEMAGOGUE:
DONALD TRUMP

(2015–Present)

[Socrates:] And amid evils such as these will not he who is ill-governed in his own person—the tyrannical man, I mean—whom you just now decided to be the most miserable of all—will not he be yet more miserable when, instead of leading a private life, he is constrained by fortune to be a public tyrant? He has to be master of others when he is not master of himself: he is like a diseased or paralytic man who is compelled to pass his life, not in retirement, but fighting and combating with other men.

Yes, he [Glaucon] said, the similitude is most exact.

Is not his case utterly miserable? And does not the actual tyrant lead a worse life than he whose life you determined to be the worst?

Certainly.

He who is the real tyrant, whatever men may think, is the real slave, and is obliged to practise the greatest adulation and servility, and to be the flatterer of the vilest of mankind. He has desires which he is utterly unable to satisfy, and has more wants than any one, and is truly poor, if you know how to inspect the whole soul of him: all his life long he is beset with fear and is full of convulsions, and distractions, even as the State which he resembles: and surely the resemblance holds?

Very true, he said.

Moreover, as we were saying before, he grows worse from having power: he becomes and is of necessity more jealous, more faithless, more unjust, more friendless, more impious, than he was at first; he is the purveyor and cherisher of every sort of vice, and the consequence is that he is supremely miserable, and that he makes everybody else as miserable as himself.

No man of any sense will dispute your words.

—PLATO, *THE REPUBLIC* 9, TRANS. BENJAMIN JOWETT

In his 2009 book *Demagogue: The Fight to Save Democracy from Its Worst Enemies*, Michael Signer surveyed the demagogues of world history, from Cleon of Athens to Adolf Hitler, and, while acknowledging American demagogues like Huey Long and Joseph McCarthy, concluded that "American history shows that the American people, for the most part and increasingly over time, have internalized a set of constitutional values that essentially short-circuit national demagogues." Not the Constitution or

political institutions but "the American people . . . prevent demagogues from rising on the national stage." Signer was the mayor
of Charlottesville during the riots that broke out after a white
supremacist rally in August 2017.[1]

It is now time to pull together the historical threads and look
at the present. The demagoguery that brought Donald Trump
to power has deep roots in the democratic culture of the United
States, above all the populist anti-elite strain that can be traced
all the way back to the founding. Indeed, populism and demagoguery are features of virtually all economically advanced
democratic societies, where the promise of political equality inevitably clashes with the rule of experts. In the United States,
institutions put in place at the founding and renewed and revised
over time have kept a demagogue out of the presidency except
during the disastrous administration of Andrew Jackson. But
those institutions have repeatedly come under pressure, especially
during periods of national crisis or distress, for precisely the reason that demagogues can portray them as devices for maintaining
elite control. It is not entirely clear what can be done about this
problem, which may well be a paradox that any democracy must
continually manage. But one thing is clear: the demagoguery of
Trump must be recognized for what it is; its risks and harms must
be understood and acknowledged.

THE STAKES

A common view, found more among intellectuals than ordinary
people, is that American democracy is a sham. Elected officials
do not represent the interests of the public but are motivated
by personal enrichment or the pleasures of power. The president, who is just another elected official, though the most important one, also neglects the public interest. People of various

ideological dispositions hold this view. On the left, the claim is that politicians serve the interests of wealthy people and organized right-wing interest groups like gun rights advocates and the Christian Right. On the right, the claim is that politicians cater to the ignorant mob, the propertyless rabble, or to unions, left-wing public interest groups, and minorities. In both versions, the general public is hopelessly bad at holding politicians to account: people are too ignorant, unorganized, and foolish, or (from a more sympathetic perspective) too busy and beaten down, too distracted from public matters by daily life, and thus easily manipulated by lies, insincere promises, campaign ads, oratory, emotional appeals, and the other tools of the politician. Around election time, ordinary people can be roused to enthusiasm and motivated to vote or make political donations but can't be bothered to ensure that politicians serve the public good. This democracy-is-a-sham view is, of course, just an updating of Plato's skepticism about self-government: the masses cannot govern themselves because they lack wisdom and virtue. That means that any politician can take advantage of them, and successful politicians are likely to be demagogues. Nothing distinguishes Donald Trump from the rest of them.[2]

This view has a distinguished (and also not so distinguished) pedigree in American intellectual history. On the right, the sham view was famously advanced in the vivid columns of H. L. Mencken but was taken most seriously by modern neoconservatives like Irving Kristol. Inspired by the émigré political philosopher Leo Strauss, neocons believed that the masses were not intellectually capable of facing the hard truths of human existence. Politicians put on a happy face for the public while intellectuals whispered those truths into their ears. On the left, countless academics and journalists—from Herbert Marcuse to Thomas Frank—have argued that capitalism and modern democratic politics have conspired to confuse and demoralize voters and to deprive them of legitimate political choices.

The sham view is tempting but too extreme. While academic studies suggest that political outcomes skew toward the political preferences of wealthier members of the public, the Constitution gives disproportionate political influence to thinly populated rural states. And though gerrymandering further skews political outcomes in favor of the party in power, and voters are rarely well informed, policy outcomes seem broadly consistent with public values and preferences.[3] As we have seen, presidents are not always truthful, and they do not always act in the public interest, which is often difficult to identify in any event. But people who believe American democracy is a sham should take a look at the real authoritarian systems in the world. They are easily distinguished from American democracy by imprisonment or assassinations of journalists and political opponents, reliance on censorship, and manipulation or outright rejection of elections. There is a surprising academic controversy over whether authoritarian states may actually, at least sometimes, govern better than democracies do, or just as well. The government of China, which has managed enormous economic growth for its vast population, is usually cited as an example (although that enormous growth began from a very low starting point for which the same authoritarian regime was responsible). But you don't want to live in an authoritarian state. Usually, a small clique at the top, often with the support of a small but powerful portion of the population, supplies leadership and reproduces itself without public involvement. These systems are also characterized by convulsions—coups d'état, purges, and political violence when people finally tire of oligarchic rule and either overthrow the government or are beaten back—that have been absent from American democracy since the Civil War.

Narrowing our focus to the presidency, we know that ordinary people have influence over the selection of presidents even if elites usually filter the candidates, and historical accounts reveal that presidents have been deeply attuned to public opinion. Not that they are always enslaved by it. Nor should they be. When we evaluate presidents, we are accustomed to grading them according to both how well they serve the public interest and how democratically responsive they are. Usually, these criteria do not diverge much. People want security and prosperity, and presidents try to deliver. Where people are divided, for example, over cultural issues, presidents normally take a position near the center—center-left, or center-right—and try to suppress rather than stir up conflict. When the public good and public sentiment diverge, presidents face considerable challenges. Roosevelt and Lincoln are two of our most celebrated presidents because they tried to advance the public interest when the public was confused, divided, or simply ignorant—as it was in 1940 and 1861—about where its interest lay. These presidents have also been criticized for being less than democratic in their approach to governance. Johnson and Nixon, two more presidents who sought to advance the public interest while deceiving the public, have gone down in history as bad presidents—Johnson because of his catastrophic military escalation in Vietnam, Nixon because most of his deception was oriented toward keeping power rather than advancing the public interest. The challenge for presidents is advancing the public interest democratically when they can and doing the least possible damage to democratic values and institutions when they can't.

The demagogue, as I have emphasized, is an extreme form of democratic failure—that is, the failure of democracy to advance the public interest. The demagogue does not try to advance the public interest, and may well be indifferent to it. The demagogue seeks only to gain and hold on to power, and his characteristic method for seeking power is to stir up divisions rather than suppress them. Even here, however, the distinction between a legitimate president and demagogue can be elusive. Andrew Jackson attacked the "money power," as did Huey Long and Franklin Roosevelt. But Roosevelt and Long offered a stronger and coherent argument than Jackson did, and Roosevelt's strategy for addressing the problem was more sophisticated and realistic than Long's was. Nixon, Reagan, and now Trump came to power by attacking the cultural elites. Nixon's and Reagan's critics accused them of stirring up hatred of minorities, but both presidents avoided the most extreme forms of demagoguery—exemplified by Tom Watson and George Wallace—by focusing on the issue of law and order. While that issue was linked in the public mind with race relations, and the two presidents were accused of linking African Americans with crime and (in Reagan's case) welfare, the two presidents did not attack African Americans in any explicit way. And the rise of crime in the 1970s and 1980s was a legitimate source of public concern. In contrast, Trump made the demonization of foreigners (Mexicans as rapists, Muslims as terrorists, and so on) the centerpiece of his campaign from the beginning.

The strategy of division is a problem for American democracy because the groups that are demonized—whether by right or left—are essential to the functioning of government. In those rare cases in American history where one group achieved a dominant political victory over another, our most celebrated presidents sought to heal the division rather than exploit it. Jefferson and his successors sought to integrate the Federalists into the Republican Party; Lincoln sought to reconcile the South to defeat and reentry to the Union; Roosevelt integrated business interests into the New Deal when he might have sought (as Long seemed to promise) to expropriate and redistribute their wealth. Using deception and emotional appeals to stir up hatred between groups, the demagogue obtains power, but only at the price of creating a polarized political environment where compromise can no longer be reached.

That is the heart of Hamilton's warning, quoted in chapter 1, about the risk of politicians "commencing demagogues, and ending tyrants." In the modern era, it doesn't seem like Trump or any other president could be a tyrant in the eighteenth-century sense—that is, what we call a dictator. But Hamilton's warning remains valid. If someone is elected president based on a platform of hatred and division, he makes it difficult for himself to rule as a democratic leader—through debate and compromise—leaving the only option coercion and manipulation, or, to the extent feasible, administrative fiat. Faced with civic, political, and legal institutions that will resist such efforts, the demagogic president faces either perpetual conflict and disorder or ultimate defeat at the hands of his enemies. In the meantime, the country can only endure.

WHY WAS TRUMP ELECTED?

The major reason Trump received so many votes in the general election was that he was the Republican candidate, and Republican voters usually vote for Republican candidates. Nearly all the voters who supported Mitt Romney in 2012 supported Trump in 2016, allowing Trump to triumph where Romney failed because Clinton lost Democratic votes relative to Obama.[4] After eight years of Barack Obama, many Americans in 2016 were ready for a change. Thus, the wind should have been at Trump's back. Yet he only eked out a victory, losing the popular vote, and winning the electoral prize because voters inclined in his favor happened to be scattered over swing states in a way that gave Trump the advantage.

The greater puzzle was Trump's success in the Republican primaries. He decisively defeated experienced, well-funded politicians, including Marco Rubio, Ted Cruz, Jeb Bush, and John Kasich. How did he defeat them? Trump was the only insurgent candidate, with only weak ties to the Republican Party, while the other candidates were firmly within the establishment. For Republican voters who had tired of the Republican establishment and no longer trusted it, Trump was the only candidate. Trump bolstered his insurgent credentials by attacking not only the other candidates but Republican leaders not in the race, including former president George W. Bush and Senator John McCain, with almost the same vehemence that he attacked "Crooked Hillary." This is the source of the notion that Trump was a populist: he was a critic of the established order, and an outsider who attacked the established party leadership.

Two theories have been proposed for explaining why Republican primary voters supported the populist candidate. The first is that many Trump voters had been economically left behind, or at least believed that they did not receive a fair share of the country's prosperity, and blamed the Republicans as well as the Democrats for their stagnant standard of living. The second echoes Richard Hofstadter's diagnosis of nineteenth-century populism by arguing that Trump voters felt status anxiety because of the expansion of nonwhite and foreign populations in the United States. The two theories share the premise that 2016 was propitious for an outsider because policies supported by both parties—financial deregulation, bailouts, immigration compromise, the Iraq War—were unpopular. There is more evidence for the second theory than the first, but neither theory seems capable of offering a full explanation. While the real wages of middle- and lower-income Americans had either fallen or stayed flat in previous years, income equality had begun to widen back in the 1970s. Many Trump voters prospered in the years leading up to his election as the economy recovered from the Great Recession. And many Trump voters had supported Obama four or eight years earlier. If they were racists, their racism did not go deep. This kind of anti-establishment theory would have been a more powerful explanation for the presidential elections in 2008 (in the midst of a financial crisis for which both parties were responsible) and 2012 (with the economy still weak), yet both of those elections involved establishment figures on both sides, other than Sarah Palin, the Republican vice presidential candidate in 2008, who—inexperienced in national politics, unprepared, and uninformed—was a harbinger of things to come.[5]

There is a better theory for why Trump prevailed in the primaries and hung on in the general election: that he was a demagogue. This theory depends on two claims: first, that the conditions were propitious for a demagogue, and, second, that Trump himself played the demagogue.

For the conditions in question, we can do no better than go back to the theories that seek to explain why Trump was elected in the first place. The economy had been stagnating; wages had barely budged; a devastating financial crisis along with unpopular bailouts was a vivid memory, as was the catastrophic Iraq War. All these failures could have been, and were, blamed on the elites—the experts in government, the parties, the snobbish commentariat. But, as I observed above, these factors were in place in 2012 and 2008, and so could hardly be a sufficient condition for election of a demagogue. They supplied the fuel for the political explosion, but someone had to ignite it. The scions of the Republican establishment in those years were hardly the people to light the match. Barack Obama did toy with populist language, railing at the elites in Washington in 2008, but, himself a senator and experienced politician, he ran as a unifier.[6]

Taking a longer-term view, the election of a demagogue to the presidency was also made likely, though certainly not inevitable, by the erosion of the bulwarks against demagoguery, first put into place by the Founders and further developed by generations of American leaders. The decline of the Electoral College, the extension of the franchise, the erosion of control by party leadership—all these institutional developments created the conditions in which a demagogue could prevail by appealing to the worst instincts of the people.

Technological change played a role as well. The development of technologies—from radio through television and now the internet—that allow a single person to communicate with the whole country, in a manner unmediated by civic institutions like the press, has made it far more possible for a demagogue to seize power by stirring up the mob. Americans have joined mobs since the eighteenth century. Mobs both organized themselves spontaneously in reaction to British repression in the years leading up to the Revolution, and were organized by American revolutionary leaders who realized that mobs could be used to intimidate British officials and provoke British soldiers.[7] Mobs would continue to play these dual roles up into the twentieth century. We have seen how southern demagogues manipulated mobs, but even in the North, mobs frequently attacked foreigners, immigrants, Catholics, and other disfavored groups, and—from time to time—government officials (for example, during the Civil War riots in New York City). Mercifully, the era in which public officials would tolerate mob action when it suited their political agenda seems to have died out, possibly a victim of the public's revulsion toward mob actions against civil rights workers in the South in the 1960s. Yet the mob is back, in virtual form, thanks to the internet.

Trump used Twitter to send blunt, incendiary, occasionally humorous, and frequently misspelled messages, which rallied his supporters, provoked his opponents, deepened divisions, and garnered free publicity by a media that reproduced the tweets for an audience far larger than the 10 million or so Twitter users who followed Trump during the presidential campaign (that number is as of August 2016).[8] Trump both benefited from the greater level of political partisanship exhibited on and enhanced by the internet—social media in particular—and contributed to it. Even when the news media was at its partisan height in the nineteenth century, it still served a gatekeeping function, excluding the very worst forms of deceit, defamation, and viciousness from public debate, though these forms certainly had their outlet in speeches, letters, pamphlets, and other more informal modes of expression. Those guardians are now gone, allowing a demagogue like Trump both to gain sustenance from and disseminate propaganda and lies that serve his purposes. We can be grateful that the virtual mob, unlike its historical predecessor, can't beat up, tar and feather, hang, or set alight its victims. But it can be whipped up by a demagogue, and used to serve his purposes.

Thus, with the conditions in place that were propitious for a demagogue to gain power, the only question was whether a demagogue would appear. Such a person would have to be an outsider, which ruled out all established politicians. But only a person with significant public recognition or great wealth could have overcome all the financial barriers to a candidacy. A celebrity or a rich person, or someone who was both a celebrity *and* a rich person. And that person also had to be shameless, lacking the scruples of a Steve Forbes or H. Ross Perot, or (to go back a ways) a military leader like Dwight Eisenhower. In retrospect, it seems like only one person in America fit the bill.

HOW DID TRUMP PLAY THE DEMAGOGUE?

PERSONAL ATTACKS

Trump personally attacked his various opponents, as well as random Americans who criticized him publicly. This rather large group included the TV commentator Megyn Kelly, who had challenged Trump for making derogatory comments about women; the Muslim father of an American soldier, who criticized Trump's anti-Muslim comments; and virtually all his political opponents. Taking a page from the southern demagogue Jeff Davis, Trump defended himself by flinging schoolboy taunts at his antagonists: "Crazy Joe" Biden, "Low Energy Jeb" Bush, "Crooked Hillary," "Slimeball James" Comey, "Lyin' Ted" Cruz, "Cheatin' Obama," "Mr. Peepers" (the former Justice Department official Rod Rosenstein), "Little Marco" Rubio, "Crazy Bernie" Sanders, "Psycho Joe" Scarborough (a TV journalist), "Mr. Magoo" (former attorney general Jeff Sessions), "Fat Jerry" Nadler, "Low-IQ Maxine" Waters, and "Little Michael" Bloomberg, among others.[9]

DIVISIVE APPEALS I

The centerpiece of Trump's campaign was the attack on foreigners, which brought along with it a range of racially tinged associations. He was clearest in his attack on illegal immigrants:

When Mexico sends its people, they're not sending the
best. They're sending people that have lots of problems
and they're bringing those problems. They're bringing
drugs, they're bringing crime. They're rapists and some, I
assume, are good people, but I speak to border guards and
they're telling us what we're getting.[10]

Some of Trump's critics have located his demagoguery in his
anti-immigrant stance, which they say is racist. But it can't be the
case that seeking to reduce immigration, or to enforce existing
immigration laws more strictly, even if the results are harsh, can
be, by itself, demagogic. All countries must make decisions about
immigration, and there are reasonable arguments in favor of more
or less generous policies. The demagoguery of the immigration
issue in Trump's hands lies in his efforts to use it to provoke fear,
anger, and hatred in a large portion of the public—by exaggerat-
ing the threats posed by immigrants, blaming them for stealing
jobs and engaging in terrorism, attributing the worst motives to
them and their supporters, and, mostly in code but clearly enough,
depicting them as hostile or contaminating because of their race
or ethnicity. Trump's tactics were on clear display in the run-up to
the 2018 midterm elections, which threatened to be a Democratic
rout. Trump asserted that a ragtag throng of migrants making
their way north from Honduras were an army, full of "very tough
fighters," "very bad people," and "criminals and unknown Middle
Easterners," who want "to invade our Country."[11] Trump sent
troops to the border even though in the normal course of things
the migrants would have been stopped by border guards and pro-
cessed for asylum requests. His approach, very much in the spirit
of McCarthy, was to lie and exaggerate in order to stir up public

fear and loathing. But unlike McCarthy, Trump could send out the military.

Trump has focused on unlawful immigration, rather than immigration per se, allowing for a coalition between nativists and people who are uneasy about nonwhite immigration but who strongly identify with their immigrant roots and continue to see America as a nation of immigrants, and who are thus able to rationalize their stance in terms of legality rather than racism. As the nation divides over immigration, political compromises over immigration questions, which were once common, are now impossible. One's stance on immigration has become a marker of one's affiliation with one of the two competing political tribes. Questions of immigration now engage primal fears in a way that they haven't since the early twentieth century.[12]

DIVISIVE APPEALS 2

Yet Trump's anti-foreigner/anti-immigrant rhetoric does not capture the full extent of his divisiveness. He has not just attacked illegal immigrants. He has attacked legal immigrants (as job stealers and criminals), Hispanics (as job stealers and criminals), Arabs (as terrorists), Muslims (as terrorists), and African Americans (as criminals and overpaid athletes)—sometimes conflating these categories, as when he told four Democratic members of Congress, three of them born in the United States and all of them members of minority groups, to "go back and help fix the totally broken and crime infested places from which they came." He was condemned after the riots in Charlottesville in 2017 for saying "I think there is blame on both sides," suggesting a moral equivalence between neo-Nazis and anti-Nazi protesters, and has been reluctant to distance himself from racist groups and individuals who have been enthusiastic supporters (like former Klan leader David Duke), or to avoid coded forms of bigotry ("Hillary Clinton meets in secret with international banks to plot the destruction of U.S. sovereignty").[13]

This division separates white Americans, on the one hand, and nonwhite people (both Americans and non-Americans), on the other. It thus explosively combines the two American traditions of racism and nativism, while adding an opportunistic dollop of evangelical Christianity, thus recalling the white Christian nationalism of Andrew Jackson and the populists. Trumpian nationalism seems hopelessly out of date to modern liberals, but it would be a mistake to ignore the unifying power of white Christian nationalism, which overcame the massive social divisions of the late nineteenth century and the first half of the twentieth (at the expense of blacks and foreigners, of course). That's why Progressives, including President Theodore Roosevelt and the journalist Herbert Croly, were enthusiastic nationalists: they believed that only nationalism could generate popular support for a strong central government, which was required to beat back monopoly, promote health and safety, and redistribute wealth to the poor. Indeed, even in recent years, quite a few intellectuals have longed for a suitably updated American nationalism, cleansed of its racist associations, but adequate for unifying the country against the centrifugal forces of multiculturalism.[14]

The problem for Trump is that the war is lost. Whites will soon become a minority of the population, and the core of Trump's supporters who are most susceptible to white nationalism—white, male, older, less educated, less wealthy, Christian—are all demographics that are in trouble. This is already obvious in the younger generations, and even to the Republican establishment, which, while terrified of Trump because of his hold on primary voters, has refused to adopt Trump's white nativist rhetoric. And Trump delivered little of value to his supporters; a tax cut that mainly benefited the rich is his most significant accomplishment. While liberals worry about Trump's judicial appointments—another area in which he has done well—the judges whom Trump has appointed are committed to a color-blind jurisprudence, which will not help whites compete against increasingly better educated nonwhites. Indeed, the dominant narrative about white people is gradually changing, as working-class whites are seen as a problem demographic—beset by declining life expectancy, dead-end jobs, rural backwardness, drug addiction, family breakdown, and obesity. They are no longer able to claim to belong to the superior race but are portrayed as victims rather than predators, clinging to "guns or religion or antipathy to people who aren't like them or anti-immigrant sentiment or anti-trade sentiment," as Barack Obama put it back in 2008, to give meaning to their empty, desolate lives. Thus, Trump's major gift to his supporters is to reassert their cultural dominance using inflammatory rhetoric against the liberal elites who no longer hate them but, worse, pity them. That may account for the sense that Trump has stirred up primal forces that cannot be appeased through realistic policy reform but only disregarded, once an anti-Trump coalition takes power, with damaging implications for the social fabric for years to come.[15]

CONTEMPT FOR THE TRUTH

Trump's mendacity has few precedents in American political history, and none among presidents or presidential candidates. McCarthy, Johnson, and Nixon engaged in fairly narrow tactical deception—they lied frequently and grotesquely, but their lies clustered about specific policy goals or personal obsessions. Trump's lying seems pathological, mythomaniacal even, unmoored to anything but his personal self-aggrandizement and the humiliation of his enemies. Trump lied plenty during his campaign, but even as a president with ample resources for vetting the truth of his planned statements, he has compiled an unsurpassed record of untruthfulness. *The Washington Post* documented 13,435 "false or misleading claims" as of October 14, 2019 (including repetitions of prior misstatements), or 13.5 such claims per day since the start of his presidency. Many of these lies were petty spin that exaggerated his administration's accomplishments, but an enormous number were deliberately misleading on a matter of substantial concern. These lies were damaging to the people, institutions, and countries referred to. Some examples, all taken from *PolitiFact*:

> "U.S. Steel just announced that they are building six new steel mills."
>
> "The servers of the Pakistani gentleman that worked on the DNC" are "missing."
>
> "I have watched ICE liberate towns from the grasp of MS-13."
>
> "Crime in Germany is way up."
>
> "We got $6 billion for opioid and getting rid of that scourge that's taking over our country. And the numbers are way down."
>
> James Clapper said "that the FBI was spying on [Trump's] campaign."
>
> The immigration visa lottery "randomly hands out green cards without any regard for skill, merit, or the safety of American people."
>
> "We have signed more legislation than anybody. We broke the record of Harry Truman."

These statements bear no relation to the truth—with no steel mills planned, and Trump last in signing legislation, not first.[16]

Commentators have scratched their heads about Trump's mendacity. Why would anyone trust a politician who so frequently and obviously lies about so many things? One theory is that when voters no longer trust even truth-telling politicians to serve their interests, any politician who distinguishes himself by violating political norms, including truth-telling norms, may stand out for his authenticity.[17] This may be why Trump not only lies, but lies in ways that are immediately verifiable as lies. If people did not know that Trump lied to them, they would not see him as authentic! But this theory produces additional puzzles, as it suggests that Trump's supporters believe statements of his that they know to be untrue, or are willing to gamble on a presidential candidate whose decisions as president are completely unpredictable. A simpler explanation is that many Trump voters believe Trump's lies despite their obviousness while others calculate that political checks supplied by the Republican Party and other institutions will keep Trump's policy choices roughly in line with their own.

THE ATTACK ON INSTITUTIONS

Trump violated a range of American political norms. In his campaign, he frequently called for prosecution and imprisonment of his opponent, Hillary Clinton ("lock her up"), which violated the norm against criminalizing political differences. Once in office, he encouraged the FBI to investigate Democrats, and threatened to withhold military aid from Ukraine if its president did not order an investigation of Joe Biden, at the time Trump's most likely rival in the 2020 election, based on the hypothetical possibility that Biden had used his influence when vice president to help a Ukrainian energy company on whose board Biden's son Hunter sat. Trump repeatedly attacked the press ("The FAKE NEWS media . . . is not my enemy, it is the enemy of the American people!") and judges who ruled against him in a private civil action (arguing that a judge was biased against him because of the judge's "Mexican heritage") and in a challenge to his travel ban ("courts seem to be so political"). After taking credit for a rising stock market during the first twenty-one months of his tenure, he immediately blamed the Federal Reserve Board ("gone crazy") when stock prices plunged in October 2018. As market turmoil continued, he leveled personal attacks on Fed chairman Jerome Powell ("not even a little bit happy with my selection of Jay"). During the presidential campaign he suggested that the election would be "rigged" against him, in this way providing himself an excuse in advance if he lost but also challenging the integrity of the electoral system without evidence.[18]

Many other presidents have challenged institutions; indeed, almost all recent presidents have pressured the Fed, and, as we saw, Franklin Roosevelt tried to pack the Supreme Court. And many American institutions—from the FBI and the CIA to the military and the press—deserved the criticism and political pressure they received. Yet no other president has made a habit of spewing out bile in such a crude and public way against so many institutions, and for such narrowly political reasons. Trump has rarely bothered to make a reasoned argument that the institutions that have displeased him should be reformed in the public interest, or even to disguise the partisan reasons for his attacks.

THE ATTACK ON THE ELITES

Trump condemned the "elites who've led us to one financial and foreign policy disaster after another." In a speech at the Hermitage, Andrew Jackson's homestead, he claimed Jackson's attack on elite power as precedent for his own. "It was during the Revolution that Jackson first confronted and defied an arrogant elite. Does that sound familiar to you?" As his lieutenant Steve Bannon put it, "The elites in our country left President Trump with disasters all across the globe, specifically in Korea, Afghanistan and Iran. He rejects the 'managed decline' philosophy of America's political class." Trump, like the populists before him, claims that the elites are "corrupt." "She is the most corrupt person ever to seek the office of the presidency," Trump said of Hillary Clinton. On Twitter and elsewhere, Trump has also called "corrupt" the media, the Mueller investigation, the Puerto Rican government, the Department of Justice, the FBI, the Clinton Foundation, the Democrats, *The New York Times*, the "deep state," the Mexican government and judiciary, Barack Obama, Joe Biden, Adam Schiff, Nancy Pelosi, and the "system."[19]

THE RECKLESS DETERMINATION OF POLICY

While Trump brought to his campaign certain core convictions, including his opposition to immigration and international trade, he did not take policy seriously. He made a large number of conflicting promises, and many of them were made because they provoked an enthusiastic response from stadium crowds rather than from experts or even voters with personal experience of the problem in question. He acknowledged that his "go-to applause line for sleepy crowds is about building a wall on the U.S.-Mexico border. . . . 'If it gets a little boring, if I see people starting to sort of, maybe thinking about leaving, I can sort of tell the audience, I just say, "We will build the wall!" and they go nuts.'" This put Trump into a bind. As he said to the Mexican president in a private conversation that was subsequently leaked:

The only thing I will ask you though is on the wall, you
and I both have a political problem. My people stand up
and say, "Mexico will pay for the wall" and your people
probably say something in a similar but slightly different
language. But the fact is we are both in a little bit of a
political bind because I have to have Mexico pay for the
wall—I have to.

Because he made promises based on applause lines. As president,
he has repeatedly tried to persuade Congress to fund a wall but
has met refusal because of the senselessness of extending the existing border fence into empty desert. Trump has gone so far as to
shut down the government over this matter.[20]

The wall is just the most egregious example. Even as president, Trump frequently makes policy through off-the-cuff remarks on Twitter, confronting his staff with a publicly articulated
presidential impulse that they must walk back, push forward, cir-
cumambulate, rationalize, or develop into policy. Trump seems
indifferent to the institutional damage and public confusion, having realized—perhaps correctly—that his unmediated tweeting
boosts the morale of his supporters, keeps him in the public eye,
and distracts his political enemies.

A MATTER OF CHARACTER

This recklessness forces us to return to the topic of motives.
Using power recklessly, for the sheer enjoyment of bossing people around, and with limited concern for the consequences, is the
mark of a demagogue. But nearly all politicians seek power and
enjoy exercising it. The distinguishing feature of the demagogue
is that his drive for power has no (or few) limits. He is hostile to
institutional constraints but, even more, contemptuous of those

political norms that enable people to compromise and live together. When the drive to power leads to the most obvious forms of emotional manipulation, the stirring up of fear and hatred to bring to the surface the social and political hobgoblins that had been suppressed for the sake of public unity, a demagogue is at work.

What type of person seeks power without regard to the social costs? A person of low moral character. A remarkable fact is that, while many such people have occupied lower-level positions in American government, none—until Trump—has reached the presidency. Even Andrew Jackson, who killed a man in a duel, adhered to a code of honor that put him personally at risk. In his book *The Leaders We Deserved (and a Few We Didn't)*, the presidential historian Alvin Felzenberg supplies a twist on the traditional presidential rankings by disaggregating a president's rating into categories corresponding to personal qualities. He includes the category of character, based on a rating from 1 (lowest) to 5 (highest). Felzenberg gives most presidents a rating of 4 or 5—because most presidents have been basically honest men. Dwelling in the basement are James Polk, Richard Nixon, Franklin Pierce, and James Buchanan, all receiving a rating of 1. Yet, aside from Nixon and Lyndon Johnson (who receives a 2), and I suppose Bill Clinton (also a 2), even these presidents were mostly honest. They had to be, because, until the breakdown of the role of the political parties in screening candidates, party officials—for obvious reasons—would support only those candidates they thought they could trust. Pierce, Buchanan, and other low scorers like Warren Harding (2) were not inveterate liars and hatemongers like Trump. They received their low character ratings because they were indecisive and showed poor judgment, but they meant well and took their responsibilities seriously.[21]

Trump gained votes by portraying himself as an outsider

and the establishment elites—Democrats and Republicans both, though the Democrats more—as corrupt. As an outsider, he was not tainted by establishment corruption. To prove his bona fides as an outsider, Trump violated the political norms that the establishment complied with—norms that forbid name-calling, deception, divisive appeals, and all the rest. These norms are important because they keep democratic competition within bounds, prevent it from degenerating into open warfare, preserve the possibilities of compromise, and depersonalize conflict, hence lowering the temperature and the stakes. Trump ignored and badly damaged this infrastructure of democracy. And Trump's opponents were helpless. They could not respond in kind—as demonstrated by Marco Rubio's futile effort to counterpunch by mocking Trump's "little hands" during a Republican primary debate—because they were all figures of the establishment, and hence could not distance themselves from it. In another era, the establishment, even the Republican establishment, would have been less halfhearted about stopping someone who posed such a risk to political norms. But the establishment was vulnerable in 2016 because of its perceived failures, as demonstrated by the financial crisis and bailouts, the Iraq War, and economic stagnation.

THE ELITES

Demagogues attack elites, but so do mainstream politicians, journalists, commentators, activists, and intellectuals—the elites themselves. From the right, the classicist Allan Bloom launched an industry of right-wing attacks on the universities with his book *The Closing of the American Mind*, published in 1987. From the left, the idea that business elites have ruined democracy can be traced back to *The Power Elite* by C. Wright Mills, published in 1956. The social critic Christopher Lasch, in his 1995 book *The*

Revolt of the Elites and the Betrayal of Democracy, blamed *all* the elites (defined as the top 20 percent, though of what is not exactly clear) for the collapse of American values, institutions, and aspirations. The philosopher Jason Stanley argues in *How Propaganda Works* (2015) that the elites "invariably acquire a flawed ideology to explain their possession of an unjust amount of the goods of society," which they (excluding himself presumably) inculcate in the masses through propaganda and education. Of course, these ideas go back further, to Karl Marx if you want, or Anytus and the other Athenians who prosecuted Socrates for corrupting Athenian youth. It is a long time since an American intellectual could say with a straight face, "The Elite, or those distinguished by ideas and talent, are the natural leaders of society," as a Stanford sociologist said in 1901. But don't the elite-hating intellectuals all have a point? Didn't the elites bring us the Vietnam War, the Iraq War, neoliberalism, inequality, economic stagnation, "alternative lifestyles," helicopter parenting, the locavore? Aren't the demagogues right, after all?[22]

The problem starts when we try to understand what people mean when they refer to the "elite." The dictionary defines the term as "a group of persons who by virtue of position or education exercise much power or influence." In a democracy, ordinary people enjoy some power by virtue of the vote, but other people—the elites—exercise more power. Who are these people? This question has vexed commentators since the nineteenth century. A few generalizations have gained ascendancy. The people who are the "elite" are not necessarily more intelligent and talented than everyone else. In a meritocratic society, the talented rise to the top, but not all societies are meritocratic. In the United Kingdom in the nineteenth century, feudal traditions still ensured that the oldest sons of the landed aristocracy would obtain powers and privileges that placed them in the elite even as society was democratizing. In the United States today, it has become common to think that wealthy people can, by investing in tutors and making donations to universities, ensure that their dimwitted children will obtain prestigious degrees that give them entry into the elite. A more pertinent point is that people might gain elite positions not because they are especially talented but because they choose to specialize in the right way—choosing to invest their time and effort to become a politician rather than, say, a farmer. The "elite" in this sense is a sociological category, referring to a group of people with a certain social status rather than an evaluative category referring to a group of talented people ("the elite paratroopers"). The elite may be more talented than everyone else, but they may not be.[23]

Another useful distinction is between the "governing elites" and the "other" elites. Both groups have disproportionate power and status, but only people in the first group enjoy formal positions of power. In America, the governing elites include elected officials in the national and state governments, judges, bureaucrats, and party officials. The other elites include people who exercise influence by virtue of their public prominence and expertise: journalists, commentators, academics, policy experts, scientists, business leaders, religious leaders. We can expand the category yet further by including people who donate money to politicians, obtain college educations, volunteer for candidates, pay attention to politics, or vote routinely. Of course, the distinction can be slippery, with some people circulating in and out of the governing elite. Some research indicates that government policies disproportionately reflect the political preferences of the wealthiest 10 percent of the population; we could call this group the elite as well.[24]

Whichever definition one chooses, if one wants to blame the elites for Vietnam, the Iraq War, and economic stagnation, then one will have to credit the elites for whatever has gone well in this country (unless you think nothing has gone well in this country). But when people talk of "making America great again," they rarely mention that old America was as much the product of elite control as present-day America is. And when people blame, say, white southern elites for establishing Jim Crow, they don't ever add that black elites led the mass movement that dismantled it, and that northern white elites provided political, legal, and financial support. That is why the people who attack the elites will sometimes add a modifier to make clear which elites they mean—"liberal elites," "legal elites," "bureaucratic elites," "coastal elites," "urban elites," or (from the left) "corporate elites" or "business elites." And then it becomes clear that the attack on the elites is not so much an attack on elite control in the dictionary sense as an attack on certain policy choices that (like all policy choices) happen to have been made by the people with power or influence.

In the right-wing fever dream, the elites inhabit universities, think tanks, and the (nonmilitary, non-immigration-service) bureaucracies in Washington and meet in salons where they hatch plans to ban guns, religion, and SUVs while concocting schemes to grease their children into the most prestigious colleges. In the left-wing fever dream, the elites chomp cigars while meeting in investment banks on Wall Street or in corporate suites of oil companies, where they dole out cash to politicians. The truth is less lurid, but it also can't be denied that the elites have more influence over public policy than the masses do. And that means that if the interests and values of the elites diverge from those of the masses, the interests and values of the elites will play a greater role in public life and government policy than those of the masses will.

In the past, when the values of the elites were considered superior to those of the masses, that was considered a good thing, and the elites wrung their hands as the masses gained power through the spread of democracy.[25] Today, a strong populist ethos dictates contempt for elite values, a contempt so powerful that elites like Lasch parrot it.

All this may be unfortunate, but it is an inescapable consequence of any organized system of governance, where the need for division of labor and specialization of functions results in a small group of people at the top. It was the contribution of democracy to put some constraints on that top group in a manner that was broadly advantageous for the public at large, but democracy has never been able to eliminate elite control, and in fact depends on elites to represent the people, staff the bureaucracy, operate the military and law enforcement, and resolve legal disputes. This is simply a fact of human organization: elite control has always existed in the United States and other democracies, and continues to this day. It is recognized by the public; it is (privately) acknowledged by politicians and bureaucrats; it is an inescapable fact of the day-to-day workings of government.[26]

It is also a feature of American public life that no one—or certainly no public or corporate official—may acknowledge that the elites are in control. The political scientist Thomas Dye suggests that the last American politician to do so was Alexander Hamilton, who said: "The voice of the people has been said to be the voice of God; and however generally this maxim has been quoted and believed, it is not true in fact. The people are turbulent and changing, they seldom judge or determine right."[27] One of the great battles in American political history has been over how to reconcile the existence of elites with the principles of self-government and political equality. The major solution has been this taboo. Of course, there have been periods when the political rights of ordinary people expanded at the expense of the elite, but there has never been a time when the elites have not maintained power, and there has never been a serious threat to elite rule. The anti-Federalists claimed to oppose elites, but they really opposed elite control from Washington, DC; they had no problem with local elites. The Jacksonians claimed to oppose elites, but they simply replaced northeastern merchant elites with agrarian elites from the West and South. The populists were a truly anti-elite movement as long as they remained in opposition, but to gain power they made peace with the elites of the Democratic Party, and they were never able to propose a theory of government that did not rely on elite rule. And in the twentieth century, the New Right backlash to liberal-elite rule meant a handover of power to business elites. Throughout, the franchise expanded, but at the same time, power was being transferred back and forth among judges, bureaucrats, elected officials, unions, corporations, and interest groups.

The big lie of the demagogue is the promise to eliminate these institutional elites and replace them with the unmediated voice of the people as articulated by the leader himself. The logic of this lie virtually compels demagogues to claim to have, in Trump's words about himself, "great and unmatched wisdom," without which it would be impossible to overrule experts in economics, military strategy, geophysics, and foreign affairs.[28] In fact, like everyone else, demagogues depend on advice, and find their own experts to rely on—frequently charlatans whose views mesh with the demagogue's political agenda. The lie is effective, especially in bad times, because it draws on the ideal of self-government, appeals to people who resent being bossed around by bureaucrats or corporations, flatters them by rejecting the pretensions of the experts, and offers an explanation as to why things are not as they should be. But a demagogue will always rely on another segment of the elite in order to achieve power, and rely on elites once he possesses power.

COMMENCING DEMAGOGUES, ENDING TYRANTS?

Trump entered office with less political experience than any other president in American history except Dwight Eisenhower, who was qualified by his extraordinary military leadership. One searches presidential history in vain for examples of presidents who were more indifferent to policy and ideas, and who were less temperamentally suited to the office. No other president in American history had left such a slime trail of personal corruption (Trump University), dubious associations (including the Mafia), philandering, mendacity, and sleazy public posturing (the birther controversy).

Yet is Hamilton right that a politician who achieves office through demagoguery becomes a tyrant once ensconced? Necessarily so? His point of reference was different from ours. In the classical era, the demagogue who sought power took an enormous amount of personal and financial risk. He made enemies who might try to kill him, and he went into debt so that he could pay bribes to lubricate the path to power. Once in power, then, he faced considerable incentives to abuse it: to obtain funds to repay his debts, to reward friends and eliminate enemies. Trump, by contrast, took no personal risk in running for president and did not even spend much of his own money. He may not even have thought he could win. He almost certainly understands that serious abuses of power while president pose more risk to his personal freedom and financial well-being than a quiet retirement on one of his estates.

At the same time, Trump's years in office have been tempestu-
ous (one might say "Stormy")—not because of any disciplined effort
on his part to establish a dictatorship but because of his intellectual
and temperamental deficits. He has continued his wild verbal py-
rotechnics, which have further divided the nation by outraging and
offending various groups. Rather than strengthening his position,
Trump's rhetorical bomb-throwing has distracted the nation from
relatively good economic times, while creating unnecessary tensions
with foreign countries and disrupting the regular course of government. Trump has also continued to assail government institutions,
including the FBI, the Justice Department, and the judicial system,
mainly as an improvisational effort to fend off attacks on the legitimacy of his election and his personal standing. He has casually
encouraged his subordinates to corrupt the legal system for partisan
purposes, as when he criticized the Justice Department for bringing charges against two Republican congressmen ahead of the 2018
midterm election. And yet these efforts have not protected Trump
from investigations and lawsuits and have instead hardened attitudes against him, deepening the legal quagmire he finds himself in.

Like Andrew Jackson, Huey Long, and Richard Nixon,
Trump has provoked a counterattack from the institutions he has
disparaged. Political appointees and career officials in the executive branch have leaked and blown the whistle. State officials
have launched investigations of Trump's malfeasances before
his presidency, while federal investigators and inspectors general have exposed his malfeasances during his presidency. The
courts have ruled against Trump again and again. The media
have put unrelenting pressure on Trump and his aides. Congressional hearings even before Democrats regained control of the
House in 2019, and especially afterward, laid the groundwork
for impeachment.

It would be wrong to call Trump a dictator, or even an incipient dictator. If he's a tyrant, it's only in the old Platonic sense of a person who is a slave to his passions. It's not clear how much he means what he says, and he has put relatively little effort into actually destroying institutions. His major political achievements— tax cuts, Supreme Court appointments, deregulation—did not involve any illegal or unconstitutional action. He obtained Congress's approval of the tax cuts and the Senate's approval of the confirmations, and he pursued deregulation using authority granted to the president by Congress in earlier statutes. If a demagogue is a politician who verbally attacks institutions and tries to shake public confidence in them, then Trump is a demagogue. But since he hasn't yet succeeded in destroying or seriously damaging public institutions, he's not a dictator, and doesn't seem likely to become one.

The cultural hostility toward authoritarianism and the dense institutional texture of the country seem adequate to prevent a demagogue from becoming a tyrant, for the time being at least. That, and the American public's peculiar tendency both to expect the president to solve all our problems and to distrust everyone in government—including the president. It is indeed this peculiarity that both fuels the demagogue's rise to power and dooms him when he tries to exercise it. No other people seems capable of being so frequently disappointed by the leaders whom it chooses. The problem is less that the presidency will become a dictatorship than that it will be rendered ineffectual by public loss of confidence in it, and by the fetters with which Congress, the parties, and the courts eventually bind it to bring it under control. That was the legacy of Andrew Jackson and Richard Nixon, and could be Trump's legacy as well.

It is tempting to argue that to prevent another demagogue

from taking the presidency, and causing even worse damage than Trump has done, we need constitutional reform. Perhaps we need to strip the presidency of many of the powers that it has accumulated over the years, so that future demagogues who are elected president will be unable to cause harm.[29] Or, to prevent a demagogue from seizing the presidency in the first place, perhaps we need to revive the Founders' ideal of an Electoral College that limits popular influence on the selection of the president, or encourage the political parties to return to their earlier system of screening candidates before unleashing them on the public, or somehow bring social media under control. It is not my purpose here to make these arguments. While constitutional reform may be justified, my goal in this book has been more limited. It is to persuade the reader that in electing Donald Trump to the presidency, we Americans really did choose a demagogue, a political figure who was able to obtain power by exploiting the inherent vulnerability of constitutional democracy: the tension between elite control of the institutions of democracy and the ideological commitment to mass self-government. We need to see Trump not merely as a poor choice for the presidency, like Franklin Pierce, James Buchanan, or Warren Harding. Most poor presidents have been forgotten, while Trump should be remembered. We need to see him as a political monstrosity who should be repudiated by the body politic, so that politicians who eye the presidency in the future will be deterred from using Trump's ascendance as a model.

ACKNOWLEDGMENTS

I received helpful comments from many people, and I am grateful for their patience and encouragement. Curt Bradley, Daryl Levinson, Martha Minow, and Lael Weinberger read early drafts of the entire manuscript and gave me valuable guidance. I presented drafts of chapters at two workshops at the University of Chicago Law School, where I received helpful feedback. I also received helpful comments from Justin Driver, Brian Feinstein, Jack Goldsmith, Aziz Huq, Alison LaCroix, Brian Leiter, Martha Nussbaum, Rick Pildes, Lior Strahilevitz, and Laura Weinrib.

I benefited enormously from a one-day conference on the book manuscript that was held at Georgia State University College of Law. My deepest thanks to Timothy Lytton for organizing the conference and providing me detailed comments on the entire manuscript, and to the participants, who also gave me valuable comments: Peter Schuck, Nick Parrillo, Anne Joseph O'Connell, Bill Novak, Dan Ernst, Julia Mahoney, David Bernstein, Ken

Kersch, Jed Shugerman, Sasha Volokh, Paul Lombardo, Eric Segall, Neil Kinkopf, David Sehat, Robert Baker, Andrew Cohen, Bill Edmundson, Yaniv Heled, and Erin Fuse Brown.

I assigned chapters from the manuscript to students in a seminar I taught in the fall of 2018 on demagoguery in American history. The students offered a fresh perspective that helped me sharpen my argument, and I greatly appreciate their insightful feedback, which was both passionate and patient. My research assistants caught errors large and small, brought my attention to stylistic infelicities, challenged my arguments, and helped track down obscure historical sources; many thanks to Michael Christ, Carly Gibbons, Eugenia Lee, Urvashi Malhotra, and Justin Taleisnik. Finally, I'm grateful to Adam Eaglin for helping me get the manuscript to press, and to Pronoy Sarkar for his early enthusiasm and insightful editing.

NOTES

INTRODUCTION

1. The quotation is from Edwin A. Miles, "The First People's Inaugural—1829," *Tennessee Historical Quarterly* 37, no. 3 (Fall 1978): 293, 303.

2. Ibid., 306–7 (punctuation altered).

3. For example, David Frum, *Trumpocracy: The Corruption of the American Republic* (2018); Yascha Mounk, *The People vs. Democracy: Why Our Freedom Is in Danger and How to Save It* (2018); Steven Levitsky and Daniel Ziblatt, *How Democracies Die* (2018).

4. Thurman W. Arnold, *The Folklore of Capitalism* (1937), 380.

5. Andrew Bolt, "Obama the Demagogue," *Herald Sun* blog, September 10, 2018, https://www.heraldsun.com.au/blogs/andrew-bolt/obama-the-demagogue/news-story/4b66e5f3b71b155

4784ab772b4176c98; see also Mark Hemingway, "Rejecting Trump's Demagoguery Means Rejecting Obama's," *Weekly Standard* Archives, June 14, 2016, https://www.washingtonexaminer .com/weekly-standard/rejecting-trumps-demagoguery-means -rejecting-obamas. The Bush headline is in *Esquire*, December 5, 2018, https://www.esquire.com/news-politics/politics /a25414794/george-hw-bush-racial-demagogue-campaign -governing/.

6. The populists' Omaha Platform (1892) is at http://historymatters .gmu.edu/d/5361; Farage's speech is at https://www.independent .co.uk/news/uk/politics/eu-referendum-nigel-farage-4am-victory -speech-the-text-in-full-a7099156.html.

7. There is a surprisingly small academic literature on demagoguery as a political concept, though it does play a role in studies of various historical periods in the United States, of classical political philosophy, and of democratic decline in foreign countries. For some general discussions, see J. Justin Gustainis, "Demagoguery and Political Rhetoric: A Review of the Literature," *Rhetoric Society Quarterly* 20, no. 2 (Spring 1990): 155–61; Wilma Dykeman, "The Southern Demagogue," *Virginia Quarterly Review* 33, no. 4 (Autumn 1957): 558–68; G. M. Gilbert, "Dictators and Demagogues," *Journal of Social Issues* 11, no. 3 (Summer 1955): 51–53; Reinhard H. Luthin, *American Demagogues* (1954); Jeffrey K. Tulis, *The Rhetorical Presidency* (1987); Michael Signer, *Demagogue: The Fight to Save Democracy from Its Worst Enemies* (2009).

8. Plato, *The Republic*, trans. Benjamin Jowett, http://classics.mit .edu/Plato/republic.mb.txt.

9. Bernie Sanders, "United Against the War on Women," *Huffpost*, last updated June 30, 2012, https://www.huffpost.com/entry /united-against-the-war-on_b_1464730.

10. Martin Gilens and Benjamin I. Page, "Testing Theories of American Politics: Elites, Interest Groups, and Average Citizens," *Perspectives on Politics* 12, no. 3 (September 2014): 564–81.

CHAPTER 1. THE FOUNDERS' VISION OF ELITE GOVERNANCE (1774–1797)

1. John Adams to John Taylor, December 17, 1814, https://founders.archives.gov/documents/Adams/99-02-02-6371; James Madison, *Federalist 10*, https://avalon.law.yale.edu/18th_century/fed10.asp.

2. Daniel J. Kapust, "The Problem of Flattery and Hobbes's Institutional Defense of Monarchy," *Journal of Politics* 73, no. 3 (August 3, 2011): 680–91, 687 quoted; Richard Beeman, *Plain, Honest Men* (2009), 130.

3. On Madison's remarks, see Beeman, *Plain, Honest Men*, 126.

4. Quoted in ibid., 127.

5. Patrick Henry quoted in Saikrishna Bangalore Prakash, *Imperial from the Beginning* (2015), 20; Philadelphiensis, *Anti-Federalist No. 74*.

6. Alexander Hamilton, *Federalist 69*.

7. This paragraph draws on Carl J. Richard, *The Founders and the Classics* (1995), chap. 1, 19 quoted.

8. Thucydides, *The Peloponnesian War* 6.11. I am using the 1982 Modern Library edition, ed. T. E. Wick. Hereafter cited in the text.

9. Ibid., 6.65.

10. Ibid., 2.65.

11. Ibid., 2.65.

12. Melissa Lane, "The Origins of the Statesman-Demagogue Distinction in and After Ancient Athens," *Journal of the History of Ideas* 73, no. 2 (2012): 179–200.

13. For helpful discussions, see Michael Signer, *Demagogue* (2009); Jeffrey K. Tulis, *The Rhetorical Presidency* (1987), 27–33.

14. Joseph Addison, *Cato: A Tragedy* (1712), act 2, scene 2; Benjamin Straumann, *Crisis and Constitutionalism: Roman Political Thought from the Fall of the Republic to the Age of Revolution* (2016); James W. Ceaser, *Presidential Selection: Theory and Development* (1979), 60–61; John Adams, *A Defence of the Constitutions of Government of the United States of America*, 3 vols. (1797), 1:101.

15. Gordon S. Wood, *The Creation of the American Republic* (1969), 409–13.

16. Robert F. Williams, "The Influences of Pennsylvania's 1776 Constitution on American Constitutionalism During the Founding Decade," *Pennsylvania Magazine of History and Biography* 112, no. 1 (January 1988): 25–48.

17. Leonard L. Richards, *Shays's Rebellion* (2002); the story about Mrs. Perry's yarn-beam is on 35.

18. For Webster, see Paul Leicester Ford, *Pamphlets on the Constitution of the United States, Published During Its Discussion by the People, 1787–1788* (1888), 131; Alexander Hamilton, *Federalist 71*; James Madison, *Federalist 10*; for Adams, see Wood, *Creation of the American Republic*, 514.

19. Hamilton, *Federalist 71*.

20. All quotations are from Gordon S. Wood, *The Radicalism of the American Revolution* (1991), 27–28, except "A choice," which is from Sean Wilentz, *The Rise of American Democracy: Jefferson to Lincoln* (2006), 9.

21. Wood, *Radicalism of the American Revolution*, 182 (Jefferson), 195 (Adams).

22. Mason quoted in Madison's notes on the constitutional debates, July 17, 1787, available at http://avalon.law.yale.edu/18th_century /debates_717.asp.

23. This was not the sole reason for the Electoral College; it was also intended to resolve conflict between large and small states over control of the national government. The Electoral College avoided the extremes of allowing state legislatures to choose the president (in the way they would choose senators) and allowing the national public to choose the president on the basis of a popular vote. See Shlomo Slonim, "The Electoral College at Philadelphia," *Journal of American History* 73, no. 1 (June 1986): 35–58. But this compromise could have been achieved without giving electors discretionary power.

24. Alexander Hamilton, *Federalist 68*.

25. Alexander Keyssar, *The Right to Vote* (2000), 25; Madison quoted in Richard K. Matthews, "James Madison's Political Theory: Hostage to Democratic Fortune," *Review of Politics* 67, no. 1 (Winter 2005): 54; Jack N. Rakove, *Original Meanings* (1996), 214–15, 225.

26. Paul D. Ellenbogen, "Another Explanation for the Senate: The Anti-Federalists, John Adams, and the Natural Aristocracy," *Polity* 247 (Winter 1996): 247–71, 247 quoted.

27. Quoted in ibid.

28. James Madison, *Federalist 62*; Robert Yates, "Notes of the Secret Debates of the Federal Convention of 1787," http://avalon.law .yale.edu/18th_century/yates.asp; Wood, *Creation of the American Republic*, 563.

29. Ellenbogen, "Another Explanation for the Senate"; Adams quoted in Wilentz, *Rise of American Democracy*, 76.

30. Saul Cornell, *The Other Founders: Anti-Federalism and the Dissenting Tradition in America, 1788–1828* (1999), 64–74.

31. Quoted in Ellenbogen, "Another Explanation for the Senate," 259.

32. Quoted in ibid., 263.

33. Pauline Maier, *Ratification: The People Debate the Constitution, 1787–1788* (2010), 71.

34. Ibid., 447.

35. This is a major theme of Wilentz, *Rise of American Democracy*.

CHAPTER 2. THE ANTI-ELITE BACKLASH OF JEFFERSONIAN DEMOCRACY (1797–1809)

1. Max M. Edling, "'So Immense a Power in the Affairs of War': Alexander Hamilton and the Restoration of Public Credit," *William and Mary Quarterly*, 3rd ser., 64, no. 2 (April 2007): 287–326. I am indebted (no pun intended) to his account.

2. James D. Tagg, "Benjamin Franklin Bache's Attack on George Washington," *Pennsylvania Magazine of History and Biography*

100, no. 2 (April 1976): 191–230, 191, 209, 213 quoted; James Callender, *The Prospect Before Us* (1800).

3. James H. Hutson, "John Adams' Title Campaign," *New England Quarterly* 41, no. 1 (March 1968): 30–39; Lance Banning, *The Sacred Fire of Liberty* (1998), 338–39.

4. Quoted in Stanley Elkins and Eric McKitrick, *The Age of Federalism* (1993), 496.

5. John H. Aldrich and Ruth W. Grant, "The Antifederalists, the First Congress, and the First Parties," *Journal of Politics* 55, no. 2 (May 1993): 295–326, esp. 302.

6. Elkins and McKitrick, *Age of Federalism*, 264–70; John Kenneth White and Daniel M. Shea, *New Party Politics*, 2nd ed. (2003)

7. Elkins and McKitrick, *Age of Federalism*, 264–70.

8. Madison quoted in ibid., 267.

9. Ibid., 451–61; Sean Wilentz, *The Rise of American Democracy: Jefferson to Lincoln* (2006), 40–41.

10. Wilentz, *Rise of American Democracy*, 62–71.

11. For the example of Pennsylvania, see ibid., 74.

12. Terri Diane Halperin, *The Alien and Sedition Acts of 1798: Testing the Constitution* (2016), 125–26.

13. Ibid., 66.

14. Ibid., 73; there were an additional three under the common law.

15. Elkins and McKitrick, *Age of Federalism*, 704, 706–11; letter from Thomas Jefferson to James Madison, November 3, 1798, https://founders.archives.gov/documents/Madison/01-17-02-0119.

16. Douglas Bradburn, "A Clamor in the Public Mind: Opposition to the Alien and Sedition Acts," *William and Mary Quarterly*, 3rd ser., 65, no. 3 (July 2008): 565–600; song quoted in Douglas Bradburn, *The Citizenship Revolution: Politics and the Creation of the American Union, 1774–1804* (2009), 180.

17. Quoted in Wilentz, *Rise of American Democracy*, 102.

18. Ibid.

19. Chris J. Magoc and David Bernstein, eds., *Imperialism and Expansionism in American History* (2015), 27.

20. David B. Frost, *Classified: A History of Secrecy in the United States Government* (1945), 140; Gaye Wilson, "Dressing Down for the Presidency: Thomas Jefferson's Republican Simplicity," *White House History* 32 (Fall 2012), https://www.whitehousehistory.org/dressing-down-for-the-presidency (quoted); Joseph J. Ellis, *American Sphinx: The Character of Thomas Jefferson* (1998), chap. 4; Jon Meacham, *Thomas Jefferson: The Art of Power* (2013), chap. 32.

21. See, e.g., Wilentz, *Rise of American Democracy*, 135–39.

22. See George McKenna, *American Populism* (1974), xiv, on Jefferson as a populist; C. B. Macpherson, *The Life and Times of Liberal Democracy* (1977), 11; Alexander Keyssar, *The Right to Vote* (2000), 36–37; Daniel Walker Howe, *What Hath God Wrought* (2009), 490 (the actual quotation refers to the "Democratic Party," as some historians do in order to avoid confusion with the rise of the modern Republican Party in the mid-nineteenth century).

23. Quoted in Reinhard H. Luthin, "Some Demagogues in American History," *American Historical Review* 57, no. 1 (October 1951): 24, discussing popular election of judges.

24. See Keyssar, *Right to Vote.*

25. "State Power to Bind Presidential Electors," *Columbia Law Review* 65, no. 4 (April 1965): 696–709, esp. 698.

CHAPTER 3. THE FIRST DEMAGOGUE: ANDREW JACKSON (1824–1837)

1. Quoted in Daniel Walker Howe, *What Hath God Wrought* (2009), 331.

2. Arthur Schlesinger Jr. originated the "man of the people" view in *The Age of Jackson* (1988). For the latest version, see Sean Wilentz, *The Rise of American Democracy: Jefferson to Lincoln* (2006); for Meacham, see Jon Meacham, *American Lion: Andrew Jackson in the White House* (2008).

3. Bray Hammond, *Banks and Politics in America from the Revolution to the Civil War* (1991), 328.

4. Robert V. Remini, *Andrew Jackson* (1999), 77, 79–80.

5. Ibid., 131.

6. Schlesinger, *Age of Jackson*, 36 (localism); Remini, *Andrew Jackson*, 76 (quoting Jackson); Edwin A. Miles, "President Adams' Billiard Table," *New England Quarterly* 45, no. 1 (March 1972): 31–43, 34–36 (other quotations).

7. Remini calls the twelve years leading up to Jackson the "Era of Corruption" rather than the usual "Era of Good Feelings," as did

Jackson himself, but provides little evidence for such an extravagant label (*Andrew Jackson*, ix). Histories of the US civil service agree that the federal civil service before Jackson was basically honest. See, e.g., Paul P. Van Riper, *History of the United States Civil Service* (1958), 20–26. The Jackson quotation is from Meacham, *American Lion*, 122.

8. Howe, *What Hath God Wrought*, 331.

9. Governor George C. Gilmer quoted in F. P. Prucha, *The Great Father: The United States Government and the American Indians*, 2 vols. (1984), 1:196.

10. Andrew Jackson, "First Annual Message to Congress," December 8, 1829, https://millercenter.org/the-presidency/presidential -speeches/december-8-1829-first-annual-message-congress.

11. The continuity of Jackson's policy is argued controversially in F. P. Prucha, "Andrew Jackson's Indian Policy: A Reassessment," *Journal of American History* 56, no. 3 (December 1969): 527–39.

12. Remini, *Andrew Jackson*, 275–78.

13. Richard B. Latner, "The Nullification Crisis and Republican Subversion," *Journal of Southern History* 43, no. 1 (February 1977): 19–38, 21 quoted.

14. See, for example, the 1840 platform of the Democratic Party, https://www.presidency.ucsb.edu/documents/1840-democratic -party-platform, which squarely commits the party to states' rights.

15. Hammond, *Banks and Politics in America from the Revolution to the Civil War*, 209–14.

16. For a recent discussion of why Jackson hated the Bank, see Meacham, *American Lion*. Jackson is quoted in W. E. Beard, "The Autobiography of Martin Van Buren," *Tennessee Historical Magazine* 6, no. 3 (October 1920): 163.

17. Hammond, *Banks and Politics in America from the Revolution to the Civil War*, 340–50.

18. Major L. Wilson, "The 'Country' Versus the 'Court': A Republican Consensus and Party Debate in the Bank War," *Journal of the Early Republic* 15, no. 4 (Winter 1995): 619–47.

19. "President Jackson's Veto Message Regarding the Bank of the United States," July 10, 1832, http://avalon.law.yale.edu/19th _century/ajveto01.asp.

20. Some commentators have identified other causes for the financial crisis; see Robert M. Whaples, "Were Andrew Jackson's Policies 'Good for the Economy'?" *Independent Review* 18, no. 4 (Spring 2014): 545–58. The best recent scholarship, however, places the blame squarely on Jacksonian monetary policy following the elimination of the Bank; see Peter L. Rousseau, "Jacksonian Monetary Policy, Specie Flows, and the Panic of 1837," *Journal of Economic History* 62, no. 2 (June 2002): 457–88. The banking crisis study is Richard Tilly, "Banking Crises in Three Countries, 1800–1933," *Bulletin of the GHI Washington* 46 (Spring 2010): 77–89.

21. Alexander Hamilton, *Federalist 68*; Carl Joachim Friedrich, "The Rise and Decline of the Spoils Tradition," *Annals of the American Academy of Political and Social Science* 189 (1937): 10–16.

22. Jeff Forret, "The United States Branch Mint at Charlotte: Superintendents, Spoils, and the Second-Party System, 1837–1841," *North Carolina Historical Review* 77, no. 2 (2000): 151–78. "Jackson did not invent patronage, but he did institute a particular

form of patronage—the spoils system—which openly acknowledged the role of democratic politics in the process of appointments" (155).

23. The quotation is from Jackson, "First Annual Message to Congress." Jackson's eventual appointees were mostly members of the elite or the middle class, with only a slight tilt toward the middle class compared to Adams and Jefferson, and very little or no representation from ordinary people; see Robert Maranto and David Schultz, *A Short History of the United States Civil Service* (1991), 33.

24. Jackson, "First Annual Message to Congress" (quoted); see Gary Hollibaugh, Gabriel Horton, and David E. Lewis, "Presidents and Patronage," *American Journal of Political Science* 58, no. 4 (2014): 1024–42, for evidence of competent appointments.

25. Leonard D. White, *The Jacksonians: A Study in Administrative History, 1829–1861* (1954), 327–42 (327–28 quoted).

26. Remini, *Andrew Jackson*, 198–99.

27. Howe, *What Hath God Wrought*, 496 (patronage opportunities); Scott C. James, "Patronage Regimes and American Party Development from 'The Age of Jackson' to the Progressive Era," *British Journal of Political Science* 36, no. 1 (January 2006): 39–60; Van Riper, *History of the United States Civil Service*, 41–44; Doris Kearns Goodwin, *Team of Rivals* (2006), 703 ("Egyptian locusts"); for an exhaustive analysis of the degraded bureaucracy, see White, *The Jacksonians*; on reform, see Sean M. Theriault, "Patronage, the Pendleton Act, and the Power of the People," *Journal of Politics* 65, no. 1 (February 2003): 50–68.

28. Another hypothesis is that the political elites were unwilling to allow a populist to take power once they had wrested back control of the electoral system.

29. See, e.g., Richard Carwardine, "Evangelicals, Whigs and the Election of William Henry Harrison," *Journal of American Studies* 17, no. 1 (April 1983): 47–75. For a useful biography, see Gail Collins, *William Henry Harrison* (2012).

30. William Henry Harrison, "Presidential Inaugural Address," March 4, 1841, in Phillip J. Morledge, ed., *"I Do Solemnly Swear": Presidential Inaugurations from George Washington to George W. Bush* (2008), 68.

31. Schlesinger, *Age of Jackson*, 46–47.

CHAPTER 4. THE POPULIST REVOLT (1865–1897)

1. Robert C. McMath, *American Populism* (1992), 4–5.

2. Ibid., 6.

3. Henry Nash Smith, "Rain Follows the Plow: The Notion of Increased Rainfall for the Great Plains, 1844–1880," *Huntington Library Quarterly* 10, no. 2 (February 1947): 169–93.

4. James Stewart, "The Economics of American Farm Unrest, 1865–1900," *EH.Net Encyclopedia*, February 10, 2008, https://eh .net/encyclopedia/the-economics-of-american-farm-unrest-1865 -1900/; Anne Mayhew, "A Reappraisal of the Causes of Farm Protest in the United States, 1870–1900," *Journal of Economic History* (June 1972): 464–75.

5. Richard Hofstadter, *The Age of Reform* (1955), 33.

6. Morton Rothstein, "Farmer Movements and Organizations," *Agricultural History* 62, no. 3 (Summer 1988): 161–81.

7. Stanley Lebergott, "Labor Force and Employment, 1800–1960," in *Output, Employment, and Productivity in the United States After 1800*, ed. Dorothy S. Brady (1966), tables 1 and 2; Hofstadter, *Age of Reform*.

8. Michael Kazin, *A Godly Hero: The Life of William Jennings Bryan* (2007), 61 (quoting the *New York World*), 62.

9. Jolyon P. Girard, Darryl Mace, and Courtney Smith, *American History Through Its Greatest Speeches* (2016), 301.

10. Jeffry A. Frieden, "Monetary Populism in Nineteenth-Century America: An Open Economy Interpretation," *Journal of Economic History* 57, no. 2 (June 997): 367–95, esp. 372.

11. Declaration of Purposes of the National Grange (1874), http://www.oocities.org/cannongrange/declaration_purposes.html.

12. Rothstein, "Farmer Movements and Organizations," 175.

13. The Omaha Platform is at http://historymatters.gmu.edu/d/5361.

14. Jeffrey Ostler, "The Rhetoric of Conspiracy and the Formation of Kansas Populism," *Agricultural History* 69, no. 1 (Winter 1995): 1–27.

15. See Jan-Werner Müller, *What Is Populism?* (2016).

16. Hofstadter, *Age of Reform*, 25, 30–31.

17. William Jennings Bryan's Cross of Gold speech, July 9, 1896, is available at http://historymatters.gmu.edu/d/5354.

18. Norman Pollack, "Hofstadter on Populism: A Critique of 'The Age of Reform,'" *Journal of Southern History* 26, no. 4 (November 1960): 478–500, esp. 487.

19. George McKenna, *American Populism* (1974), xvi–xvii.

20. Hofstadter, *Age of Reform*, 50; Rothstein, "Farmer Movements and Organizations," 117.

21. McMath, *American Populism*, 174–75, 206–7.

22. Ibid., 209.

23. The Omaha Platform.

24. Charles Postel, *The Populist Vision* (2009), 18, 139.

25. Ibid., 165, quoting Watson.

26. McMath, *American Populism*, 11; Rothstein, "Farmer Movements and Organizations," 173.

27. See Hofstadter, *Age of Reform*, 78.

28. Quoted in Kazin, *Godly Hero*, 39, who calls it a "blatantly demagogic" performance.

29. Hofstadter, *Age of Reform*, 85.

30. Ibid., 101.

31. See C. Vann Woodward, *Tom Watson: Agrarian Rebel* (1938).

32. My account follows Woodward, ibid.; all quotations are from him as well.

33. Martha C. Nussbaum, *Political Emotions* (2015).

34. Tom Watson, *The People's Party Paper*, December 3, 1891.

35. Tillman quoted in John Downing Weaver, *The Brownsville Raid* (1992), 270; Kazin, *Godly Hero*, 5, 21.

36. This account relies on Kazin, *Godly Hero*.

37. Quoted in ibid., 49.

38. Quoted in ibid., xiii.

39. Abraham Lincoln, "Cooper Union Address," February 27, 1860, http://www.abrahamlincolnonline.org/lincoln/speeches/cooper.htm.

40. Abraham Lincoln, "First Inaugural Address," March 4, 1861, http://www.abrahamlincolnonline.org/lincoln/speeches/1inaug.htm.

41. See Garry Wills, *Lincoln at Gettysburg* (1992); Nussbaum, *Political Emotions*, 231–35.

42. Quoted in David O. Stewart, *Impeached* (2010), 67.

CHAPTER 5. THE TRIUMPH OF ELITE TECHNOCRACY: THEODORE ROOSEVELT TO FRANKLIN ROOSEVELT (1901–1945)

1. On progressivism, see, e.g., Arthur S. Link and Richard L. McCormick, *Progressivism* (1983); Eldon Eisenach, *The Lost Promise of Progressivism* (1994); Michael McGerr, *A Fierce Discontent* (2003).

2. See Edward A. Purcell Jr., *The Crisis of Democratic Theory* (1973).

3. David Greenberg, "Theodore Roosevelt and the Image of Presidential Activism," *Social Research* 78, no. 4 (Winter 2011): 1057–88, esp. 1058, 1071–72.

4. Ibid., 1069, on the number of speeches; Theodore Roosevelt, "State of the Union Address," December 3, 1901, https://teachingamericanhistory.org/library/document/first-annual-message-to-congress-2/; Edmund Morris, *Theodore Rex* (2001), 474.

5. For Roosevelt's accusations against reformers, see the many references in his autobiography; Patricia Lee Sykes, "The President as Legislator: A 'Superepresenator,'" *Presidential Studies Quarterly* 301 (Spring 1989): 301–15.

6. *President* Roosevelt wasn't a demagogue. But was *Candidate* Roosevelt in the campaign of 1912? That Roosevelt was accused of demagoguery because he broke from the Republican Party to establish his own third party, the Bull Moose Party, which he completely dominated, and accused both major parties of corruption ("boss-ridden and privilege controlled"); attacked the Supreme Court; advocated radical (for the time) policies involving state control of business; disregarded the norm that presidents should not serve more than two terms; based his campaign on his outsized personality to an even greater degree than before; and, or so it was said, sought power (this time) for its own sake and for the pleasure of destroying his opponents. For an entertaining account, see Edmund Morris, *Colonel Roosevelt* (2010), chaps. 7–11. Yet Roosevelt's policy proposals were serious and well considered, and his criticisms of the Supreme Court and the parties were just.

7. Walter Lippmann, *Public Opinion* (1922) and *The Phantom Public* (1925); quotation from *Phantom Public* (rpt. Transaction Publishers, 1993), 29.

8. John Dewey, *The Public and Its Problems* (1927), 205.

9. Paul Stephen Hudson, "A Call for 'Bold Persistent Experimentation': FDR's Oglethorpe University Commencement Address,

1932," *Georgia Historical Quarterly* 78, no. 2 (Summer 1994): 361–75.

10. Franklin D. Roosevelt, "First Inaugural Address," March 4, 1933, https://avalon.law.yale.edu/20th_century/froos1.asp.

11. There remains scholarly debate about how hostile the Court really was, but there is no doubt that Progressives and New Dealers perceived it as such; see David Bernstein, *Rehabilitating "Lochner": Defending Individual Rights Against Progressive Reform* (2011); William E. Leuchtenburg, *The Supreme Court Reborn* (1996), 83; Richard T. Ely, "Economic Theory and Labor Legislation," *American Economic Association Quarterly*, 3rd ser., 9, no. 1 (April 1908): 124–53.

12. *Schechter Poultry Corp. v. United States*, 295 U.S. 495, 542 (1935).

13. Franklin D. Roosevelt, Fireside Chat, March 9, 1937, https://millercenter.org/the-presidency/presidential-speeches/march-9-1937-fireside-chat-9-court-packing; Leuchtenburg, *The Supreme Court Reborn*, 156–61.

14. John M. Schuessler, "The Deception Dividend: FDR's Undeclared War," *International Security* 34, no. 4 (Spring 2010): 154 ("foreign wars"); Wayne S. Cole, *Roosevelt and the Isolationists, 1932–45* (1983), 401 ("certain forces").

15. For a discussion of the *Greer* and related incidents, see Cole, *Roosevelt and the Isolationists*, 441–44; John J. Mearsheimer, *Why Leaders Lie* (2013), 46–47, quoting Roosevelt ("shooting war") and Churchill (engineer an "'incident"), 55.

16. Cole, *Roosevelt and the Isolationists*, 447, though this might be regarded as reasonable speculation.

17. One can read many of Roosevelt's wartime addresses here: https://www.worldwarii.org/p/mr.html.

18. Leuchtenburg, *The Supreme Court Reborn*.

19. Sykes, "The President as Legislator," 310.

20. Annette Shelby, "Jeff Davis of Arkansas," in Cal M. Logue and Howard Dorgan, eds., *The Oratory of Southern Demagogues* (1981), 39; on Bilbo and Blease, see Allan A. Michie and Frank Ryhlick, *Dixie Demagogues* (1939), 102, 271.

21. For useful surveys, see Michie and Ryhlick, *Dixie Demagogues*; Logue and Dorgan, *Oratory of Southern Demagogues*.

22. For biographical details, I follow Alan Brinkley, *Voices of Protest* (1982), and Richard D. White Jr., *Kingfish: The Reign of Huey P. Long* (2006).

23. On Louisiana politics, see White, *Kingfish*, 15, 17.

24. Gabriel Mathy and Nicolas L. Ziebarth, "How Much Does Political Uncertainty Matter? The Case of Louisiana Under Huey Long," *Journal of Economic History* 77, no. 1 (2017): 90–126, esp. 95–96.

25. Quoted in T. Harry Williams, *Huey Long* (1981), 762.

26. Brinkley, *Voices of Protest*, 72–73.

27. Ibid., 74; see also Edwin Amenta, Kathleen Dunleavy, and Mary Bernstein, "Stolen Thunder? Huey Long's 'Share Our Wealth,' Political Mediation, and the Second New Deal," *American Sociological Review* 59, no. 5 (October 1994): 678–702.

28. Brinkley, *Voices of Protest*, 20 ("thieves, bugs, and lice"); White, *Kingfish*, xi ("savage delight").

29. William E. Leuchtenburg, "FDR and the Kingfish," *American Heritage*, October/November 1985, https://www.americanheritage.com/content/fdr-and-kingfish.

30. White, *Kingfish*, 45, 146–48, 251; Brinkley, *Voices of Protest*, 26 ("lying newspapers").

31. Jerry P. Sanson, "'What He Did and What He Promised to Do . . .': Huey Long and the Horizons of Louisiana Politics," *Louisiana History* 47, no. 3 (2006): 261–76, esp. 265–66.

CHAPTER 6. THE ANTI-TECHNOCRAT BACKLASH FROM THE NEW RIGHT (1945–1989)

1. On the populist as bogeyman, see Daniel Bell, *The Radical Right* (1964); note that some of these essays were written by self-identified conservatives. Data on the frequent use of the term are from Google Ngram.

2. My account follows Robert W. Griffith, *The Politics of Fear*, 2nd ed. (1987), and David M. Oshinsky, *A Conspiracy So Immense* (2005).

3. Oshinsky, *A Conspiracy So Immense*, 109. The speech was not recorded, and contemporary accounts conflict.

4. The McCarthy-Welch exchange is at http://historymatters.gmu.edu/d/6444.

5. Oshinsky, *A Conspiracy So Immense*, 58–61.

6. Ibid., 57.

7. Ibid., 184, 189.

8. Quoted in Paul Joseph and Simon Rosenblum, *Search for Sanity: The Politics of Nuclear Weapons and Disarmament* (1984), 284.

9. Oshinsky, *A Conspiracy So Immense*, 433. Public opinion polling was in its infancy, and while politicians believed that McCarthy was extremely popular, recent analysis of the evidence suggests that they might have been mistaken: Adam J. Berinsky and Gabriel Lenz, "Red Scare? Revisiting Joe McCarthy's Influence on 1950s Elections," *Public Opinion Quarterly* 78, no. 2 (Summer 2014): 369–91.

10. Stephan Lesher, *George Wallace: American Populist* (1995), 92–96.

11. All quotations are from Marianne Worthington, "The Campaign Rhetoric of George Wallace in the 1968 Presidential Election," *Upsilonion* 4 (Summer 1992), https://inside.ucumberlands.edu /downloads/academics/history/vol4/MarianneWorthington92 .html, except *Meet the Press*, which is from Lesher, *George Wallace*, 390 (ellipses in original).

12. Oshinsky, *A Conspiracy So Immense*, 177.

13. Robert Mitchell, "'Nattering Nabobs of Negativism': The Improbable Rise of Spiro T. Agnew," *Washington Post*, August 8, 2018, https://www.washingtonpost.com/news/retropolis/wp/2018 /08/08/nattering-nabobs-of-negativism-the-improbable-rise-of -spiro-t-agnew/.

14. "As Spiro Agnew Sees It," *New York Times*, May 10, 1970, https://timesmachine.nytimes.com/timesmachine/1970/05/10 /354918052.pdf.

15. Ronald Reagan, *The Last Best Hope: The Greatest Speeches of Ronald Reagan* (2016), 3, 62.

16. A theme of Rick Perlstein, *Nixonland* (2009).

17. See, e.g., Nelson W. Polsby, *Consequences of Party Reform* (1983).

18. See Marty Cohen et al., *The Party Decides* (2008).

19. For the argument that these reforms helped pave the way to Trump, see Elizabeth Sanders, "The Meaning, Causes, and Possible Results of the 2016 Presidential Election," *Forum* 15, no. 4 (December 2017): 711–40. Another exception besides Eisenhower was Wendell Willkie, a businessman who received the Republican presidential nomination in 1940 but was crushed by Franklin Roosevelt in the general election.

20. In late 2018, the Democratic Party further weakened the influence of party elites by putting new limits on the voting power of so-called superdelegates over the selection of the party's presidential nominee at the national convention. See Reid J. Epstein, "DNC Votes to Bar Superdelegates from Convention's First Presidential Ballot," *Wall Street Journal*, August 25, 2018, https://www.wsj.com/articles/dnc-votes-to-bar-superdelegates-from-conventions-first-presidential-ballot-1535218320?mod=hp_lead_pos4.

21. Dan Balz, "Buchanan Hits Back," *Washington Post*, February 19, 1996, www.washingtonpost.com/archive/politics/1996/02/19/buchanan-hits-back/bf6f84fa-3529-4411-a9bd-5d3dfee09a02/.

22. Sara Diamond, "Right-Wing Politics and the Anti-Immigration Cause," *Social Justice* 23, no. 3 (Fall 1996): 154–68, esp. 154–55.

23. Michael E. McGerr, *The Decline of Popular Politics* (1988), 14–22.

24. David Greenberg, *Republic of Spin* (2017), 206–7.

25. "Barry Goldwater, in His Own Words," *Chicago Tribune*, May 30, 1998, https://www.chicagotribune.com/news/ct-xpm -1998-05-30-9805300125-story.html.

26. Eric Alterman, *When Presidents Lie* (2004), chap. 3; see Mearsheimer, *Why Leaders Lie*, for many examples of lying in wartime.

27. Quoted in Benjamin Schwarz, "Clearer Than the Truth," *Atlantic*, April 2004, https://www.theatlantic.com/magazine/archive /2004/04/clearer-than-the-truth/302928/.

28. Steven Brill, "Jimmy Carter's Pathetic Lies," *Harper's*, March 1976, https://harpers.org/archive/1976/03/jimmy -carters-pathetic-lies/; see also Julian E. Zelizer, Arthur M. Schlesinger Jr., and Sean Wilentz, *Jimmy Carter* (2010), 23–24; Neena Satija, "Echoes of Biden's 1987 Plagiarism Scandal Continue to Reverberate," *Washington Post*, June 5, 2019, https:// www.washingtonpost.com/investigations/echoes-of-bidens -1987-plagiarism-scandal-continue-to-reverberate/2019/06/05 /dbaf3716-7292-11e9-9eb4-0828f5389013_story.html.

29. "Transcript of Remarks by Reagan About Iran," *New York Times*, November 14, 1986, www.nytimes.com/1986/11/14/us /transcript-of-remarks-by-reagan-about-iran.html; "Did Clinton Lie?" *Analysis* 60, no. 3 (July 2000): 250–54, 250 quoted.

30. In *When Presidents Lie*, however, Alterman argues that the most important major policy lies since World War II had damaging second-order effects for the policies themselves as well as for democratic values.

31. Ed Pilkington, "Obama Angers Midwest Voters with Guns and Religion Remark," *Guardian*, April 14, 2008, https:// www.theguardian.com/world/2008/apr/14/barackobama .uselections2008; Domenico Montanaro, "Hillary Clinton's

'Basket of Deplorables,' in Full Context of This Ugly Campaign," NPR, September 10, 2016, https://www.npr.org/2016/09/10/493427601/hillary-clintons-basket-of-deplorables-in-full-context-of-this-ugly-campaign.

32. For the Kinsley gaffe, see Michael Kinsley, "The Gaffer Speaks," *The Times* (London), April 23, 1986.

CHAPTER 7. THE SECOND DEMAGOGUE: DONALD TRUMP (2015–PRESENT)

1. Michael Signer, *Demagogue* (2009), 24.

2. Ilya Somin, *Democracy and Political Ignorance*, 2nd ed. (2016), chaps. 1–2.

3. At least, that is how I read the literature, which is too large and complex to summarize. Recent contributions include Martin Gilens, *Affluence and Influence: Economic Inequality and Political Power in America* (2012); Christopher H. Achen and Larry M. Bartels, *Democracy for Realists: Why Elections Do Not Produce Responsive Government* (2016). These books, while pessimistic, do not advance the sham view described in the text.

4. John Sides, "Race, Religion, and Immigration in 2016," Democracy Fund Voter Study Group, June 2017, https://www.voterstudygroup.org/publication/race-religion-immigration-2016. The study found that in 2016, 89 percent of Romney 2012 voters supported Trump, while only 86 percent of Obama 2012 voters supported Clinton. Moreover, 9 percent of Obama voters voted for Trump ("Obama-Trump voters"), whereas only 5.4 percent of Romney voters voted for Clinton.

5. Diana C. Mutz, "Status Threat, Not Economic Hardship, Explains the 2016 Presidential Vote," *Proceedings of the National Acad-*

emy of Sciences 115, no. 29 (May 8, 2018): E4330–39, http://www
.pnas.org/content/early/2018/04/18/1718155115.short; John Sides,
Michael Tesler, and Lynn Vavreck, *Identity Crisis: The 2016 Presidential Campaign and the Battle for the Meaning of America* (2018).

6. As a former Obama aide put it, "And it was kind of horrifying to
   realize that the same type of message that we'd used in 2008 had
   been repurposed to [*sic*] essentially in 2016, albeit in a very different way." See Veronica Stracqualursi, "Ex-Obama Aide: Trump
   Repurposed '08 Message for 2016 Win," CNN, June 6, 2018,
   https://www.cnn.com/2018/06/06/politics/ben-rhodes-obama
   -trump-2016-election-cnntv/index.html.

7. See, e.g., Gary B. Nash, "The Transformation of Urban Politics, 1700–1765," *Journal of American History* 60, no. 3 (December 1973): 605–32.

8. See Marc Hetherington and Jonathan Weiler, *Prius or Pickup?
   How the Answers to Four Simple Questions Explain America's Great
   Divide* (2018).

9. "List of Nicknames Used by Donald Trump," https://en.wikipedia
   .org/wiki/List_of_nicknames_used_by_Donald_Trump.

10. "30 of Donald Trump's Wildest Quotes," CBS News, https://
    www.cbsnews.com/pictures/wild-donald-trump-quotes/9/.

11. These quotations come from Trump's tweets in October 2018.

12. To be sure, a far more harrowing period. See John Higham,
    Strangers in the Land: Patterns of American Nativism, 1860–1925,
    2nd ed. (1988).

13. Justin Wise, "Trump Tells Progressive Congresswomen to 'Go
    Back' Where They Came From," *The Hill*, July 14, 2019, https://

thehill.com/homenews/administration/452970-trump-tells
-progressive-democrats-to-go-back-and-fix-broken-and-crime;
David Leonhardt and Ian Prasad Philbrick, "Donald Trump's
Racism: The Definitive List, Updated," *New York Times*, January 15, 2018, https://www.nytimes.com/interactive/2018/01/15
/opinion/leonhardt-trump-racist.html.

14. Herbert Croly, *The Promise of American Life* (1909); "Theodore
    Roosevelt's Osawatomie Speech," August 31, 1910, https://www
    .kshs.org/p/kansas-historical-quarterly-theodore-roosevelt-s
    -osawatomie-speech/13176; on updated American nationalism,
    see Michael Lind, *The Next American Nation* (1995) and, on the
    right, Samuel Huntington, *Who Are We? The Challenges to Ameri-
    ca's National Identity* (2004).

15. Ed Pilkington, "Obama Angers Midwest Voters with Guns
    and Religion Remark," *Guardian*, April 14, 2008, https://
    www.theguardian.com/world/2008/apr/14/barackobama
    .uselections2008. The shift away from white dominance has been
    gradual, but a turning point was the work of Anne Case and
    Angus Deaton about declining life expectancy, "Rising Midlife
    Morbidity and Mortality, U.S. Whites," *Proceedings of the National
    Academy of Sciences* 112, no. 49 (December 8, 2015): 15078–83.
    Arlie Russell Hochschild, *Strangers in Their Own Land: Anger and
    Mourning on the American Right* (2018) is exhibit A on attempts to
    reassert cultural primacy.

16. Glenn Kessler, Salvador Rizzo, and Meg Kelly, "President Trump
    Has Made More Than 5,000 False or Misleading Claims," *Wash-
    ington Post*, September 13, 2018, https://www.washingtonpost
    .com/politics/2018/09/13/president-trump-has-made-more-than
    -false-or-misleading-claims/?utm_term=.078e34b9e9fa; "All False
    Statements Involving Donald Trump," *PolitiFact*, https://www
    .politifact.com/personalities/donald-trump/statements/byruling
    /false/.

17. Oliver Hahl, Minjae Kim, and Ezra W. Zuckerman Sivan, "The Authentic Appeal of the Lying Demagogue: Proclaiming the Deeper Truth About Political Illegitimacy," *American Sociological Review* 83, no. 1 (2018): 1–33.

18. Yoni Applebaum, "Trump's Promise to Jail Clinton Is a Threat to American Democracy," *Atlantic*, October 10, 2016, https://www .theatlantic.com/politics/archive/2016/10/trumps-promise-to-jail -clinton-is-a-threat-to-american-democracy/503516/; Alan Cullison, Rebecca Ballhaus, and Dustin Volz, "Trump Repeatedly Pressed Ukraine President to Investigate Biden's Son," *Wall Street Journal*, September 21, 2019, https://www.wsj.com/articles/trump -defends-conversation-with-ukraine-leader-11568993176; William P. Davis, "'Enemy of the People': Trump Breaks Out This Phrase During Moments of Peak Criticism," *New York Times*, July 19, 2018, https://www.nytimes.com/2018/07/19/business/media/trump -media-enemy-of-the-people.html; Nina Totenberg, "Who Is Judge Gonzalo Curiel, the Man Trump Attacked for His Mexican Ancestry?" National Public Radio, June 7, 2016, https://www.npr.org /2016/06/07/481140881/who-is-judge-gonzalo-curiel-the-man -trump-attacked-for-his-mexican-ancestry; Jacob Pramuk, "Trump Defiant on Travel Ban, Blasts the Courts as 'so political,'" CNBC (February 8, 2017), https://www.cnbc.com/2017/02/08/trump -defends-his-immigration-order-to-police-claims-courts-seem-to -be-so-political.html; Damian Paletta and Heather Long, "Declaring 'the Fed has gone crazy,' Trump Increasingly Takes Aim at U.S. Central Bank," *Washington Post*, October 11, 2018, https://www .washingtonpost.com/business/2018/10/11/declaring-fed-has -gone-crazy-trump-increasingly-takes-aim-us-central-bank/; Christine Wang, "Trump Attacks Fed Chairman Powell: 'I'm not even a little bit happy with my selection of Jay,'" CNBC, November 27, 2018, https://www.cnbc.com/2018/11/27/trump-attacks-fed-chair -powell-im-not-even-a-little-bit-happy-with-my-selection-of-jay .html; Dara Lind, "The Problem with Violence at Trump Rallies Starts with Trump Himself," *Vox*, May 13, 2016, https://www.vox

.com/2016/3/11/11202540/trump-violent; Melanie Mason, "Inside a Week of Trump Rallies: Talk of a Rigged Election, Biased Media and Barbecue Fries," *Los Angeles Times*, October 15, 2016, https://www.latimes.com/politics/la-na-pol-trump-supporters-20161015-snap-story.html.

19. Most quotations are taken from Trump's tweets, available at http://www.trumptwitterarchive.com/archive. A search for "corrupt" yielded 273 results as of November 29, 2019.

20. Nick Penzenstadler, "Trump: When Audiences Get Bored I Use 'the Wall,'" *USA Today*, January 30, 2016, https://www.usatoday.com/story/news/politics/onpolitics/2016/01/30/trump-when-audiences-get-bored-use-wall/79573388; Greg Miller, Julie Vitkovskaya, and Reuben Fischer-Baum, "'This Deal Will Make Me Look Terrible': Full Transcripts of Trump's Calls with Mexico and Australia," *Washington Post*, August 3, 2017, https://www.washingtonpost.com/graphics/2017/politics/australia-mexico-transcripts/?utm_term=.fd433555dfd6.

21. Alvin Felzenberg, *The Leaders We Deserved (and a Few We Didn't)* (2008); Michael F. Holt, *Franklin Pierce* (2010); Elbert B. Smith, *The Presidency of James Buchanan* (1975); Eugene P. Trani and David L. Wilson, *The Presidency of Warren Harding* (1977). Reading these biographies, one is hard-pressed to understand exactly why these presidents deserve such negative character assessments. They are probably best understood as normal politicians—pretty ordinary people—who could not handle the challenges of the presidency.

22. Jason Stanley, *How Propaganda Works* (2015), 269, 277 (the Stanford sociologist is Edward Alsworth Ross).

23. "Elite," *Merriam-Webster.com*, https://www.merriam-webster.com/dictionary/elite. The modern debate over who the elite are probably

begins with the work of Vilfredo Pareto and Gaetano Mosca, who wrote in the late nineteenth and early twentieth centuries. For a review of the historical debate, see Tom Bottomore, *Elites and Society*, 2nd ed. (1993). For a recent broadside, see Daniel Markovits, *The Meritocracy Trap: How America's Foundational Myth Feeds Inequality, Dismantles the Middle Class, and Devours the Elite* (2019).

24. Martin Gilens and Benjamin I. Page, "Testing Theories of American Politics: Elites, Interest Groups, and Average Citizens," *Perspectives on Politics* 12, no. 3 (September 2014): 564–81.

25. José Ortega y Gasset, *The Revolt of the Masses*, trans. Anthony Kerrigan (1985).

26. Some democracies are so thoroughly dominated by particular elites that they do little for ordinary people. This is particularly true for democracies that have undergone transitions from authoritarian systems, as the former authoritarian elite are frequently able to retain significant power after the transition. But even with "popular democracies," the countries that seem to do best at advancing the interests of all citizens (Sweden is frequently cited as an example) are governed by educated elites with outsized influence. See Michael Albertus and Victor Menaldo, *Authoritarianism and the Elite Origins of Democracy* (2018). On the inescapability of elite control, see, e.g., Thomas R. Dye, *Top Down Policymaking* (2001) and *Who's Running America? The Bush Restoration*, 7th ed. (2002), for a thorough articulation of this point.

27. Dye, *Who's Running America?*, 2. And since the quotation is from the records of the Constitutional Convention, where the deliberations were secret, Hamilton was actually speaking privately to his fellow elites.

28. Trump tweet, October 7, 2019, https://twitter.com/realDonald Trump/status/1181232249821388801.

29. This is not in fact my view—see Eric A. Posner and Adrian Ver-
meule, *The Executive Unbound: After the Madisonian Republic*
(2011)—as I believe that only a strong presidency can solve the
problems with the American constitutional system, which otherwise produces gridlock. But it is a popular view among academics
and may gain new support in the wake of Trump's presidency.
See, e.g., Gene Healy, *The Cult of the Presidency: America's Dangerous Devotion to Executive Power* (2008).

INDEX